Praise for The Mindful Coach: Seven Roles for Helping Others Grow

"Silsbee's approach is both practical and profound. This is a must-read for everyone concerned with people and learning."

Arthur M. Blank
PHILANTHROPIST; CO-FOUNDER, THE HOME DEPOT; OWNER & CEO, ATLANTA FALCONS

"The development of people is a key competency for business leadership. *The Mindful Coach* provides an inspiring and practical roadmap for developing masterful coaching skills on-the-job."

Karen Wunderlin
CONSULTANT, FORMER VICE-PRESIDENT/MARKETING, GE APPLIANCES

"A useful book facilitating the growth and development of individuals and groups. His approach reaches deeply into human consciousness and experience where meaningful change and growth occurs."

Harrison Owen
AUTHOR, *Open Space Technology*

"The tools of coaching that Silsbee outlines, with an emphasis on mindfulness and service, provide the fundamental basis for holistic and integrative physicians to work with patients."

Patrick Hanaway, M.D.
CHIEF MEDICAL OFFICER, GENOVA DIAGNOSTICS

"A welcome addition which teaches us that we can apply the deep spiritual knowledge of traditions like Buddhism to our modern business lives, in such a way that even our career becomes spiritually uplifting and a service to others."

Geshe Michael Roach
AUTHOR, *The Diamond Cutter*

"This book has broad appeal not only for coaches, but for managers, executives, and consultants. Leaders of all kinds can benefit from Silsbee's clear and caring process for bringing out the best in people. This is a must read book."

Diana Whitney, Ph.D.
AUTHOR, *The Power of Appreciative Inquiry*

"All of us who lead, manage or teach are often in the role of the coach, whether we think about it that way or not. *The Mindful Coach* provides a framework that works for the professional coach as well as the everyday manager."

Bill Coleman
SENIOR VP/COMPENSATION, SALARY.COM

"A clear and integrated model to assist people in understanding and applying the important skills in mindfulness and coaching. Executives from diverse backgrounds will find *The Mindful Coach* an insightful and practical guide."

Hannah S. Wilder, Ph.D., M.C.C.
PRESIDENT, ADVANTARA EXECUTIVE DEVELOPMENT WORLDWIDE

"I loved this book! *The Mindful Coach* is personal, spiritual, systematic and insightful. This is mandatory reading for anyone who has the responsibility of helping others learn and develop. My trainers will all be receiving a copy. This is Thich Nhat Hanh meets Stephen Covey!"

Barbara Fulmer
DIRECTOR OF TRAINING, JENNY CRAIG INTERNATIONAL

"In serving others, we can get overly focused on specific strategies or tactics and lose perspective of the larger, broader dynamic. *The Mindful Coach* delivers on clarifying, organizing, and contextualizing what it really means to be involved in a coaching relationship."

Joe Jotkowitz
PRESIDENT, ESSESSNET

"*The Mindful Coach* captures the very essence of what coaching can be. Silsbee marries the art and science of human dialogue, of compassionate listening and advice giving without creating dependency. He guides the reader gently through the seven distinct roles of a true helping relationship. This is a process to be internalized and lived every day."

Rod Napier, Ph.D.
PROFESSOR, CONSULTANT, AUTHOR, *The Courage to Act* AND TEN OTHER BOOKS

"*The Mindful Coach* is not just another coaching model. It is a frame of reference for anyone involved in developing people. This highly readable book should serve as a reference for anyone genuinely concerned about helping others. It has had a significant impact on the way I coach."

James N. Bassett, M.Ed.
EMPLOYEE DEVELOPMENT, INSTITUTE OF NUCLEAR POWER OPERATIONS

"In his hands-on new book, *The Mindful Coach*, replete with artful and challenging exercises, Doug Silsbee models the mindfulness depth from which he springs in order to impart a valuable new coaching model based on professionalism, integrity, and dedication to service."

Maggie Lichtenberg, P.C.C.
PROFESSIONAL COACH

"*The Mindful Coach* is warm, sensitive and intuitive, while at the same time clearly written by a scientific mind. The book provides a simple and cohesive model for the development process, coupled with practical strategies on how to become a more conscious practitioner."

Alejandro Bolaños, Ph.D.
CONSULTANT, CENTRAL AMERICA

"*The Mindful Coach* is a book that anyone who is serious about coaching must read. It is comprehensive and compelling and will give you insights that will help you be the best coach you can be."

James A. DeSena
AUTHOR, *The 10 Immutable Laws of Power Selling*

THE
MINDFUL
COACH

Seven Roles for Helping People Grow

Douglas K. Silsbee

**Ivy
River
PRESS**

Published by Ivy River Press
3717 Bend of Ivy Rd., Marshall, NC   28753
888-658-2021
info@ivyriverpress.com

Hardcover edition: ISBN 0-9745003-4-8
Softcover edition: ISBN 0-9745003-5-6

Library of Congress Control Number: 2004090252

The poems "Orioling" and "The Ten Thousand Things" are from *Orioling*, by Ann Silsbee, copyright © 2003 by Ann Silsbee, published by Red Hen Press, Los Angeles. Used by permission of the author.

The Raisin Meditation is from *Awakening the Buddha Within*, by Lama Surya Das, copyright © 1997 by Lama Surya Das. Used by permission of Broadway Books, a division of Random House, Inc.

ICF Ethical Guidelines copyright © 2003 International Coach Federation, Washington, DC. Used by permission.

Cover and interior photographs copyright © 2003
Douglas K. Silsbee; all rights reserved.

Book cover and interior design by Desktop Miracles, Inc.

Publisher's Cataloging-in-Publication Data
(Provided by Quality Books, Inc.)

Silsbee, Douglas K.
    The mindful coach : seven roles for helping people grow /
Douglas K. Silsbee.
    p.   cm.
    LCCN 2004090252
    ISBN 0-9745003-4-8
    ISBN 0-9745003-5-6

    1. Executive coaching.   2. Organizational
effectiveness.   3. Spiritual exercises—Psychology.
4. Self-actualization (Psychology)—Religious aspects—
Buddhism.   I. Title.

HD30.4.S55   2004   658.4'07124
                                             QBI33–2010

Printed in the United States of America

Orioling

You love their singing—the thrush, the orioles—
    though they don't perform for you. Theirs is a clan
song: *My bugs, my bough, my mate,* and:
    See how bright the orange and black of my feathers.
Nor do they sing for blighted love the hard
    blues of loss we would, or for joy,
but because they can't help it, because song
    blossoms from the stem of their being bird.
Human, you can't help trying to understand
    what stalk you flower from, what undertow
rises in the flutist to quicken with breath
    the arcs and dips of prior minds, or mind
itself, playing with fugue, with $E=mc^2$,
    inventing wheel, organ, flute, B Minor Mass—
Buddha—the bomb. The song you bear buds
    under your mind's tongue like a first word.

ANN SILSBEE

Table of Contents

Expanded Table of Contents

PART 1
Concepts

PART 2

The Septet

PART 3

Application

Fully formatted versions of all Chapter 13 exercise templates can be downloaded quickly and easily from http://septetcoaching.com.

Acknowledgments

It is trite but true for an author to say that but for the contributions of many people a book would never have been born. It has been a humbling experience to contemplate the family, friends, colleagues and clients who have contributed directly or indirectly to the writing of this book, and the degree to which I am indebted to so many for the experiences that led to my being able to write it.

First, I'm immensely grateful to my father, Bob Silsbee, who teaches me by example to observe the world keenly and constantly, and has an astounding ability to help me learn by asking me questions that makes me think. From him, I learned how to ask artful questions, and he, probably more than any other, represents the Teacher for me. I'm also deeply grateful to my mother, Ann, who passed away during the writing of this book. She showed me what it meant to follow her passion, and was an unbelievable fountain of creativity and inspiration. Two of her poems grace the beginning and ending of this book, shedding a special light on the subject we are addressing.

Loving thanks to my wife, Walker, for supporting me without qualification in following my aspirations to write this book, for providing me with feedback and wise counsel, and for believing in me when sometimes I faltered. She has given far more than she knows. A robust thank-you to my wonderful children Alisia, Megan, and Nathan, all of whom forgave innumerable absences when I know it cost them.

Thanks to those who read sections or the entire manuscript, and who gave me their thoughtful feedback and criticisms: Alex Bolaños, Gretchen

Cherington, Judy Futch, Bo Hughes, Chris Larson, Maggie Lichtenberg, Teijo Munnich, Rod Napier, Nancy Spence, Hannah Wilder, and Karen Wunderlin. A deep appreciation, too, for Chris Kochansky, who has convinced me that editors are God's gift to writers. She was always kind and supportive as she took my sometimes convoluted language and wrestled it into elegant and clean form. Only she and I will know what a bloodbath that required at times! And to Barry Kerrigan and Del LeMond, who took millions of bytes of electronic data and somehow turned it into a cohesive and beautiful work of art, another warm Thank you!

Thanks to all who helped in the development of the assessment tools, especially Judy Futch, Richard Garzarelli, Scott Gress, John Miles, Carrie Mozena, Paul Smith, and most of all, Anna Florey, whose patience and discerning mind are embedded deeply in the Septet Model. To my R&D group, Jim Burke, Gretchen Cherington, Candia Dye, Bo Hughes, C. J. Wilson, and Terri Zwierzynski, my thanks for being eager learners, providing me feedback, and being willing to experiment.

Thanks to Scott Ziemer for the original seed for the Seven Hats, which has since flowered into something beyond what either of us could have conceived at the time. And to Alex Bolaños, who was the one to suggest that this should be a book; it was a revelation to me at the time. Also, to my many fine coaches and teachers along the way, including Rod Napier, Darya Funches, Nancy Zimmers, Hannah Wilder, and many others, and to Nancy Spence, my dharma teacher, who has been a reliable and inspiring guide for me along the pathway that led to this book.

Perhaps most importantly, I want to thank all my clients, who over the years have honored me with their trust and willingness, and from whom I have learned far more than I have given. You appear, if not by name, in many ways throughout this book. If some of you recognize yourselves, know that it is with deep appreciation for you and your journey that I share what I've learned along the road.

Introduction

*In the case of good books, the point is not
how many of them you can get through, but
rather how many can get through to you.*
MORTIMER ADLER

*O*nce many years ago, when I was a chubby two-year-old, I was presented with the limitless opportunity and challenge of a lawn full of
dandelions. The sun shone down from a clear spring sky, making the
blossoms vibrant and inviting. Fascinated, I walked about on my plump
little legs, picking the shaggy yellow flowers until my fists were full. And
still there were so many!

Soon the flowers were falling from my hands as fast as I could pick
them. My fingers were incapable of holding more. Suddenly, faced with
the overwhelming impossibility of gathering all those dandelions at
once, I threw my hard-earned treasures to the wind and screamed in
frustration. I was so bent on picking them all that I missed both the

miracle of a great space filled with bright flowers and the beauty of those I could hold in my hand.

This anecdote isn't just a cute kid story, of course; my mother told it as an illustration of something about my character, even as a child. And I admit that even today, at age fifty, I still want it all: to embrace every experience, seize every opportunity, fulfill every obligation to the hilt. In my personal life I'm often challenged to know how much is enough. In my work as a consultant, coach, and teacher, I sometimes struggle to discern which actions and investments of energy will bring me the most professional fulfillment and deliver the most service to others. In both realms, when faced with a huge range of choices I have difficulty settling on just one; once I've chosen I tend to grasp it tightly. Understanding and acknowledging these things about myself has been important for me, both personally and professionally.

This book is designed for those of us—executives and managers, social workers, therapists, educators, organizational consultants, and members of the relatively new profession of coaching—whose work makes us responsible for the growth and development of others. It's about learning to be wiser—more mindful—in navigating the dandelion fields of our own lives, and about bringing that wisdom to those we coach.

Most of us who work in what I'll call, for lack of a better term, the human development professions have been trained in the use of a range of techniques and "tools" designed to help us teach people the skills they need—in the workplace or the wider world—to assess a situation, define their goals, and make good choices that will help them reach those goals. All too often, our training leads us to assume that those we are "developing" are the subjects of an objective process that we can engineer. We also tend to assume that using the "right" tool for a given situation will lead to a successful outcome. It follows that we often rely upon the comfortable terrain of established practice. Unfortunately, this reduces our own capacity to learn, to see the other person in an expansive rather than a reductionist way, and to provide what the other person truly needs. There are critical dimensions of learning that are not considered in a model that designates one person as the sole teacher and the other as the sole learner.

As people who seek to help others change and grow, we are in relationship with those we counsel. If we are human, we cannot be in a relationship without being affected by it: we are part of the dynamic. The people we work with affect us, we affect them. To do our part well, we must understand clearly what we bring to the relationship: our limitations and biases as well as our skills and expertise. To do this, we must know the territory inside ourselves. We, as guides, teachers, and coaches, are also subjects in the relationship. If we expect to be of service to anyone else we must develop our own self-awareness first.

In a recent workshop, I asked participants to raise their hands if they recalled seeing aspects of themselves reflected in those they were advising, in one way or another, as clients. Or if they had given a piece of advice that they knew they should have followed themselves. Or if they had felt pressure to demonstrate their expertise. Most of the people in the group raised their hands in response to all three of these questions. I would have as well. Each reflects a situation in which our own personalities, our own needs and biases and attachments, may influence our actions as professionals.

There's nothing inherently wrong with this. Most of us in the human development professions find ourselves in teaching, counseling, or advisory positions in part because we tend to be interesting people with useful ideas, skills, and the desire to be helpful. Still, the very existence of our own needs and attachments creates some level of risk that we may fail to be attentive to the real needs of the people we are working with. If we are not aware of our own often subtle biases and motivations, the relationship may become distorted by these undercurrents.

In addition, while tools and techniques are helpful, they can seduce us into the role of expert. Maintaining this expert stance not only requires energy, it also leaves the "expert" little room to learn since he or she is supposed to know it all already.

With this book I am proposing that we reconsider the nature of the relationship between ourselves and the people we are coaching, teaching, or counseling—that we reframe some of our fundamental assumptions about the nature of the work we do.

The Septet Model

First, I would suggest, we need to view our professional relationships with our clients in such a way that every interaction becomes an opportunity to practice being fully conscious, present, and effective. While we may not get it right all the time, I believe that it's important that we state and hold a strong commitment to becoming ever more mindful and self-aware. This changes the nature of our relationship with our clients; instead of seeing it as a helper/helpee or expert/learner situation, we redefine it as a partnership for learning. We have expertise and skills to offer: our learning will be different from our client's, but we are both in it together.

Second, in choosing to serve as teachers/counselors/coaches, we set ourselves the challenge of recognizing and, where appropriate, setting aside our own agendas and needs in order to better discern and provide what the other person truly needs. In order to consciously serve others, we must continually consider the following questions:

- How do we discern what the other person *really* needs from us as distinct from what we believe he or she needs?
- How do we learn to recognize, and manage, our own habits of mind in order to be fully present in every interaction rather than relying on received formulas?
- How do we integrate our own efforts to become more mindful in the development work we do with others?

The Septet Coaching Model presented in this book provides a line of inquiry based on my own experience with executives, coaching trainees, and others in the helping professions. It is a structure that has proven helpful in enabling us to be more mindful as we support others. The time-honored advice to "count to ten before responding when you're angry" works because, in the simple act of remembering to count, we are exercising the muscle of self-awareness and making a proactive decision about how to respond. Similarly, to be truly in service to those we are working with, we need to study our own minds, befriend and master our own thought processes, and learn to free ourselves from unhelpful habits of mind.

The organization of this model in seven parts is intended to provide a structure for learning more about ourselves as coaches. Each of the seven Voices we'll discuss in Part 2 represents a role that we play for our clients in the coaching process. For each role I've outlined several Aspects that comprise a specific and concrete set of skills and behaviors that can be practiced and learned. By identifying our patterns of strengths and weaknesses, and the habits of mind that lie behind them, we can develop ourselves systematically to be better at each of these critical roles.

Language

Although I've chosen to use the language of the emerging field of coaching, including the terms "coach" and "client," this book is meant for practitioners of many professions. Some of you, my intended readers, will be business managers or organizational development and training specialists. Some of you will be therapists, social workers, members of the clergy, or full-time professional coaches. Some will act as coaches in several capacities in your lives.

These scenarios provide examples of what I define as coaching relationships:

- a manager provides a subordinate with feedback on an in-house presentation,

- a social worker outlines ways an unemployed woman can become more self-sufficient,
- an executive coach helps a manager "brainstorm" ideas on how he can build support for his latest proposal,
- a therapist elicits ideas from a client who wants to work on a problem in his marriage,
- a high school principal provides feedback and suggestions to a teacher on how to make a history class more engaging,
- a pastor explores with a parishioner how she can deepen her spirituality.

You may not label yourself as a coach, and others may not call you such, but you will recognize yourself in these pages because you have accepted responsibility for developing the capabilities of others. Whatever the nature of your work, this book is written for you. We'll explore the definition of the term "coach" more fully in Chapter 1, but for now please discard any preconceptions about that term and consider it as applying to yourself in any relationship where you are interacting with another person in service to his or her learning, growth, and change.

Also, please consider the term "client" as applying to the recipient of that coaching, whether it's a manager that you're supporting, a counseling or social work client, a direct report, a paying private client, your chief financial officer, a member of your congregation, or your toddler learning to use the potty. The examples in this book are drawn from many arenas in which coaching takes place.

To avoid committing to any of the awkward and cumbersome options available—"he or she" followed by syntactic tangles of "his or her" and "him or her," "they" when the syntax calls for the singular, or "s/he" (Ugh!)—I've most often used the gender pronouns "he" and "she" alternately at roughly the same frequency, keeping a consistency regarding who's who within a passage or a chapter. Your pardon is begged in advance for any offense caused by unmindful usage!

The term "Master" is used to describe one of the Septet's Voices. I recognize that, even uncapitalized, this word comes with baggage for some people, who will hear connotations of patriarchy, "dominion over," a certification level, a controller, a male, or all of these. (Wait! Stop! Look inside. What reactions do you notice within yourself to the word? It is up to you to recognize the meanings that you attach to any word. You are invited to allow the word "master" to assume new meaning in your mind; this of course requires recognizing previous connotations. This looking within process is central both to knowing yourself and to deriving greatest value from the book. The simple act of recognizing patterns of thought and opening yourself to new ones is in itself a step toward our goal.)

Meaning is made; it can be dissolved, shifted, or created anew as well. "Master" is the word that means most closely what I intend: a gender-neutral term for a person with great skill, an artist; it links closely to the word "mastery," which we will use extensively. A master has looked inward to cultivate a high level of self-awareness, and to recognize and rise above habitual judgments, impulses, and reactions. A master has the capacity to make skillful choices about what to become and how to interact with others. The Master Voice is central to coaching.

The names of most of the clients mentioned in the book have been changed, as have any particulars that could be used to identify them as specific individuals. Where both a first and last name are provided, these are names of real people who have been a gift in my life and without whom this book would likely not have been written.

The Structure of the Book

The book is organized into three parts. Part 1 is an exploration of the foundational concepts of coaching, mindfulness, and service—a context for the Septet Model. Its three chapters focus on specific facets of that context.

- Chapter 1, "Coaching," is built around a definition of that term that is broad enough to cover many helping relationships. Here we take a look at the dynamics of power and relationship that influence how coaching works.
- In Chapter 2, "Mindfulness," we'll begin by looking at the nature of experience and consciousness, and at the origins of our habits of mind, especially those that can take us away from being present and attentive in the moment. Drawing on both Eastern and Western traditions, we'll also offer a number of practices that can support the development of mindfulness.
- In Chapter 3, "Service," we'll talk about what it means to place ourselves in service and dedicate ourselves to the benefit of our clients.

Part 2 introduces and explores the Septet Coaching Model, and describes the seven distinct Voices through which the coach does his or her work. Chapters 5 through 11 define each Voice, and offer sample dialogues to illustrate its various Aspects. In these chapters we'll also identify common pitfalls and suggest guidelines for using each Voice wisely.

- Chapter 4, "An Overview," provides a big picture of the multiple roles a coach plays in relationship with a client—the Voices in which the coach may choose to speak at different times.
- Chapter 5, "The Master." This is the role that underpins all the others. The Master is the coach practicing his or her own mindfulness and presence, listening attentively and choosing the most effective Voice for the benefit of the client at each point in their relationship.
- Chapter 6, "The Partner." In this role the coach works with the client to set up the parameters of the relationship, create a responsive structure for their work together, and involve the client in the coaching process.

- Chapter 7, "The Investigator." As an investigator, the coach asks questions about the client's situation, the outcomes he or she desires, and the possibilities for action. These lines of questioning are at the core of the coaching process.
- Chapter 8, "The Reflector." In taking this role, the coach serves as a mirror, supporting the client's self-awareness by providing feedback and helping the client develop the capacity for self-observation.
- Chapter 9, "The Teacher." As a teacher, the coach provides information to augment the client's own experience. The Teacher also challenges the client's thinking process and assumptions as a way to open up new possibilities.
- Chapter 10, "The Guide." As a guide, the coach points the way, encouraging the client to take action, or offering ideas and suggestions that have proven successful in other, similar situations.
- Chapter 11, "The Contractor." This Voice provides a bridge from the coaching conversation to the rest of the client's life, defining areas for follow-up action and translating new perspectives and energy into concrete, substantive next steps.

Part 3 focuses on the practical application of the ideas presented in Parts 1 and 2 of the book.

- In Chapter 12, "An Integrated Model of Coaching," a practical roadmap of the coaching process is presented as we look at the relationships between the Voices, the role of the coach's intuition in guiding the conversation, and the development of mastery in both client and coach.
- Chapter 13, "Development Strategies for the Coach," discusses specific and concrete strategies for developing the coach's mindfulness and competence, and presents exercises for each, including references to an on-line directory of supporting tools, downloadable and customizable formatted versions of the exercises and a self-assessment survey.

- Chapter 14, "Mindful Service: A Pathway to Mastery," ties together the concepts of self-mastery, service, and accountability to clients. The book closes with a discussion on the nature of practice and the spirit of inquiry.

I encourage you to take nothing in this book on faith. Experiment, test the ideas and exercises, try them on. *The Mindful Coach* extends an invitation to discover for yourself how to make your coaching relationships deeper and more fulfilling for both parties in the conversation. There are no prescriptions here. Some of what's presented won't suit your needs; other ideas or practices may be transformative. That discernment is your discovery work.

No coaching serves the client if it causes him to override what he knows to be true and right. The client is ultimately responsible for his own choices; the coach is a catalyst. Similarly, no coaching model serves the coach it if causes her to ignore what she knows, to give bad advice, or to disrespect the client in any way.

Please consider the material here as a series of testable hypotheses. Open yourself to these ideas, try them out as rigorous experiments, and observe the results closely. Through observation, you will quickly learn which practices suggested here enhance learning for you and your clients. You are responsible for the choices you make about using what proves itself. Let go of the rest.

Beyond this book, a community is developing around these ideas. You are invited to join this community by sharing your own reactions, ideas, new exercises, and experiences.

Finally, the creation of this book has been quite a learning process for me. Many others have shared their wisdom and ideas along the way. I've learned more from writing it, from discussing these ideas with friends and colleagues, and from watching myself in the process than I ever could have imagined.

May your own discovery process be as rewarding!

PART

1

CONCEPTS

CHAPTER ONE

Coaching

*I know not how I may seem to others, but to myself
I am but a small child wandering upon the vast
shores of knowledge, every now and then finding
a small bright pebble to content myself with.*
PLATO

*You cannot teach humans anything.
You can only help them discover it within themselves.*
GALILEO

Over the past decade or so, coaching—meaning helping others develop personal and social skills that will enable them to be more successful—has found broad acceptance in corporate culture as an essential leadership competency. With roots in the personal development movement, organizational development, psychotherapy, and learning theory, coaching has become well established as a field in itself. Many organizations have launched internal training programs to teach coaching skills to their managers, and the whole field of personal coaching for individuals has been expanding exponentially.

As in any growth industry, this profession has seen a rapid development of new concepts and approaches, as well as the adaptation of coaching to many different venues. Specialization and competition are increasing, and coaches are finding success in remarkably narrow niches. At the same time, questions have arisen about what qualifications, training, and certification processes distinguish professionals who are likely to provide useful service to their clients from people who just declare themselves to be coaches and hang out a shingle. It can be difficult to separate out what's substantive from what's fluff—frankly, there's a lot of both.

This book attempts to come back to the heart of what makes coaching powerful, to focus on the substantive—the advantages of a one-on-one relationship, the skills and insights that coaches have collectively developed and/or brought to the profession from other fields, and the application of those skills and insights in many different contexts. (It should be noted that although there is a significant body of work on "group coaching," coaching as we're addressing it here is a one-on-one process.)

The Septet Coaching Model is one view of what it takes to meet the requirements of any coaching situation. Since these vary so widely, we'll begin by outlining what we mean by coaching, and then explore how to do it.

A Working Definition of Coaching

Much has been written by other authors about what coaching is and what it isn't. For our purposes here, we'll define it quite broadly as *"that part of a relationship in which one person is primarily dedicated to serving the long-term development of effectiveness and self-generation in the other."*[1] Let's take a look at the elements of that definition.

Some relationships that involve coaching—for example between a coach and a paying client—are exclusively built around the learning, growth, and change of the client. In exchange for the coach's expertise, the client pays the coach money. In many other situations, however, coaching represents *part* of a more complex relationship.

Consider a department head with ten managers reporting to her. She has supervisory responsibility for the entire unit and is held accountable for its collective performance. A significant portion of her job involves organizing—making scheduling and budgeting decisions, delegating tasks, and monitoring the work of the whole department. That is not coaching. Coaching comes in when she works one-on-one with her direct reports to ask about their concerns, provide feedback, elicit ideas (for example, about how to increase employee "ownership" and commitment within a work unit), and discuss new challenges and opportunities for their own professional development. Coaching is a critical part of the manager's relationship with each of her direct reports; it is not the entire relationship.

Similarly, parents often coach their children in the context of a larger relationship. Whereas basic parental duties and pleasures—providing food and shelter, establishing rules and enforcing discipline, or enjoying a game of catch for its own sake—couldn't be considered coaching, other interactions, like encouraging a toddler after a successful potty visit, helping an eighth grader learn how to manipulate algebraic equations, taking a teenager out driving, would fit our definition. (Generally, as children move into their teenage years, they are less and less willing to be coached by their parents. However, even then, and sometimes especially then, opportunities for parents to act as coaches will present themselves.)

The phrase *"primarily dedicated to serving"* in our definition means that the learning and growth of the client are central to the purpose of the coach in a given situation. This is the overriding consideration. It is not, however, the sole consideration. In addition to his commitment to his client, the coach always has a responsibility to take care of himself. "Solely dedicated" would imply that whatever the client wants goes; *"primarily dedicated"* means that while the development of the client comes first, there's room in the relationship to articulate and address the legitimate needs of the coach as well.

The coaching relationship is often a professional one, in which the coach is paid by the client or a third party such as a company, an agency, or a congregation, but it is also a personal one as well. Setting up a framework that will work for both parties is important. The nature of each person's responsibilities, including keeping appointments, being respectful, and remaining truly engaged, should be made explicit at the beginning. Establishing guidelines and mutual expectations for the coaching process is central to enabling the coach's dedication to serving the client.

It is absolutely appropriate, at times, to provide quick answers to a client's direct questions or immediate needs for help. But it is also important to remain aware that this is not the only approach to supporting the client; if we always give in to the temptation to go for the quick fix we will most likely be undermining initiative and fostering dependence. Helping clients build long-term capabilities means helping them develop their own problem-solving skills. This *long-term* view needs to be kept in mind and made explicit.

Development encompasses a number of meanings. According to *Webster's New Universal Unabridged Dictionary,* to develop is "to become fuller, larger, better, etc.; to expand . . . ; to strengthen . . . ; to unfold gradually, as a bud." Development implies that the raw materials are already there, that nothing is being created from scratch. In coaching, the client's development means that she is growing into her potential, becoming increasingly intentional and proactive about what she wants to achieve and who she wants to be.

The long-term goals of coaching include both effectiveness and self-generation. *Effectiveness* means that the client becomes more competent and successful, according to her own defined standards and goals, in the content area of the coaching, be that building a business, learning a better tennis serve, getting or changing a job, or any other endeavor she and the coach have agreed to focus upon.

The second desired outcome of coaching is self-generation. In his book *Coaching: Evoking Excellence in Others*, James Flaherty notes that well-coached people understand that there is always more to learn, and a self-generative person is a life-long learner.[2] Self-generation means taking personal responsibility for enhancing one's own capabilities, and ultimately it implies an independence from the coach.

Finally, there are many formats for coaching. In my own practice, I have coached in half-hour phone conversations, half-day sessions in person, day-long conversations beside a mountain creek, and e-mail exchanges with someone on a different continent.

It's not the schedule or the setting that determines whether coaching is happening, but the nature of the work, specifically the dedication of the relationship, in whole or in part, to the development of effectiveness and self-generation in another. Beyond that dedication, the practical details are dictated by what best serves the learning process given the requirements of the individuals and circumstances involved.

Distinguishing Coaching from Other Professional Activities

It's my hope that this book will be of use not only to those who want to hone their skills as professional coaches but also to other professionals, like our department head, whose work includes coaching. Whichever is the case with you as an individual reader, taking a look at how our definition allows us to clearly identify the elements of coaching will help us all become more mindful and competent in helping others.

Table 1 on the following page provides some generalized examples of coaching and non-coaching activities in three professional venues. Its contents are intended to be illustrative rather than exhaustive. While coaching takes place in many professions not represented, the principle will be clear.

The purpose of the table is to help you consider how various activities do or don't fit the definition of coaching as we've framed it. (Please note that I've used "subordinate," "student," and "patient" in this table, as being more natural in the context of the professional realms represented here. However, throughout the book the word "client" is used in general discussions in order to reinforce the point that the coaching process is essentially the same across disciplines.)

It will also be helpful to look for exceptions to the generalizations presented, not in order to argue with the points being made but to

---

Table 1: Coaching and Non-Coaching Activities in Three Fields

Professional Field	Coaching Activities	Non-Coaching Activities
Managers/ Executives	• Career development conversations with a subordinate • Eliciting and discussing a subordinate's suggestions • Providing feedback about a subordinate's thinking • Discussing options for how to accomplish delegated tasks	• Delegating authority or tasks • Invoking authority as leverage or to get something done • Making annual review assessments and compensation decisions • Expressing personal dissatisfaction or judgment
Teachers	• Asking questions that encourage a student to think differently • Working with an individual student on test-taking strategies • Processing experiential learning activities with an individual • One-on-one tutoring	• Grading tests and homework • Lecturing and group discussions • Disciplining students • Any interaction with an individual student which uses authority as a basis to get a student to change behavior
Health Care Workers	• Asking patient to observe symptoms more closely • Helping client to see and understand his body as a whole system • Making suggestions for client self-responsibility in treatment • Discussing a diagnosis with patient	• Making an expert diagnosis • Prescribing medication, tests, or treatment • Viewing patient as a complex mechanical system with a breakdown • Practice-management activities

help hone your own understanding of the distinctions between coaching and other activities in relation to your own unique circumstances. Everything in this book is intended to invite you to do your own mindful discernment, not to constrain you with a definition imposed by someone else. The ultimate goal is learning to know in your gut when you are in service to a client's needs and when you are serving a different agenda.

Based on the examples in Table 1, we can make some further generalizations about coaching. Coaching is

- evocative, drawing upon the client's capabilities, aspirations, and resourcefulness,
- based on a partnership with clear, mutually defined expectations,
- focused on, and dedicated to, the development of the client,
- interactive and non-prescriptive.

Other activities, although they may be necessary, legitimate, and valuable parts of a professional relationship, and may result in client learning, are not, however, coaching. A person is not coaching when he or she

- uses authority or positional power to motivate the "client" by stating organizational expectations or implying consequences for non-compliance,
- makes unilateral decisions that directly affect the client,
- diagnoses the client using an "expert" system (while this is an important function in many fields, it serves a different primary agenda than the client's learning and development),
- makes decisions based on the needs of a larger system over the needs of the individual,
- communicates out of an emotional need, implicitly placing that need higher than the learning needs of the other.

Obviously, the distinction between coaching and non-coaching activities will sometimes be blurry. I encourage you to draw upon the guidelines above to define the boundaries of coaching in your particular arena. Clear distinctions about the professional activities you perform that are and aren't coaching will provide the basis for ongoing discernment and lay the groundwork for everything that follows as you expand your expertise as a coach. Exercise 1 will help you get started.

Exercise 1: Defining Coaching for Yourself

1. Write a brief summary of your job responsibilities; include those that entail coaching and describe the objectives of coaching as you do it in your context.

2. Consider again the definition of coaching I've presented—that part of a relationship in which one person is primarily dedicated to serving the long-term development of effectiveness and self-generation in the other—and think about it in relation to your job and the people whose skills you feel responsible for developing.

3. Then, get specific. Make a two-column table like Table 1 and fill it out with some specific examples of what you do in your interactions with the people you coach. Examples of interactions that fit our definition of coaching will go in the left-hand column and those that are excluded by the definition will go in the right.

The purpose here is for you to try out this book's definition of coaching and get you thinking about when you're coaching and when you're engaged in some other legitimate aspect of your professional relationship with a client, whoever that client might be in your particular professional venue. Later, based on the results of your observations and your own process of learning as you work with the ideas in this book, you can modify this definition or even create your own.

Becoming clear about what you aspire to provide for your clients is the first step toward mastery in coaching.

The Politics of Coaching: Four Dynamics

Let's look at how the structure of the coaching situation can influence the establishment of a viable relationship between coach and client. Here the focus is upon how to set up—and maintain—a healthy win/win situation.

Client-Initiated Coaching

Self-employed people, managers and executives, and people going through life transitions often hire private coaches to help them pursue their dreams and aspirations or to support them in addressing the problems they face. Many areas of specialization (executive coaching, small business coaching, creativity coaching, "life coaching," etc.) could be identified here. Usually the client finds the coach by word of mouth or other forms of referral; sometimes the coach finds the client. Either way, the client is eager to enter into the coaching relationship.

The important thing about this kind of situation is that it is a one-on-one contractual relationship, generally for an exchange of fees, between two people free of organizational constraints. Sometimes the client is paying the bill directly; other times the client is paying out of an employer's funds but has authority to do so, or can get the necessary signature, without any involvement by a third party. Since the person paying the bill is the person who is being served, the dynamic is pretty much self-regulating: if the client is getting what she believes she wants and is paying for, it's a successful relationship; if not, she will renegotiate or terminate the contract.

Third Party Involvement

A more complex situation arises if there's a third party with a vested interest in the outcome of the coaching. Consider the following scenarios.

- An executive wants a high-potential direct report to be coached in order to take on additional responsibility.
- A higher-up in a social service agency has his or her own agenda for the outcome in a particular case or cases.
- A manager is in trouble and coaching is an effort to remediate the situation. The client's job may be at stake, for instance, and the coach may be required to make progress or outcome reports to a third party who has the power to hire and fire, promote or demote within the organization.
- In health care, social work, or counseling settings, a third-party payer may place constraints on the coaching process, or may condition continued support on demonstrable results or actions taken.
- Coaching is being provided to managers by HR specialists or other line managers who are not in a supervisory relationship to the person being coached. Here the coach represents organizational interests as well as the client's interests.

In all of these situations, it may be a challenge to ensure that the coaching is truly dedicated to the long-term development of the client. The key, of course, is to put the various agendas on the table from the beginning and construct a coaching process that addresses them all. If there is to be communication about progress or outcomes to a third party, it's especially critical to be explicit about confidentiality.

A special case of this dynamic results if there are consequences to the client for not achieving the coaching outcomes expected by the third party. The bad news is that the client may well be resistant or resentful about being coached in the first place. He or she may or may not recognize the problems that the third party sees, so coaching may need to begin with determining if there is compatibility between the client's goals and those of the third party. The bottom line here is that if the client is unwilling or unable to engage in the coaching process in service to some motivation of his own—even if it's to jump through someone else's hoops in order to keep a job—the coaching cannot succeed. The good news is that the leverage provided by the dynamic can be helpful in getting results.

Finally, the third party's goals must be respected as well. For example, if I'm coaching a manager in an organizational setting, I always ask whether it will be a good use of the organization's investment if the client leaves the organization as a result of my coaching. If the answer is yes, then I feel much freer to truly serve the client's needs and not get caught between the client's needs and the organization's goals. Whatever the situation, it will be important to ensure that the client's goals aren't in conflict with those of any third party involved.

Transitioned Relationships

Another special dynamic results when a relationship of another sort (with a colleague, friend, former supervisor, business partner, etc.) becomes a coaching relationship. Generally, in any relationship with meaningful engagement, some of the mutual learning and exchange of ideas inherent in coaching will be present. This, however, is different from the explicit dedication of a portion of the relationship to the learning and development of one of the parties.

When this transition takes place, a new kind of relationship is formalized, one in which it is now understood that one person will be learning with the support of the other. This can be awkward, especially in collegial or peer relationships, because there can be an implication of inequality that challenges existing assumptions within the relationship. Recognizing this means having an open exchange of mutual expectations and frank discussion about how the other aspects of the original relationship will be affected. Bringing these issues to the surface and working on them is important. It may build comfort initially to place boundaries around the content of coaching, and to agree not to discuss this content outside of the portion of the relationship dedicated to coaching.

Supervisory Relationships

The last type of coaching situation we'll consider here is when the coach is the client's direct supervisor in an agency, business, or other organization. Here the coaching element is inevitably influenced by the power differential resulting from the authority of the coach/boss over the client, and by the potential for the interests of the supervisor to differ from the interests of the individual.

Coaching in a supervisory relationship often occurs in order to increase the subordinate's skill in meeting organizational objectives. This is generally referred to as performance coaching, and it can be very helpful to the subordinate as well. It is, however, conditioned on the assumption that the subordinate's goals are consistent with those of the employer. Performance coaching becomes more delicate when the subordinate has other career interests, or sees his performance more favorably than does his boss.

In order for coaching to be successful in a supervisory relationship, four conditions must be met.

- The goals of the boss must not be in conflict with the personal and professional goals of the subordinate, or the boss must be able to place other considerations temporarily in the background in order support the dedication of the coaching, in good faith, to the best interests of the subordinate.
- The subordinate must be motivated to make a commitment to learning and development for reasons of his or her own.
- Both parties must be able and willing to draw distinctions between the coaching aspect of their relationship and others, separating the development process from power issues and supervisory consequences.
- The boss and subordinate must trust each other that the first three conditions are present.

If any of these conditions is not present, it will be difficult for the supervisor to coach the subordinate, and a different means to provide development support for the subordinate may be more appropriate. If these conditions are met, however, the two parties can build a real coaching relationship dedicated to the client's growth.

I recommend to my clients who are coaching direct reports that they set aside a special time and circumstance for the coaching aspect of their relationship. The authority of the supervisor and other aspects of their relationship are then placed in the background and that time is dedicated to the service of the subordinate's development. When coaching is over, that is also made explicit.

Summary

In any of the relationships described above, coaching can take place in informal interactions—say, meeting by the water cooler for a brief exchange. The descriptions of coaching in this book, however, will be based on the assumption that most high level coaching takes place in conversations that are dedicated to that purpose. The book, then, presents a model of coaching that will guide any professional in structuring conversations dedicated to the development of others.

As coaches, we must remain aware of our commitment to the learning and growth of the client. The client is in charge; we are in service to the stated purposes of the client. We must also remember that while it is important to meet the short-term needs of our clients for immediate ideas and solutions, their long-term development is the ultimate goal, and therefore it's our responsibility to foster those skills and habits of mind that will enable them to make wise choices on their own in the future.

To the extent that we allow ourselves or a third party—or, more precisely, our own needs and goals or those of an organization—to drive the agenda, we risk undermining this primary mission. This is

why the parameters of the coaching situation should be discussed openly
and frankly at the outset, so that both the coach and the client—and a
third party, if one is involved—can make a determination as to whether
there's a good fit. The most challenging of those situations we've discussed above is coaching within a supervisory relationship, where both
parties must be able to place the authority differences in the background
in order to maintain a clear focus on the goals and needs of the client.

Service in coaching, then, is the process of engaging in coaching
as described here, and doing so with the fullest possible awareness of
the client and his or her opportunities. This requires recognition of
our own needs, agendas, and blind spots, and a willingness to set them
aside in service to the client. A mindful self-awareness is the essential
starting point in being able to serve one's clients well.

CHAPTER TWO

Mindfulness

If the human brain were so simple that we could understand it, we would be so simple that we couldn't.
EMERSON PUGH

When I dance, I dance; when I sleep, I sleep; yes, and when I walk alone in a beautiful orchard, if my thoughts drift to far-off matters for some part of the time, for some other part I lead them back again to the walk, the orchard, to the sweetness of this solitude, to myself.
MONTAIGNE

Mindfulness is the state of awareness in which we are conscious of our feelings, thoughts, and habits of mind, and able to let unhelpful ones go so that they no longer limit us. It is important to recognize, within ourselves, the presence or absence of this quality of being.

The cultivation of mindfulness is a lifelong process. As you read this book, please give yourself lots of permission to be a beginner and to experiment. Attachments to being "good at" mindfulness, or to being able to easily comprehend subtle new ideas, will only get in the way of this ongoing inquiry.

In this chapter we'll look at a simple architecture of consciousness and come to understand some of the habits of mind that impede access to self-awareness. We'll conduct a little experiment to get some first-hand experience with mindfulness. We'll explore a number of tools and approaches for cultivating our in-the-moment awareness of ourselves and others. Lastly, we'll conclude by tying the concept of mindfulness back into the coaching context that's the subject of this book.

I assure you that a commitment to cultivating mindfulness will provide you with a lifetime of learning opportunities. It will also greatly deepen your experience of coaching and your ability to be present and effective as a coach.

Although some of the terms I will use—including "mindfulness," "attachments," and "aversions"—come from Western translations of the formulations of Buddhist teachers, this is not a book about Buddhism. Daniel Goleman's domains of "emotional intelligence" (self-awareness, self-management, social awareness, and relationship management)[3] and other Western frameworks could also serve as platforms from which to develop the ideas presented here, but I have chosen Buddhist thought as a take-off point for several reasons.

First, for 2,500 years Buddhist teaching has described, in exquisite detail, a taxonomy of consciousness that explains how our minds work. This roadmap is practical, absolutely relevant today, and consistent with current scientific understanding. We can use it to understand more precisely what goes on inside us.

Second, being mindful often requires letting go of what we think we know and seeing the world and our relationship to it in a new way. It's been my experience that, for many Westerners, Buddhist language can be a catalyst for finding fresh perspectives and thus being more open to change.

Third, Buddhist teachings have been accepted and used extensively in many cultures around the world, while many other constructs that could provide a theoretical base for this work are purely Western. I believe that the ideas in this book are relevant and applicable in any culture. To place them in a transcultural framework can only make the book more accessible to all potential readers regardless of their cultural background and assumptions.

Last, and most importantly, Buddhism has provided an integration of everything that I have learned in decades of focused personal growth and development work. No other framework I have run across provides the same lucidity in describing what I observe as I seek to live fully and intentionally, and to be as effective as I can be as a coach in helping others develop their own skills and capacities.

The Skandhas

Central to Buddhism's taxonomy of consciousness are the *skandhas*, or "Aggregates."[4] Skandha is a word from Pali, an ancient South Asian language. While it doesn't translate precisely, it generally means a collection or a conglomeration of individual things. The skandhas together thus describe the whole of what we identify as being our selves. There are five of them.

The first *skandha* is form. Form encompasses our bodies, our sense organs, and all the physical aspects of who we are. We tend to assume that our bodies are solid and permanent, but they are simply a temporary configuration of atoms that will pass into a different form in the future. Even the very cells of our bodies are born and then die, being constantly replaced. There is nothing permanent about our bodies. My mother passed away suddenly while I was in the midst of writing this book; I had talked to her casually from the airport on the way to Asia, and a week later she was gone. Her ashes fit into a small box that was placed on the piano at the memorial service.

Second come feelings, emotions, and sensations. When form comes in contact with something, a sensation arises. The smells of my daughter fixing sautéed eggplant sandwiches downstairs for lunch, the sound of a Miles Davis CD playing as I write, the sensation of a mosquito on my arm, a feeling of contentment as I look out the window. As we look into our feelings, we recognize that they have their origins in sensations, but they are also connected to other *skandhas*.

The third *skandha* encompasses perceptions and beliefs. Here, the feelings that arise when form encounters sensations are interpreted by the discriminating mind, thus producing judgments, names for things, and concepts about what it is that is being sensed. At first perceptions are just neutral. Then, because they are conditioned by our past experiences, they bias what we are seeing and can cause us to react in either helpful or unhelpful ways. Because my wife was irritated earlier, when I left my dirty shoes in the front hall, I feel anxious as she walks upstairs to my office even though it may well be that she's coming to tell me how much she's enjoying the sound of the rain on the roof. Again, there's nothing "real" about my anxiety; it's just a temporary configuration, a skandha arising that will dissipate on its own.

Fourth come mental formations. Our usual experience of mental formations is thoughts, images, and self-talk or mental chatter. Mental formations arise from the combination of the other *skandhas*.[5] Our mental pictures of the future, combined with intention and will, determine our activities and ultimately the result of these activities, which may or may not be to our liking. The seeds, the potential for each of these mental formations, reside in our deep unconscious. When these seeds are watered—by sensory input, by an emotion, etc.—they sprout and arise into the higher levels of our consciousness where we become aware of them.

The fifth *skandha* is consciousness itself. This encompasses both an awareness of the other four aggregates and the deep unconscious within each of us in which the seeds, or potential, for all the other aggregates reside. In Buddhist belief, when a seed is watered—by us or by someone or something outside ourselves—it will spring into consciousness, and for this reason we must continually strive to be aware of which seeds are being watered. Becoming attuned to this process means that we are able to take notice as feelings, perceptions, and mental formations arise, and this enables us to choose whether to put more energy into them or simply let them go as being unhelpful.

Sound complicated? It is and it isn't. Here's a simple example of an experience that might last half a minute but shows the interrelationship of the five *skandhas*. When we learn to look deeply we can see that all experience has these components.

As I'm coaching my client on the phone, I listen with my ears (form) after I ask a challenging question. The sensory input (sensation) is that of silence. In response to that silence on the line, a feeling of anxiety and tension arises within me (perception), immediately followed by an interpretation that I have pushed her too hard, and an impulse to jump in and rescue her by saying more (mental formations). But I'm also aware (consciousness) of my own tension and judgment, and so I make an intentional decision to sit quietly for a minute until the client can process the question.

This little drama transpires in seconds, yet when I slow down and pay attention I can begin to notice how the process works and consider its elements before I decide upon a course of action.

In this instance, when I pay attention I also notice that the feeling of tension subsides and is replaced by calm. When I hear my client respond to the question with a new insight, I feel energized and my mind decides that the question was productive; my picture of myself as an effective coach is validated. Another round of form, sensation, perception, mental formation, and consciousness!

All of the *skandhas* are linked and they are constantly shifting and moving through us. Such is the flow of life. None of it is permanent. All the skandhas are within us. They are temporary phenomena that arise and dissipate. Normally, when I'm busy, I don't notice these subtleties. When I am paying attention, they arise, are observed, and then easily pass. Nothing I can do can make them permanent.

It is a simple fact that our experience of life is entirely made up of these five *skandhas,* and that there is nothing permanent or solid about them. Though they form the basis of what we think we know, these seemingly fixed patterns are always shifting and changing. To see this is to begin to become mindful. This is what it means to pay attention: we expand our experience to study and appreciate the intricate components of which it is constructed.

Attachment and Aversion

The second set of Buddhist teachings that are relevant to the work of a coach concerns the nature of suffering. While Westerners tend to think of suffering in terms of an acute crisis of pain or sorrow, in the Buddhist sense suffering is a condition of life that originates with the Eight Worldly Influences.[6] These consist of four pairs of opposites that guide our actions and condition our behaviors and choices. One of each pair is something that we desire—these represent attachments. Balancing each attachment is something that we avoid—these represent aversions. Recognizing and letting go of these attachments and aversions is the key to ending suffering.

The four over-arching pairs that underlie the specific attachments and aversions we may develop as individuals are these.

- We are drawn toward pleasure and attached to finding it / we avoid pain.
- We seek material gain, trying to get what we want / we try to avoid losing what we have.
- We want to be known and respected / we have an intense dislike for shame, embarrassment, and loss of face.
- We are attached to praise and to being appreciated and even adored / we wish to avoid blame and responsibility for negative things.

These "worldly influences" are all around us, intensified by our social experiences. Advertisements condition us to crave cold beer, telling us that we will experience pleasure, even attract a mate, by drinking it. Employers and schools, through pay and grades, seek to motivate us by encouraging attachment to rewards and praise. We are taught that it is good to be effective in getting what we want—a good job, stability, creature comforts, a loving spouse—and to fear the loss of these things.

None of this is bad. It just is. The relevance of the Buddhist perspective is the ensuing recognition that our experience of life is often controlled by these attachments and aversions. We are attached to the aspects of each of these pairs that we label as positive; we crave them and pursue them. We have aversion, or resistance, to those aspects that we label as negative; we avoid them. But as hard as we work to get what we want and to avoid what we don't want, we can never know what any experience is going to bring us.

Many of us dream about becoming rich. A casual friend of mine won two million dollars in the lottery. He quit his job, moved to a new, upscale neighborhood, stopped seeing old friends, and started a small business, but he didn't put much energy into the new enterprise. It seemed that the challenge and energy had gone out of life. He drank a lot, and he died of a heart attack a few short years later. Enormous financial gain did not bring him happiness.

Another friend had breast cancer. She went through months and months of painful treatments, and suffered greatly from anxiety about her future. Now, fully recovered, she has an appreciation of all of life's gifts that most of us feel only occasionally. She is clear about what she wants to do and how not to waste her life energy. She is much happier than before. As desperately as she might have wanted to avoid having the experience of cancer, for her it became a doorway into a more fulfilling life.

We put much of our life energy into pursuing our attachments and seeking to avoid our aversions, yet all that expense of energy doesn't guarantee us happiness. This is because, according to the teachings of the Buddha, those very attachments and aversions are at the root of our suffering. As Lama Surya Das writes in *Awakening the Buddha Within,*

It's easy to become so enmeshed in our worldly goals that we lose sight of the bigger picture. Without more foresight and perspective, we cannot help but prioritize foolishly. The ups and downs of office politics and interpersonal dynamics, for example, will overly affect the untrained mind. One minute you can feel like a winner, elated and on top of your game; the next you're in a slump, defeated, hopeless, and depressed. Buddhism reminds us that nothing lasts, not even our successes or defeats.[7]

Attachments and aversions, according to Buddhist teaching, are both the objects and the triggers of our mental formations. They are products of our minds. There is nothing real about them. For instance, the comment "You look good today!" from another person could be interpreted as praise or as an offensive come-on, depending on our perceptions and mental formations about the circumstances. There is nothing inherently bad or good about the comment itself, yet it has the potential to affect us significantly because of what we project onto it. We often get tangled up in these projections, and when we do, in our quest to fulfill illusory desires or to avoid illusory discomforts, we may miss what's truly important.

Our attachment and aversions—and the mental formations they give rise to—condition and limit us, providing tracks that we fall into. They become wired into our consciousness as habits.

Let's try a little thought experiment. First, imagine something that's particularly inviting to you: the smell of freshly ground coffee, a hug from a loved one, or a favorite memory from childhood. Look for a tiny upwelling of desire, a tinge of want that arises as you call this experience to mind. It will be fleeting and subtle, but if you pay close enough attention, you'll likely feel a slight pull of desire being triggered by your imagining. This is attachment.

Now try the reverse. Imagine instead a repulsive smell, or an argument with a loved one, or an incident in which you were wronged.

Notice the feelings that arise—that's aversion. Again, it's subtle, but as you learn to watch your mind at work, you'll notice more and more how a brief thought (whether pleasant or unpleasant) will trigger fleeting emotions and impulses.

People committed to a path of mindfulness are working toward noticing and accepting these subtle phenomena. We don't need to "get rid of" any of our attachments or aversions; it is simply helpful to become aware of them and how they influence our actions. (And it's also important to remember that becoming aware of our habits of mind can lead us quickly to self-judgment and a whole new attachment—to self-improvement!)

In my invented scenario about coaching over the phone, for instance, noticing that I have some tension around my client's initial silence in response to a tough question is sufficient. I don't have to change anything. It certainly wouldn't be helpful right then to get into a tizzy about my tension, or to fight it, or to analyze where it comes from. None of that would help me be more present for my client in the moment. It's sufficient to simply notice the tension and see it for what it is—nothing but a temporary feeling that will pass as soon as I let it go. Seeing the *skandhas* at work is the whole point.

> We might feel that somehow we should try to eradicate these feelings of pleasure and pain, loss and gain, praise and blame, fame and disgrace. A more practical approach would be to get to know them, see how they hook us, see how they color our perception of reality, see how they aren't all that solid. Then the eight worldly [influences] become the means for growing wiser as well as kinder and more content.[8]

The smell of baking bread from the kitchen triggers my desire to eat. A passing thought of an old sweetheart triggers a moment of remorse or longing. The sight of my wife fills me with joy, and I think about how good it feels to hug her. A conversation with a coaching client triggers my desire to be seen as helpful or intelligent.

These thoughts and feelings arise from the seeds in our unconscious, watered by sensory input and perceptions. Over time, they solidify into patterns of attachments and aversions that are particular to individuals or to social groups. As we become aware of these habits of mind, we can make a choice as to whether they are helpful or not. We can choose to continue to "water" them, or we can choose to let them go.

In coaching, our role is to help our clients recognize and act on the real choices that are available to them—to see the limitations in their own thinking and move beyond them to new possibilities. To be helpful to our clients in this process, we must first learn to see our own limitations. We must become familiar with our own attachments and aversions, our own drives and cravings and fears.

In my practice, I've encountered what I'd call certain attachments and aversions that are specific to the coaching profession. I offer the list below so that you can consider which of them arise in you as you work with your clients, as a first step toward determining whether they are helpful or not.

- We want to be seen as competent by the client / we want to avoid being seen as ineffective or unhelpful.
- We value a personal connection with the client / we try to avoid tension or conflict in the relationship.
- We look for a sensation of aliveness and creativity / we are impatient with rote conversation.
- We like the security of coaching according to a specific template or model / we try to avoid being seen as uncertain.
- We want to earn additional fees or appreciation/ we fear being fired or taken for granted.

To the degree that our actions and behaviors are shaped by our own attachments and aversions, we are responding to our own desires to attain pleasure and avoid suffering rather than to the client's needs. By cultivating mindfulness we become better able to make wise choices about how we can best serve our clients.

Self-Observation and the Cultivation of Mindfulness

Over the past decades, mindfulness has become a much abused concept in pop psychology, various branches of what's called the human potential movement (including the coaching industry), and the intersecting realms of commerce and merchandising. "Live consciously," "go with the flow," "get in touch with your feelings," "let go and let God," and "live in the present" have become trite and sometimes empty catchphrases. Advertisements promise serenity and peace in the luxury of your new car, access to your inner creativity in the form of a computer, and an oasis from the busyness of life in an expensive resort. It seems that our fast and commercialized world now promises to sell us what the wisdom traditions of many cultures have taught for millennia is freely and instantly available to all!

True mindfulness, however, requires attention and effort. In the Buddhist tradition, being mindful means "to be aware of our bodies, aware of our feelings and emotions, aware of our thoughts, and aware of events, as they occur, moment by moment."[9] From a Western perspective, the definition of (being) "conscious" is remarkably similar: "having . . . knowledge of one's sensations, feelings, etc., or external things; aware of oneself as a thinking being; knowing what one is doing and why; . . . an awareness of what one is thinking, feeling, and doing."[10]

It sounds simple, but people spend a lifetime trying to learn to become mindful. We have all experienced moments of mindfulness, of course. Taking communion at church, the intimacy of looking into the eyes of a loved one, saying grace before dinner, being moved by the sight of a mountain, the joy of a child—being deeply conscious of what is happening at these moments is being mindful. In coaching, we might feel a surge of appreciation for our client, ask just the question the client needs, or jointly discover a new way of looking at the challenge he or she is facing. These moments happen, but usually the heightened awareness they evoke quickly slips away. Cultivating the ability to *stay* mindful is spiritual practice of the highest order, and it represents mastery in the habits of our own minds and emotions.

Self-observation—noticing our thoughts, emotions, and impulses as they arise, and thinking about their origins—is the key practice in mindfulness.[11]

Conditioning and Habits of Mind

As we grow up, become socialized, and learn to function in society, we learn certain patterns of thought and interpretation that seem to work for us. These patterns are as varied as the world's cultures, families, and individuals. Over time they become embedded in habits of mind: automatic ways of processing information, interpreting what we see and hear, and making decisions about how to respond to life's events. Like fingerprints, our individual patterns are unique, unlike anyone else's. In Western psychology we call the process that produces these patterns "conditioning." Our conditioning determines how we experience our lives, or, as a Buddhist might put it, gives shape to the ways in which the five *skandhas* express themselves in us.

Some of these habits of mind serve us well. They help us respond effectively to life's invitations and challenges. We even come to think of them as "good" traits of character. I grew up in a family of scientists. In part because of my early experiences, I have a boundless curiosity that impels me into learning and has led me to seek out opportunities for personal exploration and reflection that have made for a fascinating journey and have helped me succeed in my professional life.

However, some habits of mind that have served us in the past may at some point become limiting, even detrimental. Because they're habits, though, our mental energies continue to follow these established pathways in our minds, like a stream following a worn groove over bare rock. Meanwhile, like seeds stranded on the bank above, new ideas, new ways of thinking, and new possibilities for our lives fail to sprout for lack of water.

In my very intellectual family of origin, we communicated about ideas but not about feelings. Much went unsaid, and strong expressions of emotion were discouraged. Then, as an adult, I married a woman who is much freer with her feelings, whatever they might be and however they might come out. My conditioned response, instilled over years of living in an emotionally unexpressive family, had always been to either shut down or flee in the face of someone else's expression of intense emotion, especially anger.

In my marriage, this didn't work so well and I had to reconsider my habits of mind. When my wife is angry about something, I still have to work hard to stay present and to resist the urge to shut her off. She, in turn, works hard to address the source of her anger without overreacting. It requires mindfulness on both our parts to be aware of, and abandon, unhelpful habits and cultivate new behaviors in their place. In all realms of life, becoming aware of the opportunity to choose new behaviors over old ones is the essential challenge of growth.

This is not what we in the West label psychotherapy, as valuable as that endeavor might be for many people. We don't need to understand all the details of where our conditioned patterns came from, or of the early experiences that imprinted unhelpful habits in our minds. We can, in any moment, step beyond our patterned responses by simply becoming aware of them and seeing instead the multitude of alternatives that are available to us. It is a simple shift in perspective, an expanded view. This, in short, is what we seek to help our clients do through coaching.

We all have habits of perception and response that impede our ability to be mindful, and in my experience many fall into certain discrete categories that I've laid out for discussion below. I know there are a lot of them, so please read these sections lightly. (Later, in Chapter 13, we'll offer some exercises to help you develop your powers of self-observation.)

The purpose here is not to overwhelm you with a litany of obstacles to mindfulness, but to develop a language for talking about them. The simple act of recognizing how any one of these types of habits of mind influences you, and accepting it without judgment or self-flagellation, is a real moment of awakening. Read, inquire into the nature of your own mind, and smile with recognition whenever you see yourself reflected here.

Self-Judgment

Let's begin by looking at what we sometimes do when we become aware that we're behaving in a less than perfect way. For example, I might notice that I'm feeling easily distracted as I listen to my client talk about an emotional experience that he's had. I notice my attention wandering; my gaze drifts out the window. By noticing my distraction I have immediately become more self-aware; this brings me back to the present and provides an opportunity to listen more carefully.

Once I notice my distraction, however, I tend to scold myself. Little tapes go off in my mind: "A sensitive coach and mindfulness author isn't supposed to be distracted," "I'm being selfish," "I'm a lousy listener," etc., etc. This sort of self-judgment is, of course, rooted in my well-intentioned desire to measure up to some artificial standard of attentiveness I measure myself against. The tendency toward self-judgment is just another habit of mind, another groove my thoughts follow. The truth is, I was distracted for a moment—that's all. No big deal.

If I launch into self-judgment, I allow my attention to shift once again. Instead of ignoring my client because of the view from the window, I'm ignoring him because I'm wrapped up in my own inadequacy as a listener. Either way, I'm still not listening.

When we really pay close attention, we find that self-judgment is nothing more than the *skandhas* doing their little dance. In this case, self-judgment is simply another layer of my own conditioning, and it doesn't help me listen to my client any more than an interesting view out the window did. It's just a different habit of mind, and equally unhelpful.

The trick, then, is simply to notice your own habits as they arise. As they do so, just smile at them. Awareness and acceptance takes the energy out of these mental formations, and they lose their grip on us, and with it their capacity to make us suffer. Any additional energy that we put into fighting them, trying to get rid of them, or analyzing them takes us away from the present just as surely as any other distraction would do.

As you read through our descriptions of other habits of mind, watch for the ones that you might yourself engage in from time to time. When you recognize something that you might do, just smile at that awareness and take a breath. Watch for your own self-judgment as you recognize yourself. Practice the discipline of observing with a neutral mind and letting go of any self-judgment that arises.

Social Identity

Our habits of mind are often rooted in social identities that we seek to preserve or strengthen. James Flaherty explains social identity in terms of two components that interact with and reinforce each other.[12] The first is the image that people have of us, which shapes how they interact with us. Clients come to us, whether we are a manager in an organization or a paid coach, with certain expectations that we can help them. Knowing this, we are more likely to respond in a way that fulfills those expectations. The other side of the coin is the image we have of ourselves, the "story" of who we are that we believe to be true. Since this story gives our lives meaning and our ego an identity, we become attached to the story and seek evidence to support and reinforce it.

For example, I sometimes seek to protect and reinforce a social identity as a knowledgeable person with good ideas and information to share. This identity is reinforced by clients who pay me for those good ideas. My own conditioning leads me to avoid appearing stupid or lacking in knowledge. This isn't a bad thing, but it does present traps of which I need to be aware. It is easy for both my client and me to default to a narrow teacher/student relationship and thus limit our work together. If my energy is going into protecting or reinforcing a social identity, I am no longer fully available to my clients.

Any role can serve as a social identity. As Flaherty puts it, to the extent that our "relationship with others . . . has become hardened through a repetition of behavior and bound by the inflexibility of expectation," we become trapped in that role.[13] It quite literally becomes a worn groove in our consciousness: the role is a manifestation of the path of least resistance through the tangle of neurons in our brains. To change such a habit requires both mindfulness and discipline. While the client often colludes and reinforces habitual, unconscious behavior on the part of the coach, the responsibility falls on the coach to do her own work in recognizing the social identity she is attached to.

Projections

Above my desk I have a picture drawn by my daughter many years ago, when she was about seven. It's one of those elementary school drawings where you trace the outline of your hand, then decorate it to turn it into a Thanksgiving turkey. Megan, however, took the assignment in a slightly different direction and drew a lovely chicken. It's done on black paper and the sky is filled with little white stars and chicken footprints. The head of the chicken is looking up at the sky, and the title at the bottom says "Chickens like star gazing!!!!" I think this drawing is both hilarious and profound.

Just as we do, Megan's chicken sees herself in the universe. Where we might see a heroic Orion—a human being—with bow drawn, the chicken sees her own footprints in the stars. We look at the world through the filters of our experiences and then interpret what is going on out there in a way that affirms who we are and confirms the importance of our existence. This feels both gratifying and reassuring. But such projections are just a mental game we play, the *skandhas* at work in our minds. Nancy Spence, author of *Back to Basics: An Awareness Primer*, puts it this way:

> At the heart of understanding projection is accepting the awareness that we are experiencing the perceptions we have about people, events and situations. What we are seeing out there is what we are doing inside. *Accepting this awareness means accepting responsibility for how we react to others.* Sometimes it is not easy to acknowledge that the difficulty we have with others is only a reflection of the difficulty we have with some aspect of ourselves. Sometimes it is not easy or pleasant to recognize we are always looking into a mirror.[14]

We project on our clients in the same way, finding ourselves reflected in them. Those aspects that we judge and resist in others are likely to reflect traits that we also have difficulty accepting in ourselves. This is both a source of compassion and a source of trouble.

For example, I might be talking to a client about how overwhelmed she feels by her inability to focus on important planning issues in the face of a hundred emails a day in her inbox, each of which must at least be glanced at. I empathize with her because in the face of countless demands from consulting projects and other responsibilities, I find it difficult to find the time to write every day. But I also feel irritated and frustrated with her at times because of her seeming inability to prioritize in order to get things done. Not so coincidentally, those feelings are simply my projection onto my client of my own failure to make time for high priority tasks; they have nothing to do with my client and everything to do with me.

This kind of projection can be useful; if I can understand the frustration my client feels, this may help me to see possible ways for her to manage the challenges she faces. But projection can also cause trouble. Both the sense of comforting intimacy and the feelings of irritation that we experience when we see ourselves in our clients impede our clear view of the client. They can easily trigger our own attachments and aversions, unconsciously steering our coaching to seek the former and avoid the latter.

Projection also makes it all too easy to assume that what works for us will work for them—which may or may not be true. Further inquiry might uncover major differences between my situation and that of the client, differences that would point to different solutions. If I'm caught in my projection, the likelihood is that I'll quickly assume that I understand and so fall into a coaching approach that is based more on my own history and needs than on those of the client.

It's important to remember that when we're projecting, we're not seeing things as they are. We have become attached to an interpretation, a mental formation, that somehow affirms something about ourselves. When we confuse ourselves with a client we cease seeing that person and her situation as fresh and unique and are therefore no longer present and mindful.

Philosophical Positions

Belief systems and philosophical positions are part of our personality and identity, but they are also arbitrary and conditioned. And, just like other aspects of who we are, they shape how we express ourselves and limit our understanding.

For example, let's say that I believe that the answers to all of life's questions reside within the individual. There are ways in which this belief may serve the coaching process; it might, for instance, lead me to ask probing questions that will in fact help the client discover her own resourcefulness. At the same time, that belief, if rigidly adhered to as a philosophical position, may also prevent me from playing one of a coach's key roles, that of a teacher. I'm far less likely to share my own experience or suggest specific alternatives if I believe that the answers to a client's questions must always come from her own experience.

It behooves us all to become increasingly aware of the philosophical positions that we hold, and to be mindful of their implications.

Emotional Triggers

Certain stimuli trigger emotional responses. These are the *skand-has* again, arising and infusing our awareness so that we are no longer mindful and neutral. As coaches, when we get wrapped up in strong feelings and reactions we cease to be present with our clients.

For example, a client with whom I worked, whose job was at risk because of some quite ineffective leadership traits, tended to view himself as a victim. He insisted that he had been "set up" by people around him, who had focused on a few minor negatives and ignored the overwhelming positives. His persistent unwillingness to take ownership of any part of the problems he was having in the workplace made me feel frustrated, even angry with him at times, and it also triggered anxiety and self-doubt about my abilities as a coach. In this case, my emotional reactions made it a significant challenge for me to remain compassionate with this client and to continue to engage with him.

Although our emotions may provide information that's useful in the coaching process—in this case, my own reactions to my client's behavior eventually led me to be quite candid about which of those behaviors might be putting him at risk of being fired—a coach must be able to recognize his or her own feelings and must work to keep them from influencing the work that is being done with the client in inappropriate ways.

Routines

We all tend to get numbed by routine. I fly frequently on business. It is an enjoyable drive from my home through the mountains to the airport. One day, upon checking in at the counter, the agent politely informed me that I had the wrong ticket. I looked at it closely. Unfortunately, although the date, time, and destination matched, the flight—which I had booked myself—left from an entirely different airport, in the other direction from home and now three hours away. Clearly I hadn't been paying attention when I turned onto the main road. My wife still laughs at me about that one.

I take some small comfort in the fact that, as Ellen Langer reports in her book on mindfulness, "William James [told] a story of starting to get ready for a dinner party, undressing, washing, and then climbing into bed. Two routines that begin the same way got confused, and he mindlessly followed the more familiar one."[15]

Routines help us get things done, but they may also put us to sleep. Because it's easiest to stay in the worn groove, take the path of least resistance, we follow a habit without paying sufficient attention to whether it is taking us where we want to go.

As coaches, we tend to follow the same line of questioning, to fall into the same pattern of conversation with a client, time after time. But when coaching becomes routine we're at risk of not paying attention. We miss openings that the client gives us, nuances of tone or wording that may represent a breakthrough. Under the influence of an attachment to the illusion of being competent and comfortable, and an aversion to exerting the energy, or taking the risk, of trying something new, we fall asleep at the wheel.

To counter this tendency, ask yourself, How can I disrupt my routines? What can I do to help me see each coaching client and conversation in a fresh way?

Distractions

Most of the professionals I know are exceedingly busy. Interruptions are constant, and the time available to focus on a single task seems to decrease daily. The fragmentation of time and experience that's become a seemingly inescapable part of our lives makes it difficult to focus on important tasks, or to feel productive at the end of the day.

But while it appears that this is externally driven, and that we have no control over the distractions that plague us, closer scrutiny shows otherwise. Yes, there are external demands, but it's an internal reaction (those *skandhas* again!) that bids us to interrupt what we're doing to take that phone call, or get lost in our emails, or attend right now to whatever else is pulling at us in the moment. We can heed that voice or not; that's a choice. Neither choice is right or wrong, but each has consequences.

Internal distractibility is a habit I call busy mind. Busy mind is characterized by rapid and often unconnected thoughts, tangents, and ideas, and it results in a lack of focus. Our minds can process information a lot faster than conversation proceeds, for example. We are at choice, then, about how to use this extra mental capacity. A mindful choice is to focus our full attention on what we're doing rather than getting distracted by unrelated matters.

As coaches, it is up to us to train our minds to recognize distractions when they pull at us, and to bring our attention back to our clients and the work at hand.

Expert Mind

Just as routine can put us in a metaphorical sleep, so can the overconfidence that comes from expertise. Once we have achieved a certain level of mastery, it's easy to believe that we know how to do something. The most perilous stage for a teenage driver isn't the very beginning, when everything seems new and the driver is careful and attentive. Rather, it comes when she thinks she has it down; she's got her license, the state has anointed her a Driver, and she experiences long-awaited freedom. Then the risk is overconfidence; the driver doesn't know what she doesn't know.

As an alternative, Shunryu Suzuki suggests that we cultivate "beginner's mind." This is the quality of attention that results when we are seeking to learn something new, and it's the antithesis of the self-hypnotism that can result when we believe we have mastered something.

> In the beginner's mind there is no thought, "I have attained something." All self-centered thoughts limit our vast mind. When we have no thought of achievement, no thought of self, we are true beginners. Then we can really learn something.[16]

When we become attached to our own expertise—when we assume we have all the answers—we cease to pay careful attention. This puts us at risk for missing something important about a client or a situation.

In my own practice, for instance, I felt quite confident when a client named Ruth asked me to coach her in developing her delegation and management skills—after all, this was one of my areas of expertise. Since coaching by phone had always worked well for me, that's how I set up our relationship. It was only later, when she told me she had auditory processing difficulties, that I realized that this was one reason why we hadn't made any progress after several long-distance conversations. But by then she had made the decision to stop working with me, and I could hardly blame her for my own inattentiveness.

The mindfulness we lose when we are attached to our expertise can be regained when we let go of thinking we know it all. Beginner's mind serves us because we are more able to see what's in front of us with fresh eyes.

Observing Our Habits of Mind

Once we become conscious of our habits of mind, we can either embrace them as being helpful or let them go so that they no longer limit us. This is one of the keys to change, which is what we support our clients in achieving. But if we are to help them navigate this territory we must first explore it ourselves.

The following exercise is a variation on a traditional eating meditation, as described by Lama Surya Das.[17] It's an excellent experiment for noticing your own habits of mind at play. (Please note: It's hard to read the directions and perform the experiment at the same time. You could read the whole thing through and then turn your attention to the raisins, or you might make a tape of it to listen to or ask a friend to read it out loud as you do the exercise.)

Exercise 2.1: The Raisin Meditation

Eating meditation is a marvelous way of putting ourselves in touch with nowness. This simple meditation with raisins can also be used with individual nuts or even tangerine sections. Later you can practice with all kinds of food, from a bowl of cereal to a plate of lasagna.

The first time I did this eating meditation, it tried my patience to the limit. I was accustomed to eating raisins by the mouthful, not one at a time. But I discovered that the chewing meditation can really slow us down and make us more aware of compulsive behavior. It helps you notice how your mind and body works. It helps us cultivate mindfulness and awareness in more varied situations.

Start by taking three raisins in your right hand. . . . Sit down, make yourself comfortable. Look at the raisins. Look at them as if you have never seen a raisin before. Turn them over. . . . We're going to direct our total attention to these three raisins.

Pick up one raisin with your left hand. Examine it closely. Feel its texture. Notice its colors and whether it's dry or moist. Notice any old associations you may have with raisins, such as like or dislike, or indifference. Smell it. Bring it to your lips. Notice any feelings of anticipation you may have about eating it.

Are you in a hurry? Do you wish perhaps that you could pop all three raisins into your mouth? Just notice whatever comes up in relation to this tiny little dried grape. Take the raisin in your mouth and chew it as slowly, as meticulously, as carefully, and as conscientiously as possible. Taste the actual taste of the raisin, but don't swallow it. Keep chewing. Notice how much you feel like swallowing. There is an impulse to swallow and get another one, but just keep chewing. Chew on that raisin until it becomes raisin juice. Chew and pay attention.

Exercise 2.1: The Raisin Meditation (cont'd)

If your mind wanders, if you hear a sound, bring your mind back to the raisin. Don't look around. Place your attention back on chewing the raisin. Point your mind, direct your attention, focus your awareness intently, intensely—like a light beam, like a laser beam. One-pointedly, focus on the raisin, on the place where your teeth make contact with the raisin; feel it directly. No need to understand why or how or what is the meaning of raisins, or meditation or of life for that matter. Just chew the raisin twenty or even one hundred times if possible, concentrating totally. Relax and enjoy the experience. Get the most out of it, as if this is the only food you're going to have all day. Chew it totally, appreciating and absorbing everything about it. Through total attention, extract the essence of every aspect of it—the taste, texture, and so on. Just keep chewing the raisin. Swallow it, and then just rest in the afterglow of this delicious experience.

Now slowly take the second raisin from your right hand with your left and bring it up toward your mouth. Look at it. Smell it. Feel it. Examine it. Resist the impulse to rush it into your mouth. Simply notice those impulses. Then put it in your mouth and start chewing it. . . . We see how long we can make it last. Simply pay attention to chewing the raisin while letting go of everything else. This stabilizes and unifies our mind. Just doing what we are doing, for a change. One hundred percent. Just sitting, and just eating. How delightful! How delicious.

Now you take the third raisin and do your own meditation on it. A new raisin, a new experience. How is it different from the other two? Does it look the same? Does it taste the same? Maybe it's sweeter. Maybe less startling. Where did your attention go? Bring it back. Concentrate.

This is a pragmatic example of meditation practice. We master meditative awareness by doing it again and again. It's always different, it's always fresh, it always develops and reveals new discoveries. We are exercising the muscles of awareness, directing our attention to precisely what we are doing.

When we chew our raisin, we are learning to thoroughly and meticulously chew over whatever task we happen to have at hand. In this way we learn to mingle mindfulness and concentrated awareness with daily life.

This exercise provides us the opportunity to notice what arises as we try to maintain mindfulness on one simple task. We may experience desire, or our aversion to raisins. If we pay close attention, we may notice a subtle impetus to eat them fast, or the impetus to spit them out. We may experience our distractibility, or boredom, or sheer pleasure, or resistance to this silly exercise, or a desire to keep doing the one thing we're doing. We may realize that millions of years of evolution and months of sunshine on grape vines in California went into creating this single raisin and giving us this delicious experience! The range of possible responses to such a simple practice is astounding. I've done this meditation with groups in workshops, and find that people are consistently surprised by what they can see clearly arising in their minds as they "chew the raisin."

This, of course, is the point. When we focus on something so simple, everything else appears in stark relief. All that other stuff is there all the time anyway, it's just that we rarely see it so clearly. Learning to be conscious and appreciative of how our own minds work is essential to becoming effective and authentic as coaches. When we coach, our coaching becomes the raisin, the object of our total focus and awareness.

Basic Tools for Cultivating Mindfulness

There are a vast number of specific tools and approaches for cultivating your own mindfulness. Conversations with your friends and colleagues, a quick search on the Internet, or a tour through the self-help and spirituality sections of a good bookstore will turn up any number of resources on the topic. (Some of these are listed in the back of this book.) You must discern for yourself which writers, teachers, or programs are useful. Do some research and try things out, but pursue only what both seems authentic and speaks to you.

At the same time, remember that mindfulness is not an esoteric pursuit, and help in attaining it can be found in many contexts—in everyday activities as well as self-help books and religious or philosophical texts. Here are four simple things you can do that may help you become more aware of yourself and your habits of mind while learning to be more focused and attentive to the moment. Cultivating mindfulness in any area of your life will be helpful in others.

Meditation. There are many forms of meditation, some secular and some connected with specific religious practices.[18] At its most basic, meditation involves sitting still, focusing on your breathing or a symbolic object, noticing the thoughts, images, and feelings that arise, then letting them go to come back to the object of meditation. As Western scientists are documenting in their most recent studies, meditation has physiological as well as psychological benefits.[19]

Exercise 2.2 is a simple breathing meditation in the form of a poem from Thich Nhat Hanh.

Exercise 2.2: A Breathing Meditation

Recite this to yourself as you breathe in and out, synchronizing it with your breath and gradually slowing your breathing down. You can do this before a coaching session. It's a great thirty-second way to become more mindful and present.

> Breathing in, I know I'm breathing in.
> Breathing out, I know
> as the in-breath grows deep
> the out-breath grows slow.
> Breathing in makes me calm.
> Breathing out brings ease.
> With the in-breath, I smile.
> With the out-breath, I release.
> Breathing in, there is only the present moment.
> Breathing out, it is a wonderful moment. [20]

Reciting this poem verbatim isn't important. Paying attention to your breath as you speak the words, and synchronizing them, is. After a little practice it can be abbreviated to "In, Out / Deep, Slow / Calm, Ease / Smile, Peace / Present moment, Wonderful moment." You *can* try this at home!

Sports and physical activity. I've been told that I'm old enough to have to take physical exercise really seriously and young enough to still be in denial about it! Yoga, jogging, dancing, walking—all of these are great stress relievers, get the blood circulating, and help us get out of our heads and into our bodies. Sports like golf, tennis, and skiing require a balance between a focus on technique and a relaxed, concentrated mind. All sports have a mindfulness aspect that's been called the "inner game."[21] (Basketball coach Phil Jackson of the NBA knew this when he taught his Chicago Bulls mindfulness techniques on their way to becoming a dynasty in the 1990s, winning seven championships.)

Physical activity provides a complete set of sensations to be aware of. Try to become conscious of your body, where it needs attention, where it feels good, what it's asking for. Practicing body awareness will also help you tune in to your own physical reactions as you're coaching, and to your client's body language as well; if you pay attention to them, these cues can alert you to your own emotional reactions, or to something that's going on with your client.

Nurturing creativity. All people are creative, but in our society we may not have been encouraged to explore this aspect of ourselves since kindergarten. The process of being expressive in some sort of physical activity—music, painting, pottery, metal fabrication, etc.—is simply a discovery of another realm of your inherent intelligence. Yes, it comes more easily to some than others, but it's available to all of us. If you already have such an outlet, pursue it and seek to become more aware of your own creative process as you do so. If you don't, find a way to tap into this realm: dance lessons, a poetry or singing class, wood-working, gardening.

Using your breath, your hands, or your body to create something in the physical world exercises parts of the brain that aren't usually activated by "knowledge work" or the routine tasks that so many of us do for a living.[22] Also, you are nearly certain to get in touch with your own attachments to "being good at it": more conditioning to let go of on the path to mindfulness.

Spending time outdoors. Natural settings put everything into perspective. There is an order in nature that is beyond us. The natural world can be experienced as dangerous or unpredictable, or as bountiful and benign, depending on one's relationship to it. But its vastness and variety—even today, when the influence of human beings threatens to disrupt its rhythms—can be restorative for someone who spends lots of time in an artificial environment, being frazzled and pulled in multiple directions by purely human concerns.

I'm lucky enough to live on sixty-three acres in the mountains of North Carolina. After a walk to the river and back I'm a different person. Of course I can fuss and obsess in the woods just as easily as I can in my office, but out there it's more obvious that it's my mind that's producing that activity rather than the environment. At the same time, the physical activity and the beauty of what I see all around me serve to reduce mental chatter and bring me into the present. Most of us can find places to walk among trees or along moving water; those who can't might bring stones or plants or other reminders of the natural world into their environment.

Summary

Mindfulness is the state of being aware of our own perceptions, thoughts, feelings, and judgments. As we become more self-aware, we learn to identify and acknowledge our own habits of mind and so prevent ourselves from becoming trapped by them; as we see and accept them, they tend to dissipate, giving us a clearer view of what is around us.

This heightened consciousness provides the best platform from which to coach others. It is unbiased by our own agendas. It allows us to be aware of the nuances of what the client brings. It is open, spacious, and accepting. This is what we cultivate through our own mindfulness practices.

CHAPTER THREE

Service

*No ray of sunshine is ever lost. But the green which it
awakens into existence needs time to sprout, and it
is not always granted for the sower to see the harvest.
All work that is worth anything is done in faith.*
ALBERT SCHWEITZER

I will act as though what I do makes a difference.
WILLIAM JAMES

*C*oaching—whether you do it as a professional coach with a client, a
manager with an employee, a teacher with a student, or a health care
worker with a patient—means placing yourself in service to another.
The underlying ethic guiding the performance of this service is that it is
done consciously, with self-awareness, and for the benefit of the client.

Much is done in the name of service. Some is not so helpful; some is
even arrogance disguised as help for others. True service means discerning and providing what is needed. This requires a high level of commitment and care.

The coach represents, and stands for, the client's higher potential. As coaches, we can sometimes see the possibilities for a client's

success more clearly than he can. It is true service to believe in someone's potential and encourage him to realize it, to help him set goals and develop strategies for achieving those goals. It is also true service to help a client acknowledge his limitations, help him work to overcome them, and accept him fully even when he can't bring himself to take the plunge into change.

Inevitably, agendas other than those of the client will influence the coaching relationship. As we discussed in more detail in Chapter 1, a coach wants/needs to feel and be seen as competent and effective, to earn fees, to get positive evaluations and/or referrals. In addition, third parties may affect both the content and duration of the coaching.

Placing oneself in service as a coach means making a clear decision that, while those considerations may come into play, they are secondary to providing what the client needs. Coach and client need to reach an agreement that works for both parties about the parameters of their relationship, including logistical arrangements, mutual responsibilities, fees, and systemic constraints. Above all, the coach must be able to respect and support the outcomes that the client seeks.

It should be noted that these parameters and issues may need to be revisited from time to time. Sometimes the nature of the coaching process changes to such an extent that parts of the initial agreement no longer apply. In that case, a renegotiation is in order. Bottom line, the relationship must be structured so that both parties feel that their underlying needs are being met. For the coach, this is key to being able to serve.

Placing Oneself in Service

The importance of mindfulness in serving cannot be overstated. The mindful coach knows, from his awareness of his own feelings and thoughts, when he is serving the client and when not. He knows if his personal agendas and judgments are in the way, and what to do with them if they are. He is able to be mindfully present with the client, and to listen and respond clearly, with acceptance, and without judgment. Mindfulness is essential to service.

To place oneself in service is a noble thing. It does not involve being subservient or putting oneself in a "lesser than" position in relation to the other. It is, rather, a dedication, a clear commitment to attend primarily to the client's needs for the time being. This is what allows coaching to happen.

Nor does being in service mean that we soft-peddle tough feedback, or dance around difficult issues—as coaches, we must sometimes participate in emotionally challenging conversations or tell our clients things that are hard for them to hear. It does mean that when we do so, we do it mindfully. We first check out what's going on for us, what needs have arisen in ourselves in response to a given situation. Only then can we speak directly, clearly, and compassionately.

If we're angry, for instance, we must ask ourselves what part of that anger comes from our own emotional baggage and what part has to do with the client. Letting our emotions go unexamined may be easier for us, but it won't serve the client. On the other hand, it may be very useful to describe how the client's behavior affects us—to say that we notice our anger arising, for instance—and to make the connection explicit between our experience and the client's learning process. If we do so, however, it must be by choice and in recognition that in this particular instance it may be helpful for the client to recognize how his behavior may affect others.

One choice is acting out our own conditioning; the second is providing difficult feedback compassionately. The difference is self-awareness.

The act of placing yourself in service is a powerful catalyst for self-awareness, because as soon as we place our needs off-limits they'll drive us crazy. If you don't believe this, try going on a sugar-free diet for a week. Or giving up coffee, if you're a coffee drinker. Or stopping just about anything that is habitual. All of a sudden, you *really* want that thing—whatever it is!

If we've become accustomed to drinking coffee to give us a little boost of energy, the desire for caffeine is an attachment that arises whenever there's an opportunity to energize our brain chemistry or, perhaps even more ferociously, when coffee is denied to us. But we can become as addicted to certain habits of mind as we are to certain foods or substances. The same attachments and aversions arise in the *skandhas* when our habits of mind are challenged.

To place oneself in service, then, is to sign on to a curriculum for self-awareness. Learning self-awareness—learning to notice and suspend one's own addictions, habits, and conditioning—is a primary requirement for being an effective coach. But it works both ways: the client benefits from being served well and the coach benefits from learning to be of service, from learning the discipline of true mindfulness.

Staying Mindful and Present

In Part 2 of this book we'll take a deeper look at the coaching process by discussing the seven roles a coach plays with a client—the Voices, if you will, in which the coach speaks at different times—and in Part 3 we'll offer a series of exercises linked to those Voices that will help you develop your self-awareness skills as a coach. First, as a bridge between the general and the specific, let's consider some basic practices for cultivating mindfulness and presence in a professional context: essential requirements for service.

Looking deeply. This is the process of "sitting with" something particularly troubling that comes up in your awareness—an emotion, a confusion, a dilemma that doesn't just go away when you recognize it. Most of us, when confronted with something painful or a difficult problem to be solved, move quickly to try to eradicate our discomfort as soon as possible. Looking deeply means probing a bit further, expanding that recognition so that we can get beyond our initial reaction to go for a "band-aid" solution.

One well-known tool for doing this is called the Five Whys.[23] When you are troubled by a situation or problem, simply ask yourself "Why am I troubled?"—but don't be satisfied with your first answer. Look at that answer and ask "Why is *that* so?" Repeat the process again until you've asked "Why" five times. Five is just an arbitrary number, of course, but each question-and-answer cycle moves you further toward getting to the root of the situation you're investigating. The goal, of course, is to come to a place of acceptance by understanding the true nature of the difficulty.

Letting go. This is a central tool for mindfulness. Letting go follows awareness. When we notice that we really want our client to do such-and-such, we need to ask ourselves why, and if we see that this is the result of our own attachments, we need to let go of that particular agenda. Letting go is a simple decision to not invest any more energy into something. It's different from actively pushing away a thought or an urge; it really means fully accepting the thought, then moving on. It's a matter of recognizing it as simply a creation of our conditioned mind, and then letting it dissipate.

Breathing consciously. The breath is the most available tool for mindfulness there is. We're never far from a breath, and our breathing patterns reflect our bodies and our emotions. When our parents used to tell us to take a deep breath and count to ten before acting when we're angry or upset, they were instructing us in mindfulness. What they didn't say is that if you have the presence of mind to remember to take deep breaths, the work is already half done: you have already noticed that you're angry, which requires being able to step away and observe yourself. That self-awareness is at the core of mindfulness.

Centering yourself. Find a practice that works for you to center yourself, a short set of steps to take that focus your attention and bring you into the present. For example, before a coaching appointment, I do the breathing practice outlined in Exercise 2.2. Then I take a few minutes to look through the client's file and create a plan for the session. Or, before I write, I light a candle, then stand straight and breathe deeply a few times. Both practices ground me in the present moment and in my body. Then, when I move into the activity I'm about to begin, I am ready and open and mindful.

There are many centering practices. Experiment to find what works for you, then make a habit of it (see Exercise 3, and Exercise 13.1). If it begins to get rote and ineffective, then change the practice. Pay attention to yourself and find something that works.

Exercise 3 asks you to consider what enables you to be present, working from your past experiences. Expanding from this, you can explore practices that can help you be more centered and mindful in situations where you are coaching. I encourage you to make this an ongoing process of experimentation to discover what works best for you.

Exercise 3: When Are You Most Present?

1. Do the basic breathing meditation (Exercise 2.2) or use any other method that works to get yourself centered and present.

2. Consider the times and places in your life when you feel most in the moment—most alive and aware of what's going on within you and around you. Don't work at it, just let them come to you.

3. Then put pen to paper to answer the following questions:

   • When have you felt most present and aware of the moment?

   • What do you think contributed to this heightened awareness in each case?

   • What might you do before and/or during a coaching session to awaken and maintain your full attention and mindfulness?

Cultivating an observer mind. As we practice self-observation, we become aware of two kinds of conscious experience, an active one and an observing one. It's as if your consciousness has two parts. The first part is the one who acts, who does whatever you're doing in the world. The second is the observer mind; this is the part who watches. For example, notice that as you are reading this paragraph you can also observe yourself in the act of reading.

In the second part of the book, we shall see that our ability to recognize and shift between key coaching roles depends upon our capacity for self-observation; developing that capacity is the point of many of the exercises that are found in the third part of the book. But you can practice self-observation at any time. Right now there's a part of my mind that is typing the words you will be reading in a different "now." There's another part that sees me typing and is also aware of the rain falling outside, the bright green of new spring leaves, and the feeling of energy that runs through me. Awareness of both of these parts simultaneously helps bring us fully into the present. Cultivate that awareness and try to bring it into your practice as a coach.

Coaching is an action-oriented learning process for the client. It should be for the coach as well. The best thing you can do for your clients is to develop yourself. Although you can always add new tools and techniques, your ability to be mindfully present is at the core of how you serve. Focusing on this should be central to your development as a coach.

There are landmarks in the territory of mindfulness. Look for these as indicators of your level of presence and use them as data points to track how well you are meeting your client's needs. Here are some examples.

- Pay attention to your energy level. Notice if you feel a charge, or a surge of energy, as you begin to talk with your client about a given issue. That good feeling may signal a moment of mutual discovery, or it may be the result of your own identity being fed. Ask yourself, "What am I getting out of telling the client this? Whose need is really being met?"
- Conversely, if you feel tired and drained during the course of a coaching conversation, ask yourself what's going on. Perhaps you're following a well-worn groove and there's nothing new or of interest to animate the coaching conversation. Perhaps you feel drained because there's an identity of yours that's not being fed, or

the client is seeking to pull you into a role that you don't want to play. A lack of energy is a clue to look inward, see what's going on, and come back to the client with a new mindfulness.

- Notice the client's energy level as well. When you give a piece of feedback or provide an interpretive framework that's a good fit, he or she will feel energized, ready to take the next step. On the other hand, if the client's energy seems low, that may be an indication that he or she is getting bogged down, that you might need to take another tack.
- Check in with the client often to see if the conversation is on track. Make it clear that it's your job to be attentive to his or her needs as they are emerging.
- Pay attention to any suspicion that you are being pulled into the same role over and over again. There may be a need in the client that seeks to keep you in that particular role, but if your dialogue is continually forced into the same narrowly defined channels, chances are your progress with that client will be limited.
- Watch for the word "should," as in "I should explain this to my client," "I should formulate a question to probe that," "She should already know how to do this," etc. "Should" connotes a position or a standard. It may represent a voice that you carry, the representative of a philosophical position that may or may not be helpful. If you notice a "should," take a breath and consider where it comes from and whether or not it's serving your client's needs.

The Coach as Learner

Coaching is a practice field, one in which the mindful coach also learns and grows. We study ourselves, constantly and gently seeking to become better at what we do.

Although it has its dangers, one of the wonderful things about coaching is what we learn from seeing ourselves in our clients. I recall discussing this with a man I'll call Marty, a highly capable engineering director. Brilliant, tenacious, and likeable, Marty grew up in a hard-scrabble working-class environment and was the first in his family to go to college. In spite of his obvious competence and the respect he had earned from everyone on his management team, he still suffered from bouts of acute insecurity, usually triggered by stress. When this habit of mind closed in on him, he often interpreted the innocent gestures of others as reflecting a lack of confidence in him. This made for more stress, which in turn made him more sensitive. He still functioned well, but he wasn't having much fun.

The experience of coaching Marty shed light on my own internal dynamics. As the son of two Ph.D.s who grew up in an academic environment, I often felt I wasn't smart enough. When insecure, I can get tense and sensitive to the cues that tell me what others think about my ideas. In other words, it was easy to project and see myself reflected in Marty, and that taught me something about myself.

Here's the rub. While we seek to be compassionate and empathetic with our clients, while we learn as much from them as they learn from us, we must remember that if we are to serve them well we need to keep the focus on their needs, not ours. If I can stay mindful, a resonance of experience with a client like Marty will lead to compassion, insight into possible practices that might lighten his load, and self-awareness about how I myself might grow. If I'm not mindful, the similarities between us may cause me to ignore the differences, or to unconsciously assume that strategies that work for me will work for him. Finally, the recognition of similarities can be the impetus that gets me to do my own work, but I need to remember to do it outside my professional relationship with a client.

I strongly recommend that, if you want to coach others, you be coached yourself. There's no substitute for the support and insight of a seasoned professional with whom you share common language and goals. Furthermore, the experience of being a client will teach you a great deal about resistance and motivation, give you a gut feel for the dynamics of change, and help you learn how to coach others with sensitivity and integrity.

Accountability and Professional Ethics

I have worked with some of my clients for years, and I know that the coaching has been valuable to them, but there have also been periods when we didn't seem to be accomplishing much. I could reassure myself by saying, "Well, So-and-so seems to be happy, so she must be getting what she needs," but while the absence of client complaints can be comforting, it's not the best indicator that good coaching is taking place. In truth, there have been times when a client and I were both, each for our own reasons, just going through the motions.

Because this kind of subtle collusion can sneak into the relationship, true service requires that although we recognize that the process of change can sometimes slow to a crawl, we build a certain rigorous accountability into our agreements with our clients.

Accountability means doing the following.

- Together with the client, we define the goals of the coaching in measurable ways, and we commit ourselves to helping the client achieve them.
- We specifically state that the coaching relationship can be ended or renegotiated at any time; we ensure that the client will feel at ease to say, "This isn't working for me," or, "I think I'm done for now."
- We make the coaching process explicit, and share as much about how we coach as our clients are ready for. This is part of helping them learn to coach themselves.
- We ask for feedback from our clients about how we are doing as coaches. This can be done informally, as in asking the client what's working and what isn't as the relationship develops. It can also be

done formally with an assessment system that allows a coach to elicit very specific feedback from his or her clients.[24]

- We understand clearly that the end result of our coaching will be that the client no longer needs us. We accept this from the outset and we make it explicit.

It is the coach's responsibility to weave these principles into the fabric of the coaching relationship. The process of doing so reminds us that we have placed ourselves in service to the client, and sends a strong message about what we stand for and the extent to which we can be trusted to look out for the client's best interests.

The International Coach Federation has published a set of ethical guidelines for the coaching profession to which its members commit to adhere. Whether or not you are a professional coach, many of these guidelines will apply to you, whatever the coaching venue may be. Coming from a leading organization in the industry, the ICF's ethical guidelines represent the definitive statement for the profession as of this writing. Making these available to our clients is one way to bring these issues up for discussion and thus ensure our accountability to them. The following are the ICF Standards of Ethical Conduct most relevant to the context of this book.

The ICF Standards of Ethical Conduct

2. I will honor agreements I make in my all of my relationships. I will construct clear agreements with my clients that may include confidentiality, progress reports, and other particulars.

6. I will accurately identify my level of coaching competence and I will not overstate my qualifications, expertise or experience as a coach.

7. I will ensure that my coaching client understands the nature of coaching and the terms of the coaching agreement between us.

8. I will not intentionally mislead or make false claims about what my client will receive from the coaching process or from me as their coach.

9. I will not give my clients or any prospective clients information or advice I know to be misleading or beyond my competence.

10. I will be alert to noticing when my client is no longer benefiting from our coaching relationship and would be better served by another coach or by another resource and, at that time, I will encourage my client to make that change.

11. I will respect the confidentiality of my client's information, except as otherwise authorized by my client, or as required by law.

12. I will obtain agreement with my clients before releasing their names as clients or references or any other client identifying information.

13. I will obtain agreement with the person being coached before releasing information to another person compensating me.

14. I will seek to avoid conflicts between my interests and the interests of my clients.

15. Whenever any actual conflict of interest or the potential for a conflict of interest arises, I will openly disclose it and fully discuss with my client how to deal with it in whatever way best serves my client.

16. I will disclose to my client all anticipated compensation from third parties that I may receive for referrals or advice concerning that client.[25]

Summary

In this chapter, we explored the notion of service and what it means to "place oneself in service" to a client. Above all, it means doing the work to ensure that the coaching relationship is set up so that the needs of both parties will be met and it remains absolutely clear that the client's development comes first.

Placing oneself in service requires mindfulness. A coach needs to maintain a relaxed and clear awareness of what is going on within her own mind and body in relation to the client and the coaching process. By being self-observant, she is able to notice her own attachments, aversions, judgments, and needs arising, deal with them appropriately, and then come back to a focus on the client. Serving makes it necessary to be mindful; being mindful makes it possible to serve.

Building accountability to the client into the partnership demonstrates our commitment to service and helps ensure that we will honor that commitment.

PART

2

THE SEPTET

CHAPTER FOUR

Overview

> *The map is not the territory.*
> ALFRED KORZYBSKI

> *What we play is life.*
> LOUIS ARMSTRONG

A septet, in music, is a group of seven musicians playing together. The Septet in this book consists of seven integrated roles that we take on as we coach. These Voices, as we are calling them, are those of the Master, the Partner, the Investigator, the Reflector, the Teacher, the Guide, and the Contractor.

In this overview chapter, I'll share the origins and purpose of the Septet framework, present a brief overview of each Voice, and offer some suggestions about what this model might mean for you in whatever venue you serve as a coach. The following chapters in this part of the book will be dedicated to the exploration of each of these Voices in depth.

This model is an artificial construct for helping us look at what, precisely, we do as coaches. Please read these chapters carefully but not obsessively; what's presented in them is intended as a framework for examining yourself in the coaching process rather than as a flow-chart to be followed to the letter. In Part 3 we'll put all the pieces back together and offer strategies and exercises for maintaining or improving your coaching skills.

It should be noted that the Septet Coaching Model is derived from my own quarter-century of professional experience with change; although mindfulness and self-observation are central to my approach to coaching, the model itself is not part of any historical mindfulness tradition.

Introducing the Septet

The Septet Model is an architecture for seeing the coaching process more clearly, and for becoming aware of the roles that coaches play in helping situations, professional and otherwise. If you are mindful in using the Voices, and consciously choose between them as you help others develop their own skills, your coaching will be enhanced. Think of the Septet as a structure to guide your own inquiry into what it means to you to be a coach.

The Voices represent the seven essential roles that a coach plays. Think of them as instruments; each has its own tone and way of expressing itself, its own place in the music. When we're in tune with our clients, when our own conditioned patterns are set aside and we are fully present, we are able to choose the Voice that's most appropriate and most helpful at a particular time. In practice, we will often shift quickly and fluidly between Voices, both shaping and responding to a dynamic, ever-changing conversation.

The Voices of the Septet are like the musicians in a jazz band. There's a basic, agreed-upon structure to a jazz tune, yet as the musicians improvise—listening and responding to what is emerging in the moment—one or another steps forward to take the lead. The same piece of music is never played identically twice. Improvisation, spontaneity, and an interplay between the members of the band assures that the music is fresh and alive, a reflection of a unique moment in time.

This takes both practice and mindfulness.

Stages of Learning

To switch metaphors for a moment, you could consider the Voices— roles you play as a coach—as being like the skills you learn in order to drive a car. In learning to drive, we begin with the mechanics. We learn the pieces, one skill at a time. We learn how to start the car, how to use the accelerator and the brakes, how much of a turn of the steering wheel produces what result. Then we begin to integrate the skills together, accelerating, braking, and steering as we navigate the landscape.We learn the rules of the road and what to expect from other drivers. With practice and attention, we become smoother and smoother. Soon we don't need to think about the turn signal, the windshield wipers, the transmission, we just know how to use them. It feels smooth and seamless because we've internalized the skills involved.

But driving is an activity that requires full attention, even at high levels of mastery. The best drivers are always alert; while they rarely think about the mechanics of driving, they're fully aware of what they're doing at all times. They're attentive to the performance of the car, to the road, to the changing positions of the cars around them, making countless minor decisions intuitively and easily as they seek the best and safest possible course through the traffic. (A short safety aside: While some people are able to drive and use a cell phone at the same time, statistics suggest that they're deluding themselves if they think this doesn't affect their ability to be mindful drivers!)

Like learning to drive a car, using the Septet Model may seem awkward and complicated at first, as you focus on one Voice at a time, seeking to understand what it means, how you do this role in your own context. You may feel self-conscious when you try a Voice that's not already in your repertoire, and it can certainly feel overwhelming to think of mastering all of them.

Over time, however, you'll become more comfortable and less self-conscious. When we've practiced and done our work around each of the roles, we come to know how and when to be the Investigator, the Reflector, or the Teacher, for instance, and how to notice when we're not doing it mindfully. We learn to shift smoothly and seamlessly between the Voices. We become more fluid and less concerned about the distinctions between the roles as we learn to integrate them, sometimes playing two or three in rapid succession.

At this point, it will be important to avoid becoming over-confident, thinking "I've mastered this." When we feel on top of our game, the temptation is to forget to be mindful. The moment we become attached to the idea that we know it all, we stop learning and paying attention. Our egos are invested in being good at one thing, and we seek to present ourselves to our clients as being good at it all. It is only by persisting, by noticing our lapses of attention, maintaining the alertness of a beginner, and bringing attention to our areas of incompetence, that we continue to stay present and to grow.

We must remember that there is always room to deepen our understanding of our own attachments, aversions, and habits of mind, and that learning how to bring our full attention skillfully to our clients is a life-long process. This is the place from which we can become truly mindful coaches, by continually seeing ourselves as learners.

A note to the perfectionists out there: learning to use this system will be much easier if you don't take it too seriously. By this I mean as you experiment with it, remember that it's only a construct. Be gentle with yourself as you try things out. See what happens; the work here is to discover what enables you to improve your skills and effectiveness.

Getting all tangled up in using a complex system perfectly will interfere with your learning process *and* make it much less fun. Let your curiosity and intelligence guide you, rather than holding yourself to an artificial and perhaps impossible standard for "getting it" quickly. Cultivate your own beginner's mind.

The Septet Model will have served its purpose when we can look back at a coaching session, see how we moved easily into each Voice as it was needed, know that we offered the fullness of ourselves as expressed in all the Voices, and didn't have to think about it.

An Overview of the Voices

The idea for the Voices originated with a client, Scott Ziemer, who was exploring the possibility of moving into coaching as a profession. In an effort to define for himself what coaching was all about, Scott came up with a list of seven roles that a coach plays, which we spent time discussing together. The roles (and the distinctions between them) have changed considerably as I've continued this line of work, and were known as the Seven Hats for years before they came together to form a Septet. But the basic ideas that emerged from my conversations with Scott provided a new and useful language for discussing the nature of coaching.

Here's a rough sketch of the seven Voices and the tasks or responsibilities—parts of the whole process—they represent.

- Master (the coordinator): staying self-aware, modeling growth and learning, being fully present
- Partner: defining, negotiating, and sharing responsibility for the coaching relationship with the client
- Investigator (the question asker): finding out what the client's true needs are, gathering information about the client's situation and desired outcomes

- Reflector: providing feedback and encouraging self-awareness in the client
- Teacher: providing information, language, and tools for addressing issues and problems
- Guide: providing impetus and ideas for action
- Contractor: encouraging mutual accountability, monitoring client follow-through.

Let's look at each of these in sequence.

The Master is the overarching role that encompasses and supports all the others. The Master is the ground from which the others spring.

Please recall from the "Language" section of the introduction to this book that I am using the term "master" with full awareness that it carries patriarchal connotations for some. I reiterate here that I intend it as an inclusive, gender-neutral term for a person with great skill, an adept, an artist, one who has attained a high level of discernment and competence, or a controller in a neutral sense—and it is to tap into all of these latter (newer) meanings, as no other word can do, that I am using it. If the word "master" carries patriarchal baggage in your mind, you are invited to shed that baggage for the time being and let the newer, more inclusive meanings of the word take precedence. After all, many words have multiple meanings; which is operative at a given time depends upon context, and the context here is inclusive and egalitarian.

A master, then, is one who has done the inner work of knowing herself and developing the capacity to use her skills wisely, artfully, and effectively. These meanings of the word are central to the Septet Model of coaching, in which the Master represents the quality of the coach being present and aware. The Master is the observant, conscious part of the mind that discerns what the client needs, when to shift roles in order to move with those needs, and how to stay present and as free as possible from the limitations of our own conditioning. Like the conductor of an orchestra, the Master pays attention to the whole, and shapes the tempo and feeling of the music being played, even when other Voices are being heard.

The six "operational" Voices—Partner, Investigator, Reflector, Teacher, Guide, and Contractor—represent more specific elements of coaching, and are identifiable by actions and choices of words. I hasten to add that we're not in the business of creating multiple personalities. There are times when two roles might be played simultaneously, and lots of areas where the lines between them blur; there's some overlap, for instance, between the Partner and the Contractor, the Teacher and the Guide. For the sake of our inquiry, however, for now we'll assume that these Voices are distinct. Let's look briefly at each.

As the Partner, the coach focuses on building a win/win structure for his relationship with the client, and on honoring and maintaining that structure. The Partner Voice involves the client in decisions about the course of the coaching relationship and supports the client in taking increasing responsibility for his or her own learning. The Partner represents the coach's commitment to the client's outcomes, and his responsibility for the maintenance of mutual trust and respect.

The role of the Investigator is to ask questions. This is the Voice that many training programs for coaches emphasize, and for good reason. The Investigator role is at the core of coaching. The purpose of the Investigator's questions is to support the client's deeper understanding, not to procure answers for the coach or to allow the coach to formulate advice. Speaking as the Investigator, the coach challenges the client to look at the situation differently, to clarify what he or she wants, and to identify what can be done to bring these outcomes closer. In this role the coach is a learning partner with the client because both learn from the questions asked.

I think of the next three Voices as "the sharpeners" because each takes the coaching process forward by clarifying and sharpening the client's answers to the questions of the Investigator. The sharpener Voices include, in increasing order of directiveness, the Reflector, the Teacher, and the Guide.

By taking the role of Reflector, the coach serves the client as a mirror: the Reflector provides feedback to the client and encourages the client to seek feedback from others as well. Speaking in this Voice, the coach promotes the client's self-awareness regarding the choices at hand and the consequences of those choices. The Reflector also encourages the client to become more self-observant and helps find ways to do this. The Reflector supports the client in discerning his or her real potential in a situation, and in paying close attention to the capabilities and resources he or she brings to the challenges of the moment.

The Teacher Voice represents the second most commonly emphasized role for a coach—that of the "expert." As the Teacher, the coach provides information, tools, and language that help the client see the situation more clearly and expansively. The Teacher provides ways of looking at things, models, and tools for interpretation. The Teacher also challenges the client's thinking process, encouraging the questioning of assumptions and the exploration of the logic of his or her view of the situation at a deeper level.

The Guide's function is to present alternative pathways forward and encourage the client to take action. The Guide helps a client commit to doing something practical and concrete, to create change on the ground. At its most directive, the role of the Guide includes recommending specific courses of action.

The Voice of the Contractor is generally heard while wrapping up a topic or concluding a conversation. The Contractor negotiates clear and specific agreements for the client to act upon, stands for accountability to action, and follows up about results in subsequent conversations. In this role, the coach is developing the client's commitment to substantive change by exploring resistance and helping to resolve doubts. The Contractor supports the client in transforming new insights into concrete actions.

Each of these seven Voices, then, represents a role of the coach. In addition, each Voice encompasses a grouping of two to five specific functions, or Aspects, of the coach. There are twenty identified Aspects in all; their relationship to the Voices is laid out in Table 4.

Table 4: The Voices and Their Aspects

Master

M1 Maintains self-awareness

M2 Listens with focus and presence

M3 Models learning and growth

M4 Embraces the client with compassion and respect

M5 Chooses which of the operational Voices to use at a given time

Partner

P1 Establishes and honors an explicit structure for the coaching relationship

P2 Makes explicit, clear choices with the client about the coaching process

Investigator

I1 Asks questions that deepen a client's understanding of the situation

I2 Helps the client articulate desired outcomes

I3 Asks the client to generate courses of action

Reflector

R1 Provides direct and honest feedback

R2 Directs the client's attention toward his/her capabilities and potential

R3 Encourages self-observation and reflection

Teacher

T1 Provides "expert" information, tools, and language

T2 Challenges and stimulates client's thinking process

Guide

G1 Encourages the client to take action

G2 Offers options and/or recommends courses of action

Contractor

C1 Establishes clear agreements about actions

C2 Explores and resolves client doubts and hesitations

C3 Follows up with client about agreed-upon actions

Of course, each of these Aspects could be further elaborated and sub-divided, and the taxonomy could become quite intricate. In describing the coaching process in detail, we could list literally hundreds of coaching behaviors, and nearly as many ways of describing the coaching process. The Septet Model is one. The important thing is to have a framework and roadmap for yourself. In identifying these seven Voices and twenty Aspects, I've attempted to draw useful distinctions while at the same time remembering that we reach a point of diminishing returns if they are parsed too finely and we get tangled in classification and taxonomy.

A Sneak Preview of the Model

Before exploring the specifics of each Voice and Aspect, let's remind ourselves that each of the roles interacts with and supports the others. Figure 4, "The Septet Coaching Model" depicts this integration—the flow of coaching—including key elements that take place outside the coaching relationship for both the coach and the client.

Take a minute to look at the figure, read the bullet lists in it, and think about how its parts relate to one another. Notice, for example, that the Masters (both coach and client) sit outside the coaching arena and are present within it. The process of seeking mastery takes place in all areas of our lives; the coaching process is simply one activity that brings it into sharper focus. Coaching takes place within the intersection of the separate worlds of coach and client, and that is the subject of this book.

The qualities of the Master as coach, as expressed in the five Aspects listed above, are cultivated by the coach outside of coaching as she does her own learning and growth in life. The Master offers this larger perspective and experience to the coaching relationship. From this larger

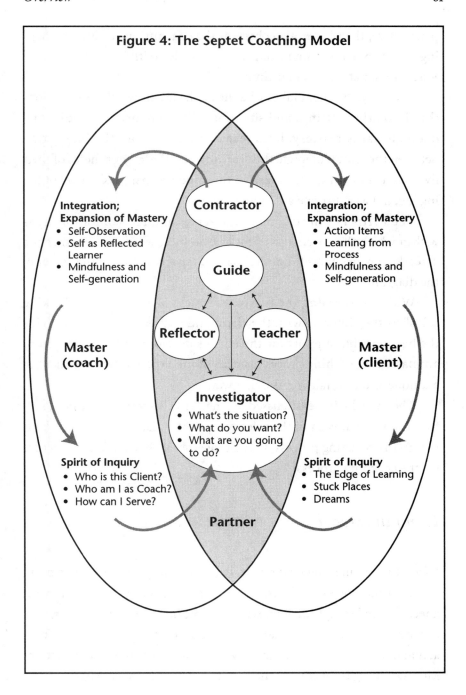

Figure 4: The Septet Coaching Model

perspective, the Master also observes the coaching as it unfolds, shaping what happens within it, and choosing which of the six "operational" Voices to use at a particular time.

Similarly, the client takes what he or she learns within the relationship into other settings and situations. Both are on their individual quests towards mastery; both learn and grow from the interaction between them and integrate this learning into the larger spheres of their lives. Coaching, in short, is seen in this model as part and parcel of living life, not as a discrete activity.

The Partner both structures and serves as guardian for the arena within which the coach and client can do their work. The Partner is a caretaker and a guarantor of the coaching space, shown in the center of the diagram.

Within this realm, the five other Voices play their parts, "taking solos" as they interact with the client and with each other to provide the best possible support for the client's development. This interplay animates the coaching process as each of the Voices serves the client in a unique and mutually reinforcing way.

The model will be discussed at length in Chapter 12. For now, suffice it to say that each of the roles comprises a distinct set of functions within the coaching process; they fit together as an overall architecture for the coaching process.

Using the Model

Each of the remaining chapters in Part 2 will begin with a description of one of the Voices. Each Aspect of that Voice is then explained, with anecdotes and sample dialogues to illustrate how it emerges in an actual coaching situation. These narratives are simplified, constructed from actual ones in such a way as to show the essence of an Aspect in action. Most coaching is, of course, more intricate than it appears here.

While the goal of including these stories and dialogues is to help you think about the roles you're playing and the purpose of each part of your coaching conversation with a client, it won't be particularly helpful to spend lots of mental energy parsing each sentence to determine which Voice or Aspect it represents. The focus of the book, after all, is on becoming mindful, not on improving our expertise at splitting hairs. Much of the professional development work that will follow in Part 3 derives from this understanding.

Work with this model to develop your awareness of what Voice and Aspect you're using at a particular time; pay attention to the distinctions between them but don't obsess about classification. Try to become intentional and conscious about shifting Voices and identifying which Aspect of the process you're focusing upon at a given time.

Each of the chapters in Part 2 closes with a description of some of the pitfalls involved in the use of a particular Voice—and guidelines for avoiding those pitfalls by staying mindful. Note, too, that the content of the coaching varies widely. This is intentional, and meant to emphasize the point that these roles are universal, and that this model is relevant to all the many venues in which coaching occurs.

CHAPTER FIVE

The Master

My music is the spiritual expression of what I am—my faith, my knowledge, my being . . . When you begin to see the possibilities of music, you desire to do something really good for people, to help humanity free itself from its hangups . . . I want to speak to their souls.
JOHN COLTRANE

Experience is not what happens to you; it is what you do with what happens to you.
ALDOUS HUXLEY

*W*e begin (and will end) with the Master. Why? Because the Master is qualitatively different from the other Voices. This role encompasses the mindfulness and awareness that we aspire to bring to our professional lives; it stands behind, coordinates, and animates the other Voices we may choose to use as coaches.

Mastery blends skill and experience with attention in the moment. We have seen the concept of the master glorified in media representations of athletes and artists, pop stars and poets, but we can also find mastery all around us, in mechanics and midwives, cooks and carpenters—in ourselves as well as in others. Perhaps we notice the fluidity and efficiency with which we flip burgers on the grill. Perhaps we deliver a perfect tennis serve or golf shot, or a strike in bowling. Or we prepare a dish in the kitchen, adding touches of this and that, knowing just how it will all fit together.

And sometimes, as coaches, we notice that we are listening attentively and fully to our clients as they speak: we are energized and engaged and able to draw upon all our skills. These are moments of mastery, and we have all had them. The role of the Master isn't about *what* we're doing, it's about how we're doing it.

The Present Moment

We have all had experiences of being fully present and alive in the moment. It happens, for example, when we listen with rapt attention to a speaker who is fascinating and passionate, or to a piece of music that soothes or energizes us. It happens when we are moved by a beautiful sight—a waterfall, a mountain, the way moss grows on a rock—or when an unexpected event jolts us out of our routines.

Of course, we will never experience this presence of mind consistently; it is the human predicament to have conditioned habits of thinking and behavior that get in the way. Our personal work, of course, is to recognize these habits, examine them, and let them go if we determine that they are unhelpful. This is simply a matter of making choices. We also support our clients in doing this work for themselves. For both client and coach, the path toward mastery we are discussing here is a path of mindfulness.

Mindfulness results from the simple exercise of the willingness to be there, to be present. It's a choice, available to us all the time, to suspend our habits of mind and mental games and just *be* there. Sometimes it's very easy. (This morning, clearing my desk was a snap, and the writing is flowing well.) Sometimes it feels very hard; our habits of mind grip us tightly and we have to work to overcome one resistance or another. (Yesterday the clutter on my desk seemed overwhelming, my writing was blocked, and I frittered away time in unimportant tasks, feeling scattered and inept.) Still, even in those moments, it comes down to a simple choice. Sometimes we feel able to focus and be attentive, at other times we don't. The choice, the opportunity for mindfulness, however, is always there, right in front of us. Making that choice, over and over, in each moment of our lives, is the first step on the way to mastery. That's the deal.

To do any kind of work well, we need to set up our surroundings to support this state of consciousness, attending to our physical comfort and reducing distractions. As I write this piece, I'm sitting at my desk in the quiet early morning. My desk is clear of the clutter that sometimes occupies it. The large window, facing east, has a view of the knoll opposite the house. The trees on the knoll are silhouetted against a sky that's just beginning to lighten as dawn approaches. The overhead light is off, and a small lamp shines a soft light upward in the corner of the wood-paneled room. I have a candle burning on my desk, a birthday present from my son. It is peaceful and quiet. Such surroundings are conducive to being present and self-aware.

In the classes and retreats that I lead about the Septet, I often ask practicing coaches for examples of the things they do in order to focus their attention for an upcoming coaching session. Read the file and prepare a plan, says one coach. Light a candle before the session, says another. Lie down and close your eyes for three minutes. Arrange the room and any relevant equipment. Do a brief breathing meditation. Listen to music. Write a plan for the conversation. Focus on the client and her capabilities. Stretch. The ways to achieve that focus, to bring yourself into the present, are as many as there are humans. The important thing is to find a practice that gets you there.

The Aspects of the Master

Let's describe again what mindfulness looks like in a coaching conversation. Being fully present means being fully engaged with the client.

We are attentive, alert, energized, and relaxed. We don't have expectations for what the client should do or where the session should go, but we are open to new possibilities and new ways of seeing the client and his or her situation. We are engaged.

We notice when urges arise within us—an urge to convey an idea, for instance, or to make a recommendation, or to make sure that the client "gets" something that we deem to be important. When these urges arise, we notice them and ask ourselves about their origins. Do they arise from our own attachments and habits of mind? Are they responsive to the client's needs? Then we either act on these urges or let them go. It's the job of the coach to ask questions, make inferences, and share ideas with the client. The key point is that as we do so we are not bound up in our own attachments; there's no judgment about whether we did it well or not, just a commitment to remaining constantly aware of the client and of ourselves.

This description makes it clear that mindfulness underlies each of the five specific Aspects of the Master role:

M1 Maintaining self-awareness
M2 Listening with focus and presence
M3 Modeling learning and growth
M4 Embracing the client with compassion and respect
M5 Choosing which of the operational Voices to use at a given time

Let's explore each of these in turn.

Maintaining Self-Awareness (M1)

Self-awareness means the capacity to observe oneself in action. This is a characteristic of human consciousness, something we all do from time to time, but in order to become more aware of this capacity, and put it to use, it's helpful to imagine that your mind has two parts. The first, which we'll call the active mind, is the part that's engaged in the action of the moment—typing, cooking, walking, reading, talking with a client. The second part, which we might call the observer mind, stands aside, in a sense, watching, noticing, ever alert. The observer mind is like a scientist: interested, dispassionate, objective. It notices what the rest of the mind is doing and—especially if we learn to pay heed to its observations—brings us a new perspective on what we are feeling and doing.

Once attentive to these observations, the active mind decides what to do with them. Generally, if what has been observed is an unproductive habit of mind, we will choose to discard it, to bring our attention back to what we are doing. On the other hand, if what has been observed is useful, we can choose to act upon it. Having noticed, we become aware of choices that take us beyond our conditioned and habitual responses.

Let's look at a fictional scenario that illustrates the operation of this dual awareness in a coaching situation.

"I really need some help with this speech," the client says to the coach. He's an executive at a large utility company who's scheduled to address an industry convention in a week's time. "I need to be convincing—all the major players will be there—but I don't want to look arrogant. Brilliant but down-to-earth. Can you help me figure out how to do that?"

Yeah, right! the coach is tempted to say, with more than a hint of sarcasm. Simple as pie. But then her training as a professional kicks in.

"Of course," she says, "that's my job." She feels a little flustered by her initial reaction of irritation to the client's request.

"Let's think about the audience," she says—always a good place to begin. "Who are these major players and why do they think *you* have something important to say?"

Whoa! says a voice in the coach's mind. There was a bit of an edge in that question. And look at his face—he's not too pleased.

"It's a group of executives," the client says more formally, with a hint of defensiveness in his voice, "getting together to discuss emerging trends in state utility regulation. They invited me, as an expert, to talk about the strategies that have served this company so well under my leadership."

So much for humble! the coach thinks to herself. But then that other, inner voice engages her in a dialogue with herself:

A little judgmental there, aren't we, coach? Might want to watch that.

But he IS arrogant.

So?

Arrogant people irritate me.

And how does that help you do your job?

Well, actually, not at all in this case. I guess I need to let it go.

It takes a few more moments, but having made that decision, the coach is able to get herself back on track, to help her client focus on the issues of concern to him.

"So tell me," she says, with new interest in the topic. "What's your message? What do *you* think about the new regulations? Let's talk about what you think needs to be done . . ."

Though the "thoughts" of both coach minds are set in italics above, I doubt that you as a reader had any trouble distinguishing the active mind, the one that reacts personally and immediately, from the observer mind—that part of the self that stands apart and represents a more objective view.

Being self-aware means being attentive to both, but this puts us in a delicate position. It's all too easy to move to a place of self-judgment as we begin to see how easily and constantly our own opinions and judgments of others arise. "There's no way I can catch all of that stuff," you may well lament. "And furthermore, how can I act at all—do my clients any good—if I'm always second-guessing myself?" It can seem a bit overwhelming.

We need to redefine our terms here. In the realm of self-awareness, success doesn't mean being perfectly attentive, or being free of feelings and attachments that arise in the course of coaching (or any other activity, for that matter). The commitment to paying attention to what's going on inside ourselves—what we're feeling, our judgments, our attachments and aversions, our distractions—is an ongoing one. Each time our ability to notice these things increases, we are, by definition, succeeding in becoming more mindful and observant.

We are conditioned beings. Every small moment of self-awareness, of noticing a judgment or an urge or an attachment or an aversion, is a small awakening. The goal, and the only measure of success, is our commitment to doing this work, to paying attention.

Listening with Focus and Presence (M2)

"Listening with focus and presence" means that the coach, whether the work being done in person or by phone (or even by email, if that's what the circumstances allow), is present in the moment—fully attentive to the client, listening carefully to what he or she has to say, and keeping the conversation open.

Darya Funches describes the requirements of this kind of presence like this:

> We cannot be present . . . when we are preoccupied with how we are being seen or experienced, or with determining the "right thing to do." We can be present only when we are in touch with our feelings, thoughts, and intuitions in the moment. The gift of presence gives [coaches] access to an area of "creative indifference," enabling them to work with clients without predetermining how things should be and what they should do. Any magic in the [coaching] process, if such a thing exists, is often attributed to this type of stance—that of an evocator—not from one's investment in a predetermined set of actions.[26]

For clients, our engagement as listeners—our interest, acceptance, and confidence—is evocative. It creates a context within which a client can find his or her own footing and move to a new awareness about the specific situation under discussion. It creates a sense of safety and possibility. In *Co-Active Coaching,* Laura Whitworth and her colleagues describe this Aspect of coaching as the promotion of "spaciousness."

> Spaciousness . . . means complete detachment from any particular course of action or any results that the client achieves. The coach continues to care about the client, the client's agenda, the client's health and growth, but not the road the client takes to get there, the speed of travel, or the detours that might take place in the meantime—so long as the client continues to move toward the results the client wants. . . . The spaciousness of the relationship requires that the coach must not be attached to whether clients take suggestions, or, if they do, whether they do it "right" or "wrong." Either way the client is right. It is a paradox that the coach often expects more of clients than they dare dream for themselves, and yet clients are unconditionally supported whatever they do. That is the breadth of the spaciousness in the relationship.[27]

Here's a real-life example of what that can mean, one drawn from my own experience.

A while ago I was involved in a personal growth group guided by my Buddhist teacher, Nancy Spence. I was committed to the group, which met for five hours monthly, but it was a very busy time for me professionally, with a lot of travel. We would meet to do our work together and Nancy would give us "homework" assignments, usually drawing from a text with which we were working. All too often I would be lax about doing the homework. In part I was dealing with some resistance to the content, and in part I was simply too busy to devote sufficient attention to it. I would come into the class—which I enjoyed and found valuable—with a certain amount of guilt. I sometimes felt as if I hadn't earned the right to be present in the group.

Nancy, on the other hand, was not judgmental in the least. She was just as warm and appreciative toward a slacker like me as she was toward anyone else. Regardless of how that might have made others in the group feel at first, Nancy's total acceptance, appreciation, and presence made it clear to all of us that any judgments and critiques about our "performance" came from within ourselves. It was, in fact, my own standards and lack of acceptance of where I was that caused me the guilt and anxiety about my adequate preparation for the group. Her neutrality or "creative indifference"—her presence as a listener—allowed me to see myself more clearly, and to see what I had to work on.

That's the essence of being present as a listener. Our full attention is available for our clients, no matter what they are going through. Our support and acceptance doesn't waver. In not reacting to their "stuff" and not projecting our own, we ensure that our interactions become a neutral and safe place in which our clients can see, and do, their own work.

Presence in this sense is experienced by others as a "deep listening," which James Flaherty describes as "not merely the engagement of the ear and the auditory nerve [but] a full engagement of the attention, thought, and intention of the coach in the conversation."[28]

The authors of *Co-Active Coaching* describe three levels of listening, and their framework is absolutely relevant to this Aspect of the coach in the role of Master. In "Level I listening," they explain, "our attention is on ourselves. We listen to the words of the other person but the focus is on what it means to us." We've already talked about how our own tendencies to be self-centered hinder our ability to serve our clients. In "Level II listening," "there is a sharp focus on the other person . . . a great deal of attention on the other person and not much awareness of the outside world." Such an excessive focus on the client's every word and desire on a superficial level is also too narrow, since it impedes our ability to be mindful of other sources of information.

"Level III listening," however, expands our awareness to include information from all sources. [29] As we would put it, at this highest level, listening includes everything that our senses experience, as well as emotions, thoughts, the environment, and the context in which the coaching is taking place. This is the essence of mindfulness.

This level of openness, of listening coupled with acceptance and support, is what we call presence. Presence is beyond the skill of listening, but is what allows real listening to take place.

Modeling Learning and Growth (M3)

The third Aspect of the Master concerns the way we lead our lives. As coaches, we "earn the right" to work with our clients by acquiring knowledge of both our specific areas of expertise and the larger territory of learning and change. Our exhortations to our clients to "create the life you want" will sound hollow and hypocritical if we have not sought to do the same. It's not that we must demonstrate mastery in everything that we touch. It's that we must be fully engaged in the *process* of mastery. In so doing, we model for our clients a way of living life fully.

Darya Funches describes the cultivation of presence as becoming "the embodiment of your message about learning and change." We experiment on ourselves, using the rich opportunities with which life presents us as a practice field for learning and growth.

> The gift of presence requires change practitioners to become more "whole" in the work they do. Although they must recognize the appropriate role to fill in relation to the client, they must also integrate themselves as whole beings into that role. If that role is considered substantially different from one's own personal identity and experience, work becomes a form of personal death, as opposed to an experience of growth and vitality.[30]

This speaks to the essential nature of integrating our entire life experience into the work that we do. Our effectiveness as coaches does not result from an academic understanding of learning and change. It requires knowing what growth and change feel like from the inside— knowing how to be successful in our endeavors *and* being familiar with the ways in which we (and presumably others) undermine ourselves and sell ourselves short.

In the end, it's our own life experience that enables us to

- understand, empathize, and offer insight into what our clients are going through;
- help our clients see their challenges and obstacles in a larger, safer, context;
- express confidence in our clients, grounded in our own experience of having faced similar challenges; and
- provide a model to our clients as people who have experienced both success and failure and maintain a robust faith in possibility and change.

While we will share our own personal experience with clients only with discretion, that experience is always there, in the background. I believe that my own encounters with both success and disappointment— and my willingness to reflect on each—have made me a better coach.

A number of years ago, I decided to finally fulfill my long-deferred desire to become a musician. In a moment of inspiration, I sat with my wife and a close friend, and we each created a plan for something major we wanted to accomplish in our lives, promising to support each other in those endeavors. Mine was to take up the saxophone. As a frequent dabbler, I knew my own tendency was to jump into something new and exciting, feel like it was going to change my life, and then slowly watch my commitment erode as the novelty wore off. I knew that for me the challenges would be to not get attached to my rate of progress and to stay with it.

All went well for a while; I bought a horn, found a teacher, and started playing. It was fun, and soon I could play the themes of a few old jazz standards. Of course I had music in my head that my fingers couldn't come close to playing, and it felt frustrating at times, but I could also see progress. I was excited that I *was* staying with it, and I felt I was stepping into a vision of myself as a more artistic, expressive person.

Then my wife and I bought sixty-three acres of land and a house north of town, and decided to open a retreat center. The process of transforming a barn into an inspiring meeting place was tremendously consuming of both time and energy. Soon the saxophone lessons became harder to schedule and I stopped finding the time to practice. Launching the retreat center had assumed more importance as the central dream in our lives; making music went on the back burner as a latent ambition.

While playing a musical instrument is something I will come back to in the future, I learned much from this whole experience that makes me a better coach. For example, I know what it is to move through long-held blocks and fears to start something new, and to experience the huge release of energy that results from making a commitment to something long resisted. I know the struggle to cultivate the discipline of practice. I know both what it's like to set goals and achieve them and what it's like to set goals and watch my own commitment erode in the face of conflicting priorities.

These dynamics are part of the reality of change. Coaches who blithely say that you can accomplish anything that you set your mind to may be speaking their belief. But that kind of statement doesn't acknowledge the struggle, the fear, and the starts and stops that often accompany significant change. To be able to relate to these struggles and to be grounded in our own experiences of success and failure makes us more compassionate *and* more knowledgeable when we coach others through their own experiences.

We must, if we wish to provide authentic service to our clients who seek to grow and change, acquire a working knowledge of the territory.

This means that we experiment with ourselves—we try new things, we're open to change. Our own life is the practice field for what we bring to the coaching relationship. We can support our clients authentically to the extent that we learn how to do this ourselves.

Obviously, we don't live our lives this way solely in order to be more credible as coaches. We do so because experimentation, self-awareness, and a willingness to change are part and parcel of living life fully. In seeking a purposeful, empowered, and meaningful way of living we come to better understand what it means to be self-generative. And this cannot fail to help our clients.

Embracing the Client with Compassion and Respect (M4)

Compassion and respect for the client are central to the coaching process and together make up this key Aspect of the coach's Master Voice. As Pema Chödrön writes,

> When we talk of compassion, we usually mean working with those less fortunate than ourselves. However, in . . . trying to help others, we might come to realize that compassionate action involves working with ourselves as much as working with others. . . . Only in an open, nonjudgmental space where we're not all caught up in our own version of reality can we see and hear and feel who others really are, which allows us to be with them and communicate with them properly. . . . To the degree that we have compassion for ourselves, we will also have compassion for others. Having compassion starts and ends with having compassion for all those unwanted parts of ourselves, all those imperfections that we don't even want to look at.[31]

Being compassionate, then, is a way of seeing that begins with an acceptance of self, with all our warts and weaknesses. When we cultivate this in ourselves, we are able to extend it to our clients and others with whom we have relationships. To the extent that we judge and think negative thoughts about ourselves, we are likely to fall into the same traps with others. And we must guard against that. But having compassion does not equate to a soft-hearted, mushy, feel-sorry-for-ourselves-or-those-less-fortunate-than-ourselves mantra. It's a clear practice, a stance that requires toughness and rigor.

As James Flaherty points out, "Many times the limitation on our respect for someone is not so much in what they're doing as it is in the imposition of our values on what they're doing."[32] We must be able to separate the workings of our own minds from what is real and true about the client, for these are two very different things. This requires sufficient self-awareness to know what our own values and judgments are, notice when they show up, and decide whether or not they are relevant.

In seeking the level of respect we need to have in order to work with someone, it will be helpful to look closely at the choices he or she has made in the past, and the context in which these choices were made. The context includes both the external circumstances within which the client operated, and his or her conditioning and belief systems. Most often, this kind of understanding makes it much easier to find a place of compassion and respect from which to operate.

Maintaining an expanded view enables the coach to be accepting and supportive of a client even in the face of significant difficulties and distress. It also is enormously helpful in assisting that client to move to a more self-accepting, empowered view of the situation he or she may face.

There's another part of the equation. Sometimes, even when we understand this fuller picture, it is impossible to respect choices made by the client that seem self-destructive or even unethical. If the client's beliefs or behaviors are such that the coach can't find this place of respect, then the coach should end the coaching relationship, or not enter into it in the first place.

Treating a client with compassion and respect does not mean that the coach needs to accept or agree with everything that the client says, does, or thinks. That would make for a relationship in which the coach would have nothing to offer and no progress would ever be made. And, we shouldn't forget, the client has every right to query us about our own values and beliefs. Respect, therefore, is not automatically conveyed. It is developed jointly. Bottom line, the coach and client must have sufficient mutual respect around the content areas in which coaching is occurring to enable them to work together.

Choosing Which of the Operational Voices to Use at a Given Time (M5)

The last major Aspect of the coach's work as Master is being responsive and flexible as the needs of the client change. It is as the Master that the coach coordinates the Voices, moving between them as necessary.

Here's an example from my own practice. I was coaching Jack, the executive director of a health care organization of two hundred people. Jack was dealing with a very critical boss, who had made a lot of negative statements about the organization's recent performance, and apparently didn't trust the data and clarifications that Jack provided. The focus of our conversation was on the boss's demands and how to best respond to them.

As I asked questions about the situation, the level of emotion rose in his voice. My observer self noticed his reactions, my own discomfort with questioning further, and my intuition that there was a significant emotional component to his reactions. We shifted gears, and took a moment to acknowledge the level of stress he was under. It became clear that the situation was very difficult for my client, and he wasn't dealing with it well. He had gotten very angry with his boss the previous week, and, it turned out, had erupted in other situations with other people as well. To me it seemed clear that his difficulty handling the boss was only a symptom of a deeper stress that was disrupting his usual steady demeanor.

We needed to look at what he could do to take better care of himself, to dissipate some of the stress that he was carrying in his body and that was coming out in unhelpful ways. Once we had done that, he felt more empowered over his own responses, and we could move back into a discussion of strategies for dealing with his boss.

This required my being light-footed in my coaching, shifting from the Investigator role to being a Reflector and a Guide. My Master paid attention to the overall dynamic of the conversation. Had I been attached to my line of questioning about a different way to work with the boss, the opportunity presented by my intuition that an underlying pattern was involved would have been missed.

If we can't be flexible in this way, "internal friction" may be generated in ourselves as coaches by the conflict between two parts of ourselves—two Voices—arguing, as it were, over which way to go. It may also be generated when a coach has agendas about what the outcome of a session should be but the client is going in a different direction. We can experience this friction as tension or confusion; at its root are our own attachments pulling us in different directions. Staying alert and self-aware—the first Aspect of the Master—is the key to overcoming internal friction.

The Master, then, maintains a watching eye over the coaching conversation. The Master is constantly assessing the needs of the client, and making conscious choices between different roles and ways of being with a client. It is the Master who chooses which of the operational Voices is most helpful and appropriate at any given time, based on a clear view of the client. Flexibility and ease, backed by confidence in the coaching process, results from the acceptance and mindfulness that are part and parcel of the practices of the Master.

Pitfalls and Guidelines

I have been asked a number of times if the Master role can be overused. My answer to this is a qualified no, because this Voice is, by definition, self-monitoring. It is the Master's practice to notice the attachments and aversions that arise in the course of the coaching conversation. Doing this means that the coach pays attention to herself, notices if she is interacting with the client in a way that isn't helpful, and modifies what she's doing to take this into consideration.

As we shall see with each of the other Voices, however, there are pitfalls to be aware of. At times the "presence" cultivated by the Master can come across as intensity beyond what the client needs or desires. If this happens, naturally enough, the client can become resistant. It is the coach's responsibility to pay attention to the client and to notice this resistance. If the Master is present and mindful, she will notice this dissonance and adjust her behavior to bring her level of intensity back to what the client is ready for. This is self-monitoring in action.

Also, as with any other Voice, there's some risk in assuming the social identity of the Master. In this case, there's a danger that we'll become attached to seeing ourselves as masterful, or to being seen by others as present and mindful. To unconsciously fish for comments like "You're such a good listener!" or "You're so wise and present," or "I feel so safe with you," or "You're a real inspiration to me" is to pursue your own needs, not those of the client. It's fine if such compliments come. It's not fine to finesse the way you present yourself in order to increase the likelihood that they will.

Here are some guidelines that may help guard against the pitfalls of the Master Voice:

- See the cultivation of your own mindfulness as a lifelong practice. Recognize that you will never perfect it, and be compassionate with yourself when you notice your attachments and aversions. Being forgiving and accepting of your own conditioning is a necessary step toward helping your clients pursue mindfulness themselves.
- Remember that noticing your distractions is success. If you find yourself absent-mindedly looking out the window as your client

tells you about the emotional trauma he experienced the other day, don't focus on your "failure"; noticing and returning to the present means you are succeeding in increasing your ability to stay mindful and aware. Accepting, not judging, your deviations from mindfulness and then moving on reduces the internal friction that can impede your practice.

- Practice deep listening and being fully present with your clients. Find ways to prepare yourself before a session, and ways to remind yourself to stay present during the conversation itself.

- Recognize that your entire life is an opportunity to practice mastery, and that as you learn and grow yourself, you become familiar with the territory of growth. All this is background and context for the coaching you provide for others; it earns you the right to work with your clients.

- Find ways to view your clients that encourage your own respect and acceptance of them. We cultivate compassion and respect when we seek to understand the behaviors and actions of our client in context and without judgment. If you are not able to find a way of viewing a client that allows you to respect him, you probably shouldn't be working with that client.

- Practice shifting flexibly and easily between Voices. Notice your own internal friction or tension as it arises. Generally, this is a sign of an attachment, which makes it less easy to be fluid in responding to changing needs.

Summary

The overarching role of the Master, then, is the ground on which we stand as coaches. It's as the Master that the coach sees what is going on inside herself and with the client; it's the Master who chooses the appropriate Voice for every particular moment in the coaching process. In support of the client, the Master

- practices self-awareness, noticing the feelings and distractions that arise, and letting go of what doesn't serve the client;
- recognizes that the quality of her attention is as important as what she does or says;
- cultivates her presence with clients, seeing them fully, listening deeply, and never making them wrong;
- uses her life as a practice field for learning and experimentation and change, and integrates her own life experiences and self-awareness into being fully present with the client;
- demonstrates acceptance and support of the client;
- chooses Voices flexibly and responsively according to what best serves the client, and with a minimum of "internal friction."

It is the Master that keeps us honest. The Master brings the mindfulness that animates the entire coaching process and places us in real relationship with our clients as co-explorers. This is where coaching begins and ends.

CHAPTER SIX

The Partner

*Only people who die very young learn all they
really need to know in kindergarten.*
—WENDY KAMINER

*Patience means allowing things to unfold at their
own speed rather than jumping in with your
habitual response to either pain or pleasure.*
—PEMA CHÖDRÖN

The Partner is the Voice in which the coach works closely with the client to establish a productive relationship, the container or arena within which the coaching process can take place. In the model portrayed in Figure 4 (page 81), the Partnership realm is the center section, the intersection between the circles of coach and client, representing where the lives of the two individuals overlap.

Building the Relationship

It's the Partner Voice that speaks most often in the beginning, when the initial agreements that guide the work are formed. Some of those agreements—regarding schedules, format, outcomes, etc.—are developed within the relationship. Others—about professional ethics, for example—are brought in from the outside. In either case, it's the coach speaking as Partner who makes them explicit; this Voice also comes forward if the agreements need to be revisited. The framework of these agreements is the structural basis for the relationship.

The coach is consistent in following through on agreements and thereby demonstrates commitment to the client. Coaching invariably involves encouraging the client to stretch and try new behaviors, and this commitment is one of the things that allows him to feel safe enough within the relationship to do so. The Partner recognizes this and consistently seeks to reinforce it.

It's the Partner Voice that the coach uses to make the coaching process explicit and to share responsibility with the client for guiding the direction of the coaching, thus supporting the client's competence at being a client, and ultimately his ability to coach himself. The Partner shares responsibility with the client for the guiding of the coaching process.

The Aspects of the Partner

The Partner represents those Aspects of coaching that involve both the practicalities of the relationship and its maintenance. It's as the Partner that the coach keeps the relationship clear and its boundaries explicit, addressing any confusion or misunderstandings that arise about fees, about the involvement of a third party, or about expectations by moving quickly to put the issue on the table with the client and reach a new understanding. When we are mindful as Partner, the client experiences the coaching relationship as safe, welcoming, and solid even when he or she may waver or at times feel anxious or overwhelmed.

These are the two main Aspects of the Partner:

P1 Establishing and honoring an explicit structure for the coaching relationship
P2 Making explicit, clear choices with client about the coaching process itself

Establishing and Honoring an Explicit Structure for the Coaching Relationship (P1)

Being clear about the goals of coaching and about how we will work together is the first step in establishing the partnership between coach and client. These understandings may change later, but only by agreement of both parties.

Some coaches feel comfortable simply discussing the details of this partnership with the client until both are clear about them, and feel no need to put these details into a written contract. Others prefer to spell them out in a letter of understanding or formal contract. If a third party is involved, certain parts of the agreement may be dictated by that party (by company policy, for example, or the client intake protocol of a social services agency).

Generally, the partnership agreement, arrived at after one or more conversations between the coach and the client, will include the answers to the following questions.

- How often and by what means (face to face, by phone, by email, etc.) will we meet?
- How long will our coaching sessions last?
- For how long are we committing to this structure?
- Who else, if anyone, is involved? (When a third party is a stakeholder in the coaching relationship, it's important to identify how that party will be involved and to discuss where the boundaries of confidentiality lie.)
- What will a coaching session consist of and what is each person committed to doing in preparation?

- For a relationship where fees are set by agreement between the client and the coach, what will they be and how will they be paid? What happens if either party needs to reschedule or doesn't show up for an appointment?
- What are the outcomes for coaching, how will success be measured, and how will the coach and the client know that it's time to end their partnership?

The last of these questions is particularly important, as defining the outcomes or goals for coaching is what animates the entire process.

Here are four imagined dialogues to illustrate this Aspect of coaching. Here we'll refer to the coach as the Partner, since that's the primary Voice he or she is using. In the first, a coach is talking to a prospective private client.

CLIENT: So what would this arrangement look like?

PARTNER: Well, since you're three hours away I'd say we'd have to do most of our work by phone. But we might want to meet in person every so often, say, for a morning or an afternoon. I've always found that works better if we want to look at something in more depth, or if there's something complicated you want me to help with. Or if you want to get other people involved.

CLIENT: What do you mean, "get other people involved"?

PARTNER: Well, I told you a minute ago that what happens in this relationship is confidential. But sometimes clients ask me to come and watch them on the job for half a day, to see how they interact with other people. Or even interview their staff to get some feedback from them about things to pay attention to. But you may not want that. I just want to give you some idea about the kinds of things we could do to get additional perspective into our work.

CLIENT: That makes sense. But I'm not ready to have you come in to the office and meet my people. In fact, I'm not entirely sure I want to be coached at all.

PARTNER: I don't blame you. This is our first conversation. I often work with clients I've never met in person. It can work that way. It's up to you. I just wanted to let you know what's possible.

CLIENT: I'm open to getting together at some point, but first I need to know more about what I'm getting into.

PARTNER: I'd want the same thing. The first thing about coaching is that you're in charge of where we go with it. Let's take a few minutes for me to tell you a little more about coaching, and for you to tell me what it is you want to work on. Then for now, if you decide to try it out, we'll talk on the phone once a week for half an hour. Once you know me better and you start seeing results, you can decide if that's enough or you want us to try other approaches. Does that work for you?

CLIENT: Yes, that seems fine. Let me tell you about the situation I'm facing, and then you can tell me how you'd work with me on it if I decide to hire you. Okay?

Note that in this dialogue, the "client" isn't actually a client yet. She's considering trying out coaching, but isn't fully on board. The coach is beginning to establish the safety on which the relationship would rest by acknowledging her concerns and telling her that she's in charge of where it goes. The coach's aim is to give the client the room she needs to explore what coaching might look like and how it could serve her.

Here's an imaginary dialogue in which the coach and client are working together to define the client's goal in concrete terms. This may or may not be the first major discussion in the coaching relationship, but it most certainly must happen before coaching begins in earnest.

PARTNER: Last time we talked, you said you wanted to focus on giving your people more feedback, at least to begin with. You said you were having trouble doing that.

CLIENT: Yeah. Here's the problem. I know I need to be up-front and honest about the negatives, but I don't know how to do that without making people defensive. And their reactions make me anxious, which doesn't help.

PARTNER: Well, some people get defensive whenever they think they're being criticized, and it has nothing to do with how you say it. Some people will react defensively if they walk into a fence-post. But you *can* learn to say what you need to say in a way that makes it easier to hear.

CLIENT: Okay. So how do you help me do that?

PARTNER: Well, to begin with, it's up to you to define what you want to accomplish. What would success look like?

CLIENT: Hmm. I guess I'd want to think about what I wanted to say, and I'd try not to get anxious—I do know what I'm talking about, after all. And I'd just say it calmly and try not to worry about how the person reacts. But what if they do get all bent out of shape?

PARTNER: Hold on. Let's begin at the beginning. I hear that if you can provide tough feedback without getting anxious, and know that it's valid and you've done your best to state it well—that's what we're shooting for in our work together?

CLIENT: Yeah, that's it.

PARTNER: Okay. Let's get very clear about how you'll know when you've done that, and then we'll work on a strategy for how to get there. . . .

Here the coach is encouraging the client to define her goals in very measurable terms. This serves both the coach and the client. Both should want to know when the coaching process has been successful, and precisely defined outcomes make the development of a coaching strategy relatively simple. This example is similar to an Investigator Aspect that we'll discuss in Chapter 7, but here the inquiry process is fundamental to establishing the coaching framework itself, so is considered as part of the Partner Voice. Without defining goals, coaching tends to lose focus as well as accountability. This, of course, lets the coach off the hook, but doesn't serve the client.

Now let's look at a situation in which an earlier agreement needs to be revisited. The coach is acting ethically and consistently with the ICF guidelines listed in Chapter 3 (2, 11, 13, 14, and 15 are especially relevant), but since significant trust issues are involved it's important that she and the client talk it through together. In this scenario, the client's boss (we're calling him Rob) has a close and longstanding relationship with the coach. In fact, it was Rob who suggested that she work with this particular sales director (we're calling her Claire). Rob is paying the bill.

PARTNER: I was in the office the other day and Rob asked me how we were doing with the coaching.

CLIENT: Oh? And what did you tell him?

PARTNER: I said I was enjoying it. He wanted me to say more, but I reminded him that what you and I talk about is just between us and he'd have to judge the results for himself. But he knows that's the deal.

CLIENT: I was hoping that he'd seen that things are going better with the manufacturing people. That he'd notice I've been working pretty hard at it and that not all the problems we've been having are my fault.

PARTNER: I need to say again that my relationship with Rob gives us a potential conflict of interest. That's why I wanted the three of us to talk before we began—to get us all on the same page about confidentiality and what you and I are doing. If you ever have questions or doubts about that, let's talk, okay?

CLIENT: Sure. I trust you on that.

PARTNER: Thanks. [pauses] You know, Claire, I think it might be a good idea to get together with Rob again—the three of us. He obviously wants some reassurance about how you're doing. He can't get it from me. What if you take the lead here and ask for a meeting? I can give you some support if you want to ask him if *he* sees any progress in the last few weeks.

CLIENT: What would I tell him about the purpose of the meeting?

PARTNER: You could say that you want to fill him in on what you've been doing.

CLIENT: What would you say if he asks you what you think about how I'm doing—with the coaching?

PARTNER: Well. Getting specific about anything you and I have been working on would mean changing our understanding about confidentiality, but it might be useful here. I could talk about whatever you and I agree is fair game. I can be as vocal or as tight-lipped as you want. I can say that you've worked very hard to bridge a gap with a couple of people that you don't particularly like or respect. I know it's important to you that your boss sees that. I'm willing to play whatever role you want me to, but you should take the lead.

CLIENT: Okay. [pauses] That all makes sense. But how I can approach this without it seeming just self-serving?

PARTNER: Well, first of all, it's not all bad to be self-serving. I think you'd be showing Rob that you're addressing what he wants you to address. I think you're being proactive and account-able by letting him know what you've already done to try to solve the problems he's worried about.

CLIENT: Yeah, thanks for that. I think you're right.

PARTNER: And what can you ask Rob to do for *you?*

CLIENT: Ah! Now that you mention it, I've been wanting to ask him for his support on the supply chain project we talked about last week. Hey! I think that's the pitch in the meeting with Rob. I want to update him and ask for his support.

PARTNER: Great idea! That's perfect. Progress report plus you're asking him for something. That's good because it gives him an opportunity to demonstrate his commitment to you. Now let's get clear about what you're giving me permission to talk about—or not. . . .

Notice that in this dialogue the client and coach are working from an existing agreement about confidentiality. The coach, speaking mainly in the Partner Voice, uses her encounter with Rob to bring potential conflict of interest issues to the fore in such a way that the client is alerted to an opportunity to be proactive on her own behalf. At the same time, the coach is acting ethically and maintaining the integrity of both her primary relationship with the client and her obligations to a third party to whom she has some loyalty and whose company is paying the bills. Transparency and clear communication are the keys here. Both the coaching partnership and the coach's relationship with the third party are strengthened by reaffirming their agreements, by the coach's clear commitment to both of them, and by the importance placed on being explicit about priorities and expectations in a potentially sticky situation.

Mutuality is a third key to keeping the structure of the coaching relationship in good repair. Here the coach as Partner protects his own interests while giving the client a gentle reminder to that effect.

CLIENT: I'm so sorry I missed our call the other day. I had an emergency meeting that came up at the last minute.

PARTNER: I understand. It happens. No problem here. But you understand, of course, that I'm going to bill you for that session anyway.

CLIENT: Yes, I understand. I'm sorry. I would have let you know, but it came up at the last minute.

PARTNER: Just to be clear about our agreement—if you need to reschedule, as long as you let me know *before* our appointment, I'm willing to reschedule without charging you. But if I don't hear from you, it means that I'm here reviewing notes, thinking about you, and sitting at the phone waiting for your call. And not doing other things. I know you understand.

CLIENT: Yes, of course. Thanks for going over it again.

PARTNER: Well, it's important for both of us to be willing to be held accountable. [takes a short pause] So what would you like to talk about today?

Here the coach hasn't just gone over his cancellation policy with the client, he's also reminded him of the mutuality of commitment that's in place in their relationship.

Making Explicit, Clear Choices with the Client about the Coaching Process (P2)

The essence of this Aspect of the Partner Voice is this: the coach brings the coaching expertise, but the client is the expert on what he needs from coaching. Focusing now and then on how we're working together and how we're using our time makes the coach more accountable to the client, and it makes the client more responsible as well.

This interchange occurs on a couple of levels. First, we discuss with the client what he wants overall from the coaching relationship. In general, is he looking for a supportive listener, or someone willing to challenge his thinking, or someone to give him guidance about alternatives? On a micro level, we also ask our clients what they want out of a specific session or at a particular moment. Often the client doesn't know at first, but in pausing and asking himself the question, he gets more clarity about what he's seeking from the coach. (I sometimes ask my clients to fill out and email me a brief form with a few questions in advance of each session; one of the questions addresses what the client wants from that particular session.)

Here are some questions that can help us encourage the client to take responsibility for shaping the course of a specific conversation: What would be the best use of our remaining time? How can I help you with this? What question are you asking yourself right now?

The process of shaping the coaching strategy and tactics may involve the client to a greater or lesser degree, but the guideline I've found useful is to involve the client in mapping the coaching strategy to a slightly greater extent than he asks for. In handing off more and more responsibility to the client for managing the coaching relationship, we encourage him to stretch and increase his ability to take the initiative. Part of the message here is that the client is capable of developing himself; we seek to reinforce this message by operating from the assumption that he knows how he needs to be coached if we just ask the right questions.

It's part of our commitment to our clients that we celebrate and support the development of their own competencies, even when (especially when!) the end result is that they no longer need our services.

Secondly, taking the role of Partner in this sense relieves us of the delusion that we can, or should, always know what our client needs. It should be okay for the coach to not know where to go. Although we sometimes put pressure on ourselves to create an effortless pathway for our clients, being authentic and present means sometimes feeling stuck. If we are willing to acknowledge this both to ourselves and to our clients, not knowing what to do next means we share responsibility and ask the client for help; this can open new directions. In doing so, we create choice points for the client, trusting that they will articulate most clearly what they need at a particular point.

Let's go back to Claire and Rob. She's decided to ask for a meeting with her boss and her coach together, and she and the coach have talked about the boundaries of confidentiality.

PARTNER: Okay, sounds good. So then which should we talk about first—questions for Rob, or points that you want to make with him?

CLIENT: Let's start with me asking him some questions. Maybe that'll break the ice, and that's what's important right now. I need a few really good questions that'll get him to say what he's worried about. Then I can talk about what I've been doing, and if that goes well I can ask him to give me some support on the supply chain thing.

PARTNER: Okay. . . . How about if you take a crack at some questions, and I'll let you know what I think and throw out a couple of ideas? Does that sound right?

CLIENT: Sure. . . .

Notice who's directing the course of the conversation here. The coach is placing herself at the service of the client by asking her to articulate the direction to take; the client is in charge. When the coach asks the client to make a conscious choice about what will be most helpful, she helps the client develops the capability to look inward and discern what *she* needs. This is central to creating independence and the capacity to be self-generative.

The dialogue above focuses on how best to use a few minutes of a coaching session, but the Partner Voice is also in play whenever we ask the client to make choices about the overall direction of the work. Here's what that might look like.

PARTNER: You've been talking about finding more time for your poetry. Let's go back to that. What do you think is standing in the way?

CLIENT: Well, I guess I need some support. Someone to remind me that writing is important and worthwhile, not just an indulgence. At this stage, it's really hard. I'm trying to recover a level of creativity which has been buried for years under piles of other responsibilities. I don't know if my poems are any good or not. I just know I really need to write them. But I also have to make a living, do my job.

PARTNER: I can do that, give you support. I think it's important for people to follow their urge to be creative. We can talk about why that is. What else could I do?

CLIENT: I know there must be a way to just get better organized so I can free up some time.

PARTNER: So what would be helpful with that part? I might have some suggestions, but I think you may already have some ideas.

CLIENT: I think it would be very helpful to talk about how I use my time at home. But I don't want to lose our focus on writing either. They're related. It seems like I write best when I'm feeling uncluttered and organized at home.

PARTNER: That doesn't surprise me.

CLIENT: It's like a loop. When I feel organized and on top of things, I don't feel guilty about writing. And when I write something I feel good about I have more energy for getting all my chores done, which is very easy for me to put off. I guess that's the key. Maybe for the next couple weeks you could help me talk about time. Help me try to do both.

PARTNER: So be it. I'll ask you each time what you've done to get organized, and how it's going with the writing. And I'll help you think about what you can do about snags when they come up.

CLIENT: Great. That sounds like a good direction.

PARTNER: Notice that when I asked you what you needed from our work together, you came right back with clear ideas about how I could support you. You're already getting better at asking yourself what you need, and finding answers.

Out of this dialogue comes a new "contract," a new agreement for how coach and client will work together. As the Partner, the coach is working with the client to shape the overall direction of their relationship, and pushing the client, through questioning, to become clearer about what she wants from the coach. The coach, in the final comment, also makes the cognitive connection for the client that she had, in fact, been shaping the coaching process herself.

This, obviously, is a skilled client. Not all people will be as aware of what they need as she is. It's easy to see that it's our job as coaches to help our clients become more competent in the content areas in which they are being coached. Less obvious is our responsibility in helping them develop the skill of being clients. Taking on that responsibility is how we nurture client independence and self-generation.

It can be a useful strategy to ask the client how she would coach herself through a specific situation. Doing this periodically provides a good check for both of you about whether she's understanding and internalizing the coaching process. It also strengthens the partnership.

Sometimes the client doesn't have a clue about what she needs from the coach; if so, other Voices (most probably the Reflector and the Guide) will be helpful in making suggestions and clarifying possibilities for their work together. Discerning what is needed always takes place in the light of the outcomes that the client wants to achieve.

Pitfalls and Guidelines

As a role for the coach, the Partner is always present in the background, looking out for the relationship. It's possible, however, to overdo the visibility of this Voice. Discussing what you're doing as a coach over and over may get in the way of actually doing it. There's a point at which too much attention paid to how we're coaching makes the process self-conscious and cumbersome. That said, it's my opinion that more coaches should err on the side of making their coaching process explicit; the tendency to overdo this is, I suspect, rare.

Coaches, of course, may enjoy having their skills appear "magical." Making the coaching process more visible makes it less magical, but it also makes it significantly more useful to the client.

Here are some guidelines for the effective use of the Partner Voice.

- Ensure that understandings about fees, the logistics of coaching, and expected outcomes are clear and explicit. (While a formal contract may not be necessary, I recommend that these understandings written down in some form.)
- Be clear about your own ethical guidelines and boundaries. The ICF's guidelines provide a good starting point, but there will be situations that they do not directly address. Talking about these issues with another experienced coach will be helpful. It's also wise to discuss any potential sticky areas with your client before a situation arises that causes discomfort.
- In particular, if the coaching discussion strays into areas in which you are not trained (whether technical or psychological) it is important to recognize that from the standpoints of professional ethics, commitment to the client, and emotional safety, you must stay within defined boundaries. You may need to openly discuss with your client whether a referral is appropriate.
- Give your client evidence of your integrity. When situations occur that challenge your agreement or your ethical standards, even if you resolve them yourself, it can be reassuring for the client to hear how you handled them.
- Seek opportunities to present the client with choice points— opportunities to follow either of a couple of different alternatives. Making choices puts the client in charge of the session.
- Push the client to tell you how to coach her or to define what she needs from you. Doing so even when she herself may feel unready to make demands on the relationship will help her learn how to

discover for herself what she needs, whereas always staying within the client's comfort zone creates little movement.

- Make it explicit when the client is taking responsibility for shaping the coaching process. The client's awareness of this sub-text of the coaching relationship is key; the cognitive awareness on the part of the client that she is doing this is empowering.

Summary

The Partner is the ever-present Voice that ensures that the coaching relationship is guided by clear, explicit understandings in a way that reinforces the safety of the client in that relationship. The Partner is responsible for the maintenance and shaping of the relationship context in which coaching takes place. The structure of this relationship must be such that the needs of both parties are addressed; this is a prerequisite to the coach being able to place himself in service.

The Partner function encompasses two main Aspects of coaching. The first is the establishment and honoring of agreements about the nature and logistics of the coaching relationship, including a commitment to the outcomes agreed to at the outset and amended as necessary. The coach's visible and demonstrated commitment to the client and his or her outcomes provides a clear sense of being on the same team.

It's also as the Partner that the coach makes the process itself as explicit with the client as possible. Decisions about the direction and emphasis of coaching are made jointly, and the coach seeks to support the development of the client's ability to take an active role in these decisions. This fosters client independence.

CHAPTER SEVEN

The Investigator

> *Be patient toward all that is unresolved in your heart.*
> *Try to love the questions themselves. Do not now seek*
> *the answers, which cannot be given because you would*
> *not be able to live them. . . . Live the questions now.*
> *Perhaps you will then gradually without noticing*
> *it, live along some distant day into the answers.*
> —RAINER MARIA RILKE

> *The answers to many questions are already with us.*
> *Often we just need some help to bring them out.*
> —MAE JAMISON

*W*hy does a coach always answer a question with a question? This has become a standard joke opening in more than one coaching workshop I've led or attended. While the jokes are often funny, there actually are several straightforward answers to the question.

Occasionally the coach truly has no clue, and answering a question with another question is a way to avoid having the client find that out. Sometimes the coach has defined a very limited role for herself and thinks that answering a question directly would be shortchanging the client, undercutting his ability to resolve his own dilemmas. "The answers always lie within the client; it's the coach's job to ask such masterful questions that they elicit these answers." That's certainly what many of us have been taught. Most often, though, it's because the Investigator Voice, the role of the question asker, is truly the best way to support the client in a process of discovery.

How do we, as coaches, discern which of these is the truth for us in a particular situation? *That* question takes us into the heartland of mindful coaching.

The mindful Investigator asks questions with an engaged curiosity. She is attentive, evocative and curious. First, as she enters a new area of inquiry with a client, she asks questions to gather basic information about the client and the situation. Then she asks questions designed to help the client see new possibilities and new choices within that situation. Both of these lines of inquiry are important, but we will largely bypass the first, which is relatively obvious, and place our focus on the second—the role that questioning plays in the coaching process as a tool for helping the client think about his situation, goals, and options.

It is important to understand that the Investigator is an action-neutral role. While speaking as the Investigator will often elicit possibilities for action from the client, the goal is simply for the client to come to see things more deeply as they truly are—first the situation and then desired outcomes and strategies. The Investigator role, in the Septet Model, is the very core of the coaching process; the questions posed by the Investigator evoke the fundamental architecture of change for the client. Let's explore why.

Artful Questions

"Because questions are intrinsically related to action, they spark and direct attention, perception, energy, and effort, and so are at the heart of the evolving forms that our lives assume."[33] As an action-oriented process, coaching relies on questions both to evoke new understandings and to generate a movement towards action and change.

The asking of artful questions—questions that create movement, that open a door, that lead somewhere—is at the center of the Investigator role. The proof is in the pudding, of course, but here are three characteristics that make a question more likely to advance the coaching process toward real change.

- The client doesn't know the answer to the question before the coach asks.
- The question fosters curiosity in the client.
- The question invokes new perspectives or possibilities.

Let's look at each of these.

First, the client doesn't know the answer until the question is asked; this means that the client will learn something from thinking about it. If the only one who learns from the answer is the coach, the question might still be important, but it's not going to open any doors for the client. An artful question goes beyond a simple search for facts or descriptions. The very process of considering and answering the question causes the client look at his situation in a new way.

Secondly, implicit in the question is that the client is engaged in a discovery process, and is a researcher in the arena of his own life. Artful questions are asked in a way that assumes that there is something interesting to learn here. While the coach may also be curious about the answer, the question stimulates the inherent curiosity of the client. This curiosity is usually light and fun; asking the question invites the client into a neutral observer stance, one which is somewhat detached from the content of coaching and corresponding emotions and offers a view of that content from a larger perspective. (Think mindfulness!)

Finally, an artful question is asked in such a way that finding an answer requires the client to shift perspectives or discover new possibilities. These, as we shall see, could include a new and more empowering way of viewing the situation, an optimistic goal for the future, or previously unseen choices that are available. To quote Albert Einstein,

"A problem can't be solved from the same state of mind that created it."
Artful questions invite clients into a new state of mind, a new and more
expansive way of looking. Since we, as coaches, ask questions out of the
separate world of our own experience, we are in fact often inviting the
client to view his situation from the distinct perspective from which we
might view it.

The Aspects of the Investigator

I1   Asking questions that deepen a client's understanding of the
     situation
I2   Helping the client articulate desired outcomes
I3   Helping the client generate courses of action

The three Aspects of the Investigator Voice are centered on three
areas of questioning—What's the situation? What do you want? What
are you going to do? The many variations on these basic questions are
diagnostic in that they increase the coach's understanding of the territory
through which the client wishes to navigate, but far more importantly,
when skillfully designed they serve to expand and deepen the client's
understanding. The coach may contribute new perspectives about that
territory, and use other Voices to deepen and enrich the conversation,
but it is the questions themselves that drive the process of discovery.

The three core questions, taken together, establish the creative
tension described by Robert Fritz, Peter Senge, and others as critical
to change.[34] Situation questions clarify what Fritz would call current
reality. Questioning about outcomes elicits from the client a graphic
statement of his future vision in relation to that specific situation. The
gap or felt tension between what the client has now and what the client
wants provides the motivation and direction for change. Once this tension is established, the third area of questioning, around what the client
will do, then provides a channel for the client to act decisively to resolve
that tension.

There's a certain progressive logic to the three Aspects in this Voice: the first line of questioning clarifies the situation and the client's part in it; the second clarifies the outcomes that the client seeks; the third surfaces possibilities for new actions and behaviors. But coaching is an artistic, not an engineering activity. In real life, the three Aspects don't necessarily follow each other in a predetermined sequence; a client may be primed to start in any one of the areas, and that's where the coach will need to begin, opening new lines of inquiry as the need arises.

That said, let's explore each of these Aspects and the lines of questioning they represent.

Asking Questions that Deepen a Client's Understanding of the Situation (I1)

The first Aspect of the Investigator involves exploring the situation that the client faces. This situation could represent an opportunity, a fear, a dilemma, or the need for a plan. To begin with, the coach asks questions that illuminate its *external* aspects: What did he do next? Who do you need to involve in this decision? What have you tried before that has helped? What are the major factors that you need to consider? But while these are important questions, there's another level of questioning the coach can provide that's even more likely to be helpful.

"The situation," of course, does not consist simply of factors external to the client. The second level of questioning has to do with how he *influences* what is going on. The client himself, of course, is a central element in any situation that he is able to perceive. A clear picture of the whole requires that the client understand how he contributes to, or even creates, that which he seeks to change. So another level of questioning might involve questions focused on the client: What might you be doing that makes it more difficult for him to support your decisions? What do you do that makes her mad? What entrenched patterns do you have that make it more difficult to change this habit? These questions get at the contributions that the client makes to the situation, and therefore to what he can do to affect its outcome.

A third level of questioning has to do with the *interpretations* and *underlying assumptions* that guide the client's behavior: What limiting assumptions might you be making that preclude other possibilities? What non-obvious motivations might you have? What do you get out of the status quo—how does it benefit you? These last questions get to the root of behavior, and they're even more likely to help a client discover opportunities for lasting change.

The asking of artful questions is not as hard as it might seem from the discussion above, as I hope the following dialogues make clear.

INVESTIGATOR: So, Ella, tell me why things are so difficult with your boss.

CLIENT: Well, Jim didn't really want to hire me. I was pretty much forced on him by his boss, who thinks I have a lot of good experience. And he's right. But Jim hasn't really wanted me here since the first day.

INVESTIGATOR: What do you notice that makes you think that?

CLIENT: Well, he's just cold to me. Jim's mostly pretty friendly to the other people in the department, but not to me. And he criticizes me publicly, he gives me only negatives when we meet, and I can't remember if he's ever said a single good thing about me or anything I've done.

INVESTIGATOR: Sounds pretty grim. Any good news about Jim? Any hints he might not be such a bear?

CLIENT: Hmm. [pause] When he first came in he asked me to take on a big new project. I was pleased. I was supposed to submit a plan for how I would approach it, so I did. But he sat on the plan for months and never got back to me about it until I asked him about it. And even then he just put me off. This hasn't been an easy ride.

INVESTIGATOR: Can you think of any ways you're contributing to this bad dynamic?

CLIENT: Well. I have gotten pretty shut down to him. I'm sure he knows I don't have much respect for him. I tried hard for a while, but I'm looking for a way out at this point. I don't need the hostility.

INVESTIGATOR: What do you think it is about Jim? What assumptions are you making about him? Have you really given him a fair chance, or did you just get off on the wrong foot?

CLIENT: Hmm. About Jim. [pauses] I suppose he's insecure. He knows I've got more experience in software than he does. Maybe that makes him nervous. And I know he's mad at Alex [Jim's boss] for making him put me on the team; I would have resented the way he handled it if I were in Jim's shoes. . . .

In this dialogue (we'll continue it later), the coach as Investigator asks questions at all three levels. Initially they concern the boss and the circumstances. They're about the lay of the land, external to the client (though based on her subjective view, which is of course inherently limited and biased). Then the Investigator's line of questioning changes to focus on Ella's response to Jim. The coach supports Ella in looking at how she contributes to the situation. In the end, the coach questions the assumptions that Ella holds about Jim. This is where the leverage is. Helping Ella see how she views Jim will help her think more clearly about the situation, what she contributes to it, and her options for resolving its difficulties.

Helping the Client Articulate Desired Outcomes (I2)

In clarifying what the client wants, we want significant detail. The definition of outcomes is key to the coaching process, and animates everything that follows. It's important that the client be invested enough in the outcome to surmount both internal resistance and external obstacles; a clear vision of that outcome helps the client stay motivated toward achieving it. Robert Fritz defines vision as "the inner crystallization of the result that you want to create, so that the result is conceptually specific and tangible in your imagination—so tangible and so specific, in fact, that you would recognize the manifestation of the result if it occurred."[35] The definition of outcomes helps us channel our energy in a focused direction.

INVESTIGATOR: So, Ella, let's play with those assumptions. If you're right, does that say anything about how your relationship with Jim could be different?

CLIENT: Well, I suppose it's conceivable that he could come to see me as a help to him and not a threat. But that's a stretch right now.

INVESTIGATOR: I'm not asking you to believe that it's possible right away, but let's spend a little time thinking about what it would look like. What would it mean to be a help to Jim?

CLIENT: He'd feel like I was helping him to reach his own goals. Helping his department look good. Helping him look good. For the most part, I'm already supporting his agenda, but there's been so much tension that he doesn't get it.

INVESTIGATOR: Let's stay with the possibilities for a minute. How would you know if he thinks you're being supportive?

CLIENT: Well, when I do good work he'd acknowledge it somehow. He'd give me public credit for my contributions, and he'd call on me when tough issues come up. He'd use what I have to offer.

INVESTIGATOR: And how would that make a difference for you?

CLIENT: Well. [pauses] Obviously I'd feel like we were working together, instead of at odds. We'd be able to share ideas. We'd support each other. It would go both ways. I'd enjoy work again.

INVESTIGATOR: Can you see that as at least a possibility sometime in the future?

CLIENT: I don't know. . . . But I don't like to give up on things. I don't think it's likely, but I do see how imagining how it could be different opens things up a bit. . . .

INVESTIGATOR: Yes, it's important to understand what you want to be different . . . knowing the outcome you want is what will shape your strategy.

Notice that in this dialogue the coach isn't asking the client to commit to the outcome yet. There's too much they don't know about what that would entail. As the Investigator, the coach is just asking the client to try on some possibilities—to be willing to consider that things could change.

The next dialogue concerns a very specific, job-related situation where the coach is the client's supervisor in a manufacturing environment. To keep that clear we'll call them the supervisor and the employee, but here the supervisor is coaching in the Voice of the Investigator.

SUPERVISOR: What seems to be the problem?

EMPLOYEE: My scrap is getting out of control. There's too much of it and Eric isn't picking it up often enough.

SUPERVISOR: What do you think it should look like at this workstation?

EMPLOYEE: Better than this.

SUPERVISOR: But how. What should it look like?

EMPLOYEE: Well, the scrap should be piled up over there, or in the bin.

SUPERVISOR: If you kept it piled up over there or put it in the bin, would that solve the problem?

EMPLOYEE: Yeah, for a while. Until the bin is full.

SUPERVISOR: If all the scrap is either in that pile or in the bin, how would that help you do your job?

EMPLOYEE: Well, I could walk around my press without tripping on all this stuff underfoot.

SUPERVISOR: Will that solve the problem?

EMPLOYEE: Yeah, that'll be better.

In this dialogue, the supervisor (coach) supports the employee (client) in articulating what his work area should look like. It's not a complicated problem. Both the employee and the supervisor know what the solution is, and that the employee is basically whining. The supervisor could just tell the employee to do a better job of cleaning up after himself. That would be an authority-based interaction, as opposed to a coaching interaction. But here the supervisor doesn't want to be adversarial, and so he chooses to ask a lighthearted series of questions—to use the Investigator Voice—to get the employee to define the desired outcome. This bypasses the need for a confrontation. In this case, defining the desired outcome is about all that's necessary; once that's done the steps are obvious.

This is obviously a mundane example. But that's part of the truth about coaching—it's sometimes mundane. We're all provided with any number of situations to help others learn, whether we call it coaching or not. The principles outlined here aren't magic or rocket science. They work because the way in which we interact with the people we're supposed to be helping makes a critical difference in whether we really help them or not.

Asking the Client to Generate Courses of Action (I3)

It's as the Investigator that the coach asks the client directly for ideas on courses of action or behaviors that could bring the desired outcome into being. It is important to understand, however, that in the Investigator role there is no bias for action coming from the coach. Any impetus towards action derives from the client and not from the Investigator. In this role the coach's purpose is to support the discovery of the client's ideas about how to move forward. The Investigator is detached, and does not advocate action. (To suggest ideas, or to provide an impetus towards action, is a function of the Guide Voice, to be discussed in Chapter 10.)

Once the outlines of the desired outcome are clear, however, the client is often ready and eager to get to work on them. Articulating a picture of what the client wants can release a lot of energy that was formerly bound up in confusion about alternatives.

Let's go back to Ella, whom we left at a critical juncture. We'll repeat the last thing she said, just before the coach interrupted to discuss the importance of defining outcomes.

CLIENT: I don't know. . . . But I don't like to give up on things. I don't think it's likely, but I do see how imagining how it could be different opens things up a bit. . . .

INVESTIGATOR: Yes, it's important to understand what you want to be different . . . knowing the outcome you want is what will shape your strategy. So, what do you think *you* could do differently if you kept this new perspective?

CLIENT: I thought you'd put it back on me! To tell the truth, I think I know. I think the opportunity is to try to start from scratch. I need to make more of an effort to get to know Jim. To find out how he sees things and what his goals are.

INVESTIGATOR: And what will you do with this information?

CLIENT: I have to take the initiative. I need to figure out what Jim needs from me, I guess. And that'll help him know I'm on his side, that I'm really not out to undermine him. Or replace him. It won't be easy, and I'm not too optimistic that he'll change, but it's worth a try.

INVESTIGATOR: What would be your first step?

CLIENT: I'll call him tomorrow and set up a time to meet. I think that if I take the initiative, he'll do lunch with me. I'll need to really think through my agenda so I'm ready when I go in, but I think I know how to get there.

A couple of things are notable here. First, Ella already has an impetus for action. As soon as the outcome became clear to her, the creative tension between the current unpleasant situation and a potential resolution provided its own urge for resolution. New energy for action arose in Ella and came out when she said, "I don't like to give up on things." The coach is simply staying present, asking artful questions. Ella is generating her own ideas and her own commitment.

Second, Ella pretty much knows exactly what to do. The shift of perspective the coach's questions provoked released the energy that she'd been bottling up for some time. With a clearer and more expansive view of the situation, and a clearer idea of what the outcome she wants would look like, the coaching session practically runs itself. Ella is a skilled person, and she's able to come up with specific possibilities for action on her own. Other people might need more guidance or ideas, which would require a different Voice than that of the Investigator. For Ella, the Investigator provides just what she needs to generate a plan of her own.

Pitfalls and Guidelines

While a healthy curiosity on the part of the coach animates the conversation, the coach must remain clear that the conversation isn't for the coach's benefit. This seems obvious, but when the coach is interested in the client's story (and clients are inherently fascinating!), it's easy to get wrapped up in just pursuing that story, even when it leads into areas that aren't relevant to the coaching. The skilled Investigator designs questions that tap into the *client's* curiosity, to that the client begins to drive the discovery process.

Secondly, we may fall in love with our social identity as a brilliant question asker. It's fun to ask questions that resonate and provide the seeds for new client understanding, fun to watch the light bulbs go on. To the extent that we identify with that role, and are invested in ourselves as the artful Investigator, we may stay in that role beyond the point that it is helpful.

Third, we may get over-invested in the idea that asking questions is what a coach does. If we believe, as a philosophical stance, that the answers are always within the client, we'll be tempted to do nothing but probe until those answers are found. Sometimes, though, the answers are *not* within the client, and he or she needs additional information or guidance in order to move forward. In this situation, the Investigator role will cease to be helpful. As the old saying goes, You can't get blood out of a turnip. (On the flip side, our own identification with the Teacher or Guide Voices may cause us to underuse the Investigator role. When we do this, we tend to drive or guide the process in a more directive fashion. While this is sometimes necessary, if we go there too easily we will be depriving the client of the opportunity to think independently, and may undermine his or her sense of ownership in the process. The dependency this can create is very unhelpful.)

The following guidelines will help you maintain mindfulness in the Investigator role:

- Be clear in your own mind about why you are asking a particular question or following a line of questioning. The questions should relate to the larger context of your coaching, and they should move the client toward new understanding. Remember that it is the relationship between the questions of the three Aspects that enables the experience of creative tension and the resulting energy for change.
- Make yourself more accountable for grounding your questions in the client's agenda by explaining the rationale for your line of questioning. This also sets the context for the client, and reinforces the discipline of ensuring that you have a rationale for what you're doing.
- Maintain awareness of which Aspect of the Investigator you are using. Each of the three core questions of the Investigator is useful, and each has a lot of variations. It will support your mindfulness to

be attentive to which line of questioning you're pursuing in a given conversation.

- Remain mindful that the Investigator Voice is just one of the possibilities. Don't get overly attached to it. Remember that other roles or Voices may be more appropriate in a given context.

- Be aware and let go of your own need to get to resolution, to ask "just the right" question, or to follow a certain line of questioning to the end. Also, watch your judgments about the client's answers or his or her inability to answer a question. These judgments and needs will only get in the way. Ask your questions with presence and with a belief in the capacity of the client to see things differently.

- Pay attention to the nuances in the client's responses to your questions. Is she opening up? Is he defensive and stuck? Are there light bulbs going on in her mind? As we discussed in the Master chapter, while the client's reaction—hesitation, defensiveness, excitement—shouldn't be the sole determinant of how we move forward, maintaining a broad awareness and emotional sensitivity to body language and emotional tone will increase our understanding.

- Make the coaching process explicit; this is the best way to hold yourself accountable to the client.

Summary

The Investigator Voice is a central one in the coaching process. It's largely through asking questions that we support our clients in seeing a situation anew, formulating the outcomes they want, and developing new strategies for getting there. The three areas of Investigator questioning provide the backbone of the coaching process; in a very real way, the remaining voices simply deepen the client's search for answers to these three questions, and anchor the results of the learning process in clear action steps. Done well, the three lines of Investigator questioning enable the client to develop a creative tension that motivates action and change.

A hallmark of an artful question is that the client doesn't know the answer before being asked. Through questioning, we evoke the process of learning and expansion that takes place whenever we try to answer all but the simplest questions. (Socrates was on to this a long time ago.) And whether or not the coach has an answer in mind, he or she needs to remain open to what the client generates; this learning process is one of shared discovery.

As with any Voice, we must learn to be aware of when we are over-identifying with, or resisting, the role of the Investigator. Both of these are recipes for trouble. In maintaining our self-awareness, we are able to recognize these attachments and aversions as they arise, and to let them go. Our goal is to be as fully and completely present for the client as possible.

CHAPTER EIGHT

The Reflector

The greatest personal limitation is to be found
not in the things you want to do and can't,
but in the things you've never considered doing.
RICHARD BANDLER

In times of rapid change,
experience is your worst enemy.
J. PAUL GETTY

As the Reflector, the coach provides honest and timely feedback to the client and encourages him to develop his own ability to observe himself and consider the consequences of the choices that he makes. Ideally, for the client, listening to the Reflector Voice is a bit like looking in a mirror.

The Reflector is the first of the three "sharpener" Voices, supporting the client in developing a clearer understanding of himself, his behaviors, and his opportunities. The Reflector is often called into play to help the client refine his responses to the lines of questioning the coach pursues as the Investigator.

A Rare Invitation

The Reflector Voice must be taken on mindfully. It is a privilege to share such intimate territory as our perceptions of a person. We have been invited into an inner room, within which many of the usual barriers and defenses are gone. In this room, we are allowed to speak honestly, to tell the truth, to support another human in seeing himself in a more accurate and expansive way. This is a privilege, and requires of us the utmost respect and compassion.

The mindful Reflector maintains an awareness of his or her own judgments and agendas as they arise, coming back to a deep appreciation and acceptance of the client, and of how the client approaches the work that they are engaged in together. There is no hurry. The client's awareness will unfold, but only as the client is ready.

Never does the coach use this Voice to make the client feel put in the wrong or inadequate. Rather, he or she employs it to share perspectives and encourage the client to do the work of becoming self-aware.

The Aspects of the Reflector

R1   Providing direct and honest feedback
R2   Directing the client's attention toward his/her capabilities and potential
R3   Encouraging self-observation and reflection

Each of these three inter-related Aspects for coaches using the Reflector Voice supports the others, and collectively they support the rest of the coaching process. Before we present our dialogues, a few words about each.

First, the client counts on the coach to tell the truth, to be candid and direct. Coming from a trusted and supportive person who is outside of the politics of the immediate situation, a new perspective on ourselves and our involvement can be invaluable. Because the coach is a valued and trusted support person, his or her perspective carries weight and is more likely to be heard without the defensiveness that might be triggered by comments from someone who has his or her own agenda within that situation. This means that taking the Reflector role requires mindfulness, considering deeply what to say, and keeping our comments as free of our own biases and judgments as possible.

In the second of our theoretical Aspects, the Reflector encourages the client to acknowledge his own strengths, capabilities, and potential. This aspect of the Reflector is optimistic: the coach infuses energy into the process by providing evidence of the client's inherent wholeness and ability to make a difference.

In the third Aspect, the Reflector encourages the client to look in the mirror. Here the coach encourages the client to be self-reliant by helping him to develop the capacity to observe himself clearly in action. This capacity for self-observation is one of the keys to wise action. The Reflector supports the client in considering the implications of his feelings and behaviors. It is essential to be able to see clearly the choices that one is making and to understand how those choices affect others and one's own possibilities.

Providing Direct and Honest Feedback (R1)

As the Reflector, the coach will sometimes provide direct feedback to the client. This is appropriate when the client seems to be missing a piece of information about himself, whereas if he had that information he could perhaps understand why he's getting the results he's getting.

The basic rules of feedback apply in this context: provide comments that are very specific, timely (that is, close in time to the relevant event), and descriptive of behaviors that the person you're addressing has control over.

CLIENT: I want to spend some time here talking about an interaction that I had with George yesterday. He was *way* out of line after our meeting. I know my presentation was a bit rough, but he jumped all over me. There was no call for that!

REFLECTOR: You sound pretty upset about what happened.

CLIENT: It's his job to give me feedback. But he didn't acknowledge that I'd been up until midnight working on the slides and Jerry didn't get me what I needed. And he didn't even warn me that Ruth was dead set against the project in the first place and was going to be loaded for bear! George is supposed to be on my team here! I feel set up.

REFLECTOR: Sounds like an impossible situation. I can understand why you might feel a little beaten up.

CLIENT: Yes, that's how I feel. Except run over is more like it.

REFLECTOR: And also you sound a little defensive. I'm guessing you don't feel appreciated for all the work you put into this.

CLIENT: Yeah, I am feeling defensive. I really care about this project.

Here, the coach is providing feedback to the client by reflecting back what he hears in the client's comments. This level of feedback is often described as a component of "active listening": the coach's comments are rooted in solid attention and in staying present as the client vents his frustration. Ideally, this helps the client articulate and understand his experience.

Before this exchange, the client was wrapped up in the injustice of the situation. If we can take the client's account at face value, it *was* difficult and he was set up in some sense. Certainly several circumstances seem to have contributed to a meeting not going very well from his point of view. However, as long as he's wrapped up in the anger and emotionality of it, as long as his field of view encompasses only the negativity and a perceived injustice, it's very difficult to move forward. The coach as Reflector supports him in voicing his emotions in the moment, acknowledging them, and then moving on to the next stage. This increases the client's mindfulness about his own emotional state.

Sometimes it's useful for the coach to use this Voice to provide feedback about the coaching relationship itself. For example, a coach could tell a client about an issue that affects their ability to work together, for example being consistently late to sessions, or using the session to defend a behavior or decision when the stated desire is to identify more effective alternatives. Again, there's no judgment or evaluation, just a clear statement about choices and consequences. The feedback to the client offers an opportunity to step back and see more clearly how he could better use the coaching session. Awareness creates the possibility of new choices; feedback is a key component of awareness.

In the next dialogue the client's behaviors do not appear in the actual session, but behavioral or performance issues are definitely on the table.

CLIENT: I think there's a lot of resistance to my new dress code initiative—some of it not so subtle. Everyone's poking holes in it, or joking about it, but nobody's talking to me about it. There's even a cartoon up in the break room that someone drew. I wish they'd just bring their concerns to me.

REFLECTOR: Jack, maybe your people are intimidated by how strongly you feel about professional dress.

CLIENT: I do see it strongly, but I really am open to modifying a couple of the specifics.

REFLECTOR: Do you remember the feedback from your subordinates on your evaluation about shooting the messenger?

CLIENT: Yes. I disagreed with it, because I've never done that. But obviously some people believe that's what I'm like, even if they're wrong.

REFLECTOR: Seems to me that may shed some light on the dress code issue. People who feel intimidated by you are much more likely to post cartoons in the break room than they are to come to you.

CLIENT: Oh. [pauses] Yeah, you're right.

REFLECTOR: Is that what you want?

CLIENT: No, I don't want to be intimidating. I really don't. But I guess this is further evidence that I am. Or at least that's how people see me.

REFLECTOR: Yes, I think it is. And you might have some work to do in that area. If you want, that is.

The light bulb goes on as the client recognizes how others see him. He's able to step back and see himself, for a moment, as others do. This gives him a larger perspective on an issue that bothers him.

Particularly in coaching clients where relationships with others are part of the focus, it's often helpful to have additional data sources. A wide range of self-assessments, values and style inventories, and "360 degree" feedback processes are available to help the coach support the client's self-awareness. In addition, with the client's permission, a coach can interview others who interact with him, or observe him in the workplace as he deals with others. Without these additional sources, the coach will have to rely solely on what the client brings to the table, but even if that's the case, as a "sharpener" Voice, the Reflector can provide invaluable perspective.

Directing the Client's Attention Toward His/Her Capabilities and Potential (R2)

Personal or professional development often requires a leap of faith and a commitment to trying new and unaccustomed behaviors. Fundamental to a client's readiness to take this leap is his belief in his capacity to be successful. A client may hold in his mind a picture of failure, of the dire consequences of not doing something well. If this is the dominant image in his mind, then indeed failure is more likely. It's a self-fulfilling prophecy.

Success is much more likely, on the other hand, if we cultivate a positive attitude. Recent research suggests that in fact what we think of as luck has a major component that is influenced by our choices and attitudes.[36] Even without luck, we all need occasional support in remembering or believing that we can be successful at something; it's certainly important that a client have faith in his own capabilities. Questions like, Which of your skills will help you in this situation? or, When did you face a similar challenge successfully? will go a long way towards kindling—or rekindling—that belief in relation to a current challenge.

The Reflector is the particular Voice that supports the client in aligning his beliefs and skills and energy behind what he is about to do. In this connection, the field of appreciative inquiry (AI), pioneered by David Cooperrider and others, has much to offer the coach.[37] The principles of AI are central to coaching and to the Reflector Voice in particular. Sue Annis Hammond, in writing about AI, describes the basic concept this way:

> The [clients] stir up memories of energizing moments of success creating a new energy that is positive and synergistic. [Clients] walk away with a sense of commitment, confidence and affirmation that they have been successful. They also know clearly how to make more moments of success. It is this energy that distinguishes the generative process that results from Appreciative Inquiry. There is no end, because it is a living process. Because the statements generated by the [clients] are grounded in real experience and history, people know how to repeat their success.[38]

By helping clients to identify their strengths, the coach as Reflector is able to mirror this back to them, even as they work to cultivate or discover these strengths within themselves. What a gift this is to offer to another human! And, as the following story from my own experience shows, what a wonderful gift to be able to receive.

Early in my consulting career I was preparing to teach a ten-day course in group facilitation and experience-based training to a group of high-powered Latin American business school faculty members in Costa Rica. They were highly skilled in the case method and relied on a didactic, "expert" model of teaching. Many had Ph.D.s. It was easy for me to feel that my background was inadequate next to their credentials. I had a good design for the program, but I was inwardly terrified.

My mentor and coach at the time, Rod Napier, had worked with me on the design of the course but would not be involved in the program. When we talked for one last time before I flew to San Jose he knew I was anxious, and he told me to trust what I knew and to trust the design. Rod reminded me that the participants were brilliant and successful, but that I deeply knew the material and concepts we were going to be working with—that the essence of experiential learning was to learn from what happened, and that my expertise lay in facilitating this process. As long as I worked with the emerging needs of the group, there was no way to go wrong. We would all be learners together. I felt better and I got on the plane.

Five minutes into the first hour of the program, it was apparent that two of the participants spoke almost no English. This had not been communicated to me and I was momentarily stunned. I knew Spanish reasonably well, but I was used to working through simultaneous translation, which was not at all suited to the intense group process work we would be doing. How could I deliver ten days of finely tuned training without the aid of an interpreter?

Then I remembered Rod's reminder that the entire premise of the program was teaching these bright people to use what emerged from the group and to be flexible in their own designs for future projects. I knew in a flash that this was my first opportunity to "model" what we were talking about. I knew without a doubt that I could seize the moment and change my plan. I switched languages and we conducted the rest of the program in Spanish. Those ten days became one of the most enjoyable, satisfying, and successful experiences of my professional life, but in order to make it so I had to keep the faith that Rod had helped to instill in me.

In identifying and honoring the client's strengths, the coach is supporting the client in his capacity to be successful. The coach may do this by directing the client's attention to prior successes and current skills, either through questioning or by making more direct statements. Alternatively, she may encourage the client to develop a reminder system to use in a moment of anxiety, as Rod did with me. Whatever the approach, the outcome is that the client feels empowered and will have more confidence in his ability to navigate the challenges ahead.

Here's a sample dialogue that addresses this point.

CLIENT: It seems like every year my team is just drowned at budget time, and I get overwhelmed and stressed. There's too much to do and too little time.

REFLECTOR: We talked last time about creating a back-out schedule ahead of time, so you can clear the decks for some of the activities that have to happen in the budget process. That way, you can schedule that work more proactively so it doesn't all pile up before the deadline.

CLIENT: Yeah, that's a good idea, but we always seem to get crazy.

REFLECTOR: So how could you prevent that? Let's look at the pieces. You've told me that you and your team know what's involved in putting the budget together—all the steps.

CLIENT: Yes, we certainly do. Everyone on this team has been through the process at least twice.

REFLECTOR: And, you know how each of those pieces fits into the picture. You could probably map out the whole process. Right?

CLIENT: Well. [pauses] We've never done that, but it wouldn't be hard. It's a logical process; there are certain steps. They just go one after the other.

REFLECTOR: And does your group have the skills to do each of these well? Are they competent?

CLIENT: Yeah, we do a great job. The end result is world-class. It's just the stress level . . . it takes a big toll.

REFLECTOR: It seems like you're about ready to change that. You don't have to do it the same way next time around. Do you believe it can be easier than it has been?

CLIENT: Yes, I do. I know it can be easier. It has to be.

REFLECTOR: So. Now's your chance to get ready for the next time so it *will* be easier. You and your team obviously know what the pieces are, and how they fit together, and how to do them. And so you're working from a strong position if you want to change this pattern.

CLIENT: Well, when you look at it that way, I guess we are. So you're saying we just need to think about the sequence and plan the activities better.

REFLECTOR: Yes, that's the part you haven't done yet. Will it be hard to sit down with your people and map out the whole process from start to finish on a more relaxed timeline? That's the piece that's missing.

CLIENT: No, that won't be hard. [pauses] We know how to do that.

REFLECTOR: You're right, it isn't too complex—you absolutely *can* do it. And if you do it now, you've got your roadmap ready for the next budget cycle.

Notice that in this dialogue, the focus of the coach as Reflector is to direct the client's attention to all the capabilities that he and his team can bring to bear on a situation that has previously been very stressful. The client already has most of what is needed to solve the problem, and when the coach helps him see that this is the case he ends up believing in his ability to work with his team to take care of the rest.

Here's a scenario in which the client is making a bit more of a leap.

REFLECTOR: It sounds like you're having doubts about committing your-self to run in the marathon.

CLIENT: Yes. I enjoy running, but I've never tried to do anything that big. The most I've ever run is three miles, and I'm not in great shape. I don't have much confidence about being able to run that far.

REFLECTOR: Well, then, why are you even thinking about it? Maybe, even without proof, there's something that tells you *can* run twenty-six miles.

CLIENT: Okay. Let's take a look at it. First off, it would mean a lot to me.

REFLECTOR: How so?

CLIENT: Well, it would be a huge confidence booster to do something that major. I've never been an athletic person, particularly. But I have taken running seriously. Still, twenty-six miles is a very big leap. I think I could do it—I'm tempted—but truly I don't know.

REFLECTOR: What if you trained, and got in really good shape, and then decided at the end you didn't want to go for it? Would that be a bad thing?

CLIENT: Well, no it wouldn't. I'd still be in good shape, whether or not I actually ran the marathon. Just the training would be good—it would move me up to the next level.

REFLECTOR: Exactly. And if you knew you'd done your best to train, I bet you wouldn't beat yourself up for not running in one par-ticular race.

CLIENT: I might a little, but you're right—it wouldn't be the end of the world.

REFLECTOR: No, it wouldn't. So you could register for the marathon, not knowing exactly how the training would go, and see what happens.

CLIENT: Yeah, but I want to be really committed. Anything else would feel like I'd be giving myself an out.

REFLECTOR: Sounds like you're making it all or nothing.

CLIENT: Well, it is all or nothing. Either I reach my goal or not.

REFLECTOR: I agree that commitment is important. The real commitment, though, is to just enter into a process fully and find out what you're capable of. Getting ready to run the marathon is doing just that and only that—it's not a pass/fail test. It's the getting in shape and feeling good and having all that energy that's the real goal here, don't you think? You *know* how to do all that; you've done it before.

CLIENT: Yes. [takes a deep breath] I can see that. Maybe I don't need to worry so much about the race itself.

REFLECTOR: That's right. But I *do* think you can do it. People run first-time marathons all the time; none of them know for sure until they try. If you work hard, like I know you always do, and keep doing longer and longer runs, you'll see your stamina develop. At some point, maybe when you can do fifteen miles, you'll believe that you can do twenty-six. You don't have to believe that now. Just get started.

CLIENT: That makes sense. I can be committed without setting the marathon up as the whole enchilada.

REFLECTOR: Exactly.

Here the coach believes that the client has it within him to do the training and complete a twenty-six-mile run, and reflects that belief in his comments. The client doesn't have to take it on faith, or be convinced. In order to demonstrate to himself that he does indeed have this potential, he has only to enter into a process; the evidence will follow.

For now, the coach is holding the confidence for the client until he can develop it for himself.

This Aspect of the Reflector supports the client's ability to see himself as successful—within reason, of course. It's not the coach's responsibility to get the client to feel differently. The coach accepts where the client is now, while holding out the belief that the client can move through the current situation to a successful outcome. The coach holds that belief because the client, temporarily, may not be able to hold it for himself. This provides the psychological space for movement on the client's part. This applies not only to marathons, but to any arena of work or life in which the client has yet to demonstrate his capability to himself.

Encouraging Self-Observation and Reflection (R3)

Self-awareness is critical to the client's ability to be self-correcting, and it's part of the coach's job as Reflector to provide encouragement and tools that facilitate the client's self-observation skills. (Several of the self-observation exercises offered in Chapter 13 can be of use to clients, either as they are or in modified form.)

Although other Voices may also come into play, it's as the Reflector that the coach will seek to elicit from the client his beliefs about where his current choices are leading. Sometimes the client is unable or unwilling to do this; if that's the case, the coach must decide whether to share her own perspectives on what the future trajectory is likely to be, given what the client has told her so far. There is nothing inherently wrong with doing this; however, as coaches, we must always consider the implications when we step out of a facilitative mode into a "telling" mode. We seek a balance between asking clients to draw from their own resources and the sharing of our own insights and suggestions.

CLIENT: I'm concerned that when I get stressed out it spills over into work. I see people looking at me; it's easy to assume they're thinking the worst, and that they see me as incompetent. I know that's silly, but that's what it feels like.

REFLECTOR: So how do you recognize that you're feeling stressed? And how does it affect your work?

CLIENT: I feel more anxious and more self-conscious. Of course, I'm more likely to come across as unsure to other people—well, to act unsure—at work, when I feel like that. Then the stress increases.

REFLECTOR: So if you keep feeling this way, where would it lead?

CLIENT: Seems like I'd get more and more stressed, and I know that makes me less effective. Which, of course, feeds the anxiety. It's kind of a vicious cycle.

REFLECTOR: Is that a future you look forward to?

CLIENT: No, I don't like that picture at all.

REFLECTOR: I hear you saying that you see what's happening pretty clearly, and you want to change it. So let's start talking about how you could do that. . .

In a context like this one, it's important not to stay with a negative future for long; it is, however, a possibility that the client may need to look squarely in the face in order to be motivated to choose new behaviors, and helping him do that falls to this Aspect of the coach as Reflector.

Having done that, in moving forward with this dialogue the coach would support the client in articulating a clear alternative outcome centered around his sense of competence and the positive aspects of his relationships with others. That positive future would then provide the motivation for moving forward.

This Aspect of the Reflector, then, is oriented towards "connecting the dots" for the client. The coach helps the client see alternatives based on what is happening right now. It loosens the tight restrictions of the client's way of thinking about the current situation, and frees him up to consider that he is at choice about what the future brings.

In the next dialogue, the Reflector encourages the client to develop his capacity to observe and reflect on his own behavior. This capacity is central to the client's capacity to become self-correcting. It is not that coach feedback isn't useful, but as the client learns to observe himself, the coach becomes less critical to the ongoing development of self-awareness. Encouraging this independence is a responsibility of the coach.

CLIENT: My people seem to have a lot of gripes about me, and I need to do something about it. It's pretty clear from my feedback that they see me as snappy, reactive, and—what is it they put down here?—sometimes quick to anger. That's what they said in the evaluation.

REFLECTOR: Maybe you need to get a little better at observing yourself in action. If you can notice when you're doing the things that all these people say you're doing, maybe you could change a few things about how you behave.

CLIENT: That makes sense. But if I could notice all this minor stuff, I wouldn't need to be talking to you about it. That's the problem; sometimes I don't even know what they mean by this or that. I do blow up once in a while, sure, but it's rare.

REFLECTOR: Well, we all have ingrained habits that make us do things we don't even know we're doing. Maybe the key here is paying attention to how you're feeling and how that leads you to behave. Maybe you don't even notice it when you're being snappy. If we become more self-aware, we can get better at choosing what works best—for us and for other people too.

CLIENT: I don't have a clue how to begin with this. But I guess I want to. I'm tired of being seen as some kind of ogre.

REFLECTOR: I can get you started with a self-observation exercise. It's simple. Twice a day take a minute and jot down some notes about times in the last couple of hours when people might have thought you were being snappy or short. They won't be dramatic examples, usually. I'm asking you to look for examples of how you're reacting to things and how that might come out. I'm asking you to not judge yourself, just to notice. Are you willing to try it?

CLIENT: Sure, I'll give it a try for a few days.

REFLECTOR: Good. After you observe yourself in action for a while, I'm going to ask you what you see.

Here the Reflector is issuing an invitation to self-awareness. First she offers the guidance that it's important to be able to notice what's going on inside oneself, then she suggests a process for doing so. Again, the ability to see ourselves clearly helps us get beyond our habits, in particular our self-defensive behaviors and routines. (We'll talk about tools for increasing self-awareness through self-observation extensively in Part 3 of the book.)

Drawing from Chris Argyris's work, Peter Senge describes defensive routines as

the entrenched habits we use to protect ourselves from the embarrassment and threat that come with exposing our thinking. Defensive routines form a sort of protective shell round our deepest assumptions, defending us against pain, but also keeping us from learning about the causes of the pain. . . . The most effective defensive routines, like that of the forceful CEO [someone Senge used as an example], are those we cannot see. Ostensibly, the CEO hoped to provoke others into expressing their thoughts. But his overbearing behavior reliably prevented them from doing so, thereby protecting his own views from challenge. If expressed as a conscious strategy, the defensiveness is transparent: "Keep people on the defensive through intimidation, so they won't confront my thinking." If the CEO saw his strategy presented in such bald terms, he would almost certainly disavow it. The fact that it remains hidden to him keeps it operative.[39]

The Reflector, in this Aspect, is an advocate for client self-observation and reflection. She represents the value of doing this, and supports the client as he develops trust in both the usefulness of observing himself and his ability to do so. In most cases, it will take time for the client to cultivate this trust, and to see that he really can increase his self-awareness. While he goes through this developmental process, the coach provides tools and structures while being consistent and supportive in encouraging him to keep at it.

Pitfalls and Guidelines

The Reflector is a key role in supporting the client's enhanced awareness of the choices he or she is making, and of their consequences. Well played, the Reflector role can shine light into the dark corners of a client's blind spots and defensive routines. The more firmly a behavior or a defensive routine is entrenched, the more likely it is that it's protecting something deep and tightly held.

The Reflector, then, helps the client to become more honest with himself or herself. The coach must be mindful and sensitive in filling this role, and must do it with respect, acceptance, and caring.

Let's look at some pitfalls in the Reflector role.

The social identity in which we have invested ourselves as a coach may, to some extent, rest on our ability to lift the client out of his or her current emotional state into a more optimistic one. This is a limited understanding of our role. It's wonderful when a client leaves a session feeling more optimistic. It feels good to both parties. Ultimately, however, it is not up to us to "fix" our client's mood or perspective. We are not responsible for the emotional well-being of our clients. In fact, for all of us as human beings, feeling discouraged for a while may be part of the process of working our own way out of a dilemma; people must discover their own readiness to change things. To lose sight of this is to create another attachment for ourselves and a confusing message for the client.

Another pitfall of the Reflector role is that the coach's "belief in the client" may come across as false or too easy. To superficially prop someone up does them a disservice. We believe in the fundamental capacity of every person to grow and change. What we do as coaches is provide space for our clients to develop their own realistic assessments of their unique capabilities, including those they may not have been aware of previously. That doesn't mean we believe that everyone can become a whiz at calculus or a concert violinist. We need to be able to be honest and direct when we suspect that our clients are biting off more than they can chew. If he or she is establishing a goal that seems way beyond the realm of possibility, it's our job to state that simply and non-judgmentally. "Jerry, let me suggest that your experience and skills haven't yet prepared you to run for President."

For a client to rely excessively on the coach, in any role he or she plays, leads to a kind of dependency in which the client is always looking to the outside for a sense of self. This is counter to the notion of coaching, as it ultimately undermines the client's ability to be self-generating. The mindful Reflector must be alert for this dependency. If there is a feeling that the client is pulling at the coach's energy, and the coach feels drained at the end of a conversation by the need to reassure and "carry" the client, these are red flags that some form of dependency is taking place.

Again, we can sometimes feel anxious about telling the truth. We fear the client's defensiveness. We have projections about what it might feel like to hear what we are about to say. We desire to protect the client's feelings. All of these may lead us to soft-peddle or avoid speaking the truth. Here, as always, we must be aware of our own aversions and fears, and let them go in order to be present with the client.

Finally, if serious warning signs are present, or if the client appears to be incapable of mustering sufficient optimism or belief in himself to take action toward something that he clearly wants, there may be therapeutic issues involved. Unless you are a trained clinician, referrals to other professionals with the requisite skills may well be in order.

These guidelines will be helpful in maintaining your mindfulness as the Reflector:

- Ask permission from the client before providing feedback. Ensure that there is a clear understanding between you about the purpose and the client's readiness to receive it.
- Mean what you say. Be clear about what you see. Be a good enough observer that you have concrete and specific examples of your client's unhelpful behaviors or skills and capabilities. A fuzzy, generalized belief in someone will mean less than specifics that the person can understand and relate to.
- Pay attention to your own need to be the "fixer," one who needs to be needed. If you and the client cooperate to prop up your social identity as a Reflector, this may undermine his ability to provide a positive perspective for himself. This is another opportunity for mindfulness, and for recognizing your own attachments and ego needs.
- When reflecting back the implications of a client's behaviors and choices, remain mindful that this is just a snapshot or a possibility. Any time we change something in ourselves, the entire web of relationships and consequences also changes; we determine the future starting now. There is a tendency for all of us to feel that it's too late, that we've already set things in stone. Our job as coaches is to support the client's sense of empowerment around changing himself and the course of events.

Summary

The Reflector Voice is central to helping the client in determining what he's doing well and what choices he's making that are creating consequences not to his liking. The Reflector does this through several Aspects. Sometimes we provide direct feedback to the client on what he's doing either inside or outside the coaching relationship. This can be very helpful, but this feedback must be based on clear observations or data.

The Reflector also encourages the client to observe himself in action. This is a core element of the client's developing the capacity to self-correct and to perform independently. The Reflector may suggest that the client use self-observation exercises to practice this important capability, and always urges the client to increase his self-observation skills.

The Reflector helps the client "connect the dots," by recognizing the consequences of both helpful and unhelpful behaviors and choices. This includes both the current consequences of those choices and the extrapolation of the present into the future. This aspect of the Reflector role is key in helping the client recognize multiple alternatives to what he's doing right now.

The roles that the coach plays in this Voice are delicate because they can lead us into the tender realm of the client's defenses and unconscious patterns of behavior. Mindfulness is key. The coach must maintain awareness of her own agendas and judgments as they arise, and work toward being steady and accepting, even when (especially when!) the conversation is focused on ways in which the client might be undermining himself or in pain. The unshakeable presence of the Reflector is invaluable as she gently helps the client open doors to seeing.

CHAPTER NINE

The Teacher

The test of a first-rate intelligence is the ability
to hold two opposed ideas in the mind at the same
time, and still retain the ability to function.
F. SCOTT FITZGERALD

It is a good morning exercise for a
research scientist to discard a pet hypothesis
every day before breakfast. It keeps him young.
KONRAD LORENZ

The Voice of the Teacher is, I confess, my personal favorite, the one I go
to most easily, the one I am most likely to hide behind or overuse.

I grew up with a mother and father who were educators professionally, as well as being my own first teachers as my parents. I was the
product of a public school and liberal arts college education, in which I
spent countless hours with at least seventy or so teachers (that may be
an under-estimate). I've also participated in innumerable workshops,
trainings, conferences, etc., where I was in a learning mode with people
who purported to teach something. The exposure to all of these people,
who ranged in their teaching skills from world class to sub-mediocre,

socialized me into what it meant to be a Teacher, and for me that arche-type is a very positive one.

Coach as Teacher

The word "teacher," of course, means many things to many people. Styles of teaching vary widely, and teaching often incorporates elements described in this book as belonging to other Voices of the coach. The Socratic method of teaching, for example, is the ultimate source of the Investigator behaviors of asking questions to prompt the client to dis-cover his or her own answers.

I am using the word "teacher," however, to describe a very specific set of roles and behaviors within the overall approach to coaching that we are using here. Other wisdom and perspectives on what teachers do are just as well informed and valid as this one, but they pertain to dif-ferent contexts. The Teacher role as described and differentiated within the Septet Model is a specific subset of teaching behaviors.

In the Septet, the Teacher Voice provides information, language, and frameworks that will help the client analyze his situation and take action. The Teacher is also the second of the three Voices that we describe as "sharpeners," in that they clarify and sharpen the client's responses to the Investigator's three lines of questioning. The new lan-guage and models provided by the Teacher can be immensely helpful in helping a client see new opportunities, and it's part of the Teacher's role to challenge and help expand his thinking.

It is important to be aware that, as an "expert" role, the Teacher is prone to overuse. The more easily a role can make a coach look good in his own eyes or those of others, the more likely it is to become the basis for a social identity. The giver of answers, the provider of knowledge, the wise person—these are tempting social identities into which to fall. As always, being mindful is the way to avoid the temptations and pit-falls of this role.

Used mindfully, the Voice of the Teacher offers something to the client. The nature of an offering is that the other person is truly free to accept or decline it. The Teacher may know that the information provided is likely to illuminate a pathway or a particular set of choices for the client. The mindful Teacher, however, has no attachment to the client's acceptance of the information or model being offered, nor is it his goal to get the client to move in a particular direction. The information is only provided to support his ability to see the situation differently. The translation of the information into an action orientation is up to the client.

The Teacher must be clear on how playing this role will support the client in achieving his stated outcomes. If you are not sure just how what you are offering serves the client, then it probably doesn't need to be shared. For example, if a client has mentioned, just in passing, that he's thinking of getting an MBA someday, it may not be useful for the coach to jump in and provide information about specific programs. On the other hand, if the client announces that he's just about decided to go for a degree but doesn't know what's available to him, he needs information that the coach as Teacher can provide either directly or by pointing him to other resources. The discernment for the coach is about how a specific piece of information or model will serve the immediate needs and outcomes that the client wants.

The Aspects of the Teacher

T1 Providing "expert" information, tools and language

T2 Challenging and stimulating client's thinking process

The first Aspect of the Teacher begins with the simple sharing of knowledge or information. This is "expert" knowledge, provided from the coach's experience. The knowledge is in the form of facts, information, or resources that the coach can point to. It is neutral.

This Aspect also involves the sharing of tools or language that the client can then use to draw new distinctions or to describe a situation differently. The tools and language are enabling, in that they support new ways of seeing. This, in turn, leads to new alternatives for action. There is no impetus for action, nor recommendation of an explicit course of action. The Teacher simply provides the means to see and discern more clearly.

The second Aspect of this role involves getting the client to reflect on his own thinking process and supporting him in finding new ways to analyze a situation. This is sometimes an encouragement, sometimes a challenge. Either way, the desired outcome for the client is the possibility of a cognitive shift and/or new perspectives on the assumptions and values that shape his actions. I say "possibility" here because the aim is not to have the client think like the coach, but to help him see things in new ways that will be useful to him.

Let's explore each of these in turn.

Providing "Expert" Information, Tools, and Language (T1)

Sometimes a client just doesn't have some of the information he needs in order to develop a new skill or embark on a new project. The Teacher, then, provides "neutral" information and concepts, expanding the client's view and understanding. Presented without bias for action, this information gives the client a more solid basis for making decisions and taking actions. The coach as Teacher does not direct the client toward a particular way to use the information presented, however, or recommend a course of action.

CLIENT: I need some help on how to find out about more advanced accounting training.

TEACHER: Well, King University and Reynolds School of Business both have executive programs that are well respected; they also have specialized accounting courses that you can attend as stand-alones. There are also a number of on-line programs that might cover the kind of specifics you're looking for.

CLIENT: Which would you recommend?

TEACHER: I think that both the local programs are good, and I don't know any details about the on-line ones. With a little web searching you should be able to find several you can check out. Then you can compare them all.

CLIENT: Okay, I'll give myself that assignment.

Note that the coach is not recommending a course of action here. The impetus is coming from the client; the Teacher is simply offering what he knows and pointing the client toward other sources of information.

The Teacher also provides conceptual tools and language that support the client in understanding and interpreting his situation. Without such tools, we often tend to be stuck in habitual ways of seeing things. A relevant and clear model, or new language, on the other hand, can provide new means for communicating about, and interpreting, phenomena.

For example, my client Terry had committed himself to a major diet/ exercise plan. All went well until Thanksgiving dinner, when he politely declined the mashed potatoes and gravy because of the unwanted calories. Terry's wife, a wonderful cook who was proud of her Thanksgiving spread, was taken aback by this refusal. It was a reasonable decision for Terry to make; it was also reasonable for Terry's wife to have made the mashed potatoes. The Thanksgiving menu was dictated by tradition; neither had thought to raise the question of whether Terry's diet would require changes. The result was only a minor strain in the relationship, but Terry's diet/exercise plan was one of the things I was coaching him on, and he wanted to talk to me about the incident at our next session.

The concept of interests vs. positions that Roger Fisher and William Ury present in their influential book *Getting to Yes* leapt immediately to mind.[40] It took two minutes to explain, and then we applied it to the situation. Terry's position was that he didn't want to eat extra calories; his wife's position was that she wanted people to enjoy what she had worked so hard to prepare. Beneath those different stances lay their common interests: both wanted Terry's program to succeed, both wanted a holiday dinner with the kids to be special, both wanted a sense of tradition. If they could focus on these underlying interests, it seemed clear, there would be lots of possibilities for creating a win/win solution.

While this may seem like a trivial example, it illustrates the point beautifully. Armed with that mental model, and the distinction between interests and positions, Terry saw the event in a whole new context. The information was neutral, the model just a way to think about any situation in a new way. The result, however, was very important for Terry. He was able to apply the distinction between interests and positions in a variety of situations, both at work and at home; he felt it greatly enhanced his on-the-job skills as a manager. And that year he and his family approached Christmas dinner very differently. After a discussion about what each of them wanted, they decided on a collaborative approach that had each person—including the kids—preparing something special for the meal. Terry's wife was thrilled at having more help than ever before, Terry stayed on his diet, and the experience was enjoyed by all. Acting as the Teacher, I had simply provided a language and a way of seeing; Terry did the rest.

Here's another example.

CLIENT: I just don't see why Brad would feel so put out in that situation. I was just voicing a different perspective. I was direct, but, come on! He's a grownup!

TEACHER: Jennifer, I can suggest a way of looking at what happened in a different way. It might be helpful. Would you like to hear that?

CLIENT: Sure.

TEACHER: Think of the available energy in an interaction between two people. Ultimately, there's only a certain amount, and it gets used in several ways. Quantity of airtime is part of it, but not all. Forcefulness of expression also uses up energy. Think about it for a minute. Can you see how, when they're interacting with others, some people tend to take more energy than others?

CLIENT: Yeah. [pauses] Some people are pretty assertive. I guess I'm one of those. Others are more laid back. They wait for someone else to take the lead.

TEACHER: Exactly. What does Brad usually do?

CLIENT: He's usually pretty outspoken.

TEACHER: But in this case, your opinions about the database were strongly held.

CLIENT: Yeah. [laughs] You could say that!

TEACHER: So one way to look at what happened when you met the other day is that, of the available hundred percent of the energy, you were taking up maybe seventy-five. If that's right, it leaves him with twenty-five. For someone who's used to being outspoken, twenty-five might feel a bit suffocating. Perhaps, in your desire to press your point, you were simply a bit overwhelming. Does this make any sense to you?

CLIENT: Yeah, it does. I do have strong feelings about the database, but Brad does, too. He probably felt I didn't bother to listen to what he had to say. I want to be direct, and I want to argue my case, but maybe I need to try not to get so carried away.

TEACHER: I think that's a good way to put it, Jennifer.

In this dialogue, the coach is providing a model and a context for interpreting an event.[41] Again, the tool is neutral; tools and frameworks are not inherently action-oriented. This one does, however, enable Jennifer to step outside her view of what happened with Brad and see it from a larger perspective. Once she sees the picture through a new lens, the client often spontaneously knows what she needs to do differently.

Describing his own, similar example, Flaherty writes,

> Each person's actions were fully consistent with the interpretation he brought, an interpretation that will persist across time, across events, across circumstances. Our job as coaches will be to understand the client's structure of interpretation, then in partnership alter this structure so that the actions that follow bring about the intended outcome. As coaches we do this by providing a new language that allows the client to make new observations.[42]

Providing new tools and language, then, allows the client to interpret events in very different ways; this can offer options for changed behaviors and actions that would have previously been inaccessible to the client.

Challenging and Stimulating Client's Thinking Process (T2)

It's sometimes helpful to make the assumption that each of us does the best we can, given the information and choices we perceive. In theory, if we had all the necessary information, we'd always make the optimal choices in our lives. But of course there are other factors that limit the choices we can see and are able to act upon, and many of these have to do with our conditioning.

As we know from our earlier discussion about conditioning, humans tend to process information in predictable ways. We get caught in limited ways of seeing and thinking about the situations that we face, which in turn limits the options we see for our lives. The coach, of course, is in the business of supporting the client in expanding her options.

This second Aspect is focused on the thinking process itself, the underlying mechanisms that the client uses to process information, draw inferences, and ultimately to determine courses of action. The

Teacher's job, then, in this Aspect is to challenge the client in her thinking process, and to help her get to a deeper and more accurate level of understanding. This can involve exposing the client's leaps of abstraction as she moves from simple observations to complex generalizations that may or may not be true. Or it can mean helping the client examine her assumptions, which may or may not support what she says she wants.

In our next example, the client takes a simple situation and makes significant inferences without testing them. By challenging the inferences she's made, the coach helps her see how her mind works.

CLIENT: I think Susan [the client's immediate boss] really has it in for me.

TEACHER: Why do you say that?

CLIENT: Well, she barely says hello to me in the morning when she comes in. And she criticized my presentation in the staff meeting the other day.

TEACHER: So tell me about what happened in the meeting.

CLIENT: I was presenting our sales projections for the next quarter. She said they were overly optimistic, and I should go back to the market data and be less starry-eyed. That's how she put it.

TEACHER: Starry-eyed, huh? Well, it has been my experience with you that you sometimes see things in a rosy light. Maybe she's right.

CLIENT: Well, maybe she was. My projections were a bit on the optimistic side. I didn't think it was appropriate for her to say that in the meeting, though.

TEACHER: Maybe not. Is that typical of the way she responds to people?

CLIENT: Well, she can be pretty tough. Her expectations are high. I don't think she means to be hurtful, but she can be a bit cutting.

TEACHER: So it's not really about you. Sounds like it's just her style.

CLIENT: Yeah. It is her style. But it rubs me the wrong way.

TEACHER: You can't change her style, but you can choose how think about it. Beyond style, though, it sounds like Susan's committed to accurate projections. So are you—you both want the same thing in the end.

CLIENT: Yeah, we do. She's just so tactless.

TEACHER: Is she tactless with other people too?

CLIENT: Well, she really cut down Don the other day over a pretty small detail. I guess she's just not a friendly person.

TEACHER: You mentioned how she acts in the morning. Does she say hello to everyone else? Is it just you she ignores?

CLIENT: Well, she actually just kind of brushes in, grabs her in-box, and goes into her office. I do respect her, I just wish she was a nicer person.

TEACHER: Well, from this discussion, it sounds to me like she doesn't really have it in for you in particular. It sounds like she has high expectations and sometimes isn't as diplomatic as you'd like her to be. Is that a more accurate way to describe the situation?

CLIENT: Yes, I guess it is. I think sometimes I blow things up out of proportion. And sometimes I take them too personally. When she called me starry-eyed, though, it really set me off.

TEACHER: So—you have a challenging boss! Let's talk about how you can work with her more effectively.

Here, the coach as Teacher challenges the client's thinking process. It was a set of inferences that led the client to the conclusion that she was being singled out, that her boss had it in for her, but when these inferences are challenged the client comes to the conclusion that her initial reaction was probably unjustified.

People jump to conclusions all the time. This results, of course, from our conditioned mind responding to a limited set of data and piling on interpretations. Untangling the mess that our minds sometimes make of a situation is a key part of coming to see the situation more clearly and thus being able to identify a useful course of action within it. The Teacher does this by exposing the line of thinking, the extrapolations the client makes. This allows the client to come back to what is really observable and respond to it more directly, rather than responding from a set of inferences that go way beyond the data, are likely inaccurate, and may lead in a totally wrong direction.

Chris Argyris has spent an illustrious career studying organizational learning and how defensive routines block the ability of even highly successful people to learn and change. Argyris calls this tendency to operate from the same framework "single-loop" learning. In this kind of learning, people respond to setbacks with new action strategies, but do not question the governing variables: the underlying values, assumptions, and goals that the person holds but may not even be aware of. When the new strategies fail (as they often do, because they're based on the same flawed and limited thinking) the person becomes defensive and even less able to learn.

> Because many professionals are almost always successful at what they do, they rarely experience failure. And because they have rarely failed, they have never learned how to learn from failure. So whenever their single-loop learning strategies go wrong, they become defensive, screen out criticism, and put the "blame" on anyone and everyone but themselves. In short, their ability to learn shuts down precisely at the moment they need it the most.[43]

When people hire coaches, it's often because they want to change the game and approach their lives with new strategies that are more likely to be effective. Coaches encourage "double-loop" learning, meaning they invite the person faced with a setback to examine the fundamental assumptions and goals that led to the ineffective action strategy in the first place. By assessing the underlying thinking process, the client engages in a deeper level of learning, one more likely to lead to new solutions. With double-loop learning, as Argyris and coauthor Don Schon explain in *Theory in Practice,* "individuals are . . . able to examine their values and assumptions in order to design and implement a quality of life that is not constrained by the status quo."[44]

TEACHER: So, Jessica, how did your conversation with Michael go?

CLIENT: I guess it went pretty well. We ended up talking about other things for the most part.

TEACHER: What did he have to say about your new marketing idea?

CLIENT: Actually, we didn't really talk about it much.

TEACHER: Wasn't that the primary purpose of the meeting?

CLIENT: Yes, but I didn't feel ready to bring it up.

TEACHER: When we talked last time, you felt that it was an important time to get an outside perspective, and that Michael was the one who could give you that.

CLIENT: Yeah, I did feel like that. But I'm just not ready to share it yet. I think I have to think it through a little more.

TEACHER: Jessica, you've worked on this idea a lot! Sounds like it has to be close to perfect before you're willing to share it with others.

CLIENT: Well, it reflects on me!

TEACHER: It's very important to you for Michael to see you as competent, isn't it?

CLIENT: Of course, wouldn't it be for you?

TEACHER: It would, if I were in your shoes. May I share an observation?

CLIENT: Of course.

TEACHER: I think there are two things you're trying to act on at the same time, but they conflict. The first is that it's a good thing to be getting another perspective on your idea, bouncing it around and getting it in as good shape as possible. That would make you want to talk with Michael about it as soon as possible, because you respect his opinion.

CLIENT: Yes, that's right. I think he could help me work on it.

TEACHER: Yes, but the other thing appears to be winning out.

CLIENT: What's that?

TEACHER: The other thing is that it's important to you to appear competent, to have worked out all the kinks before you share something. Maybe that's what held you back when you met with Michael.

CLIENT: Hmm. [pauses] I see your point. Yeah, it's a tradeoff. I can't do both at the same time. But maybe by trying to make myself look good, I actually get in my own way.

TEACHER: Exactly. You made the defend-your-competence thing more important than the refine-your-thinking piece. It's not what you say you value most, but that's the way you acted.

CLIENT: Yeah, you're right! I do that a lot. I usually lay low until I'm very sure of myself. But maybe that holds me back sometimes. That's a big one. I'll have to think more about that.

Here the Teacher exposes the contradiction between Jessica's stated value of refining her idea and the way she acts in order to protect Michael's perception of her as competent. It's an "aha" moment for Jessica, as it often is when we first see the unconscious assumptions that we operate from. In this example, Jessica's overriding concern in the end is to appear competent. In her conversation with Michael, that "governing value" won out over her stated goal of refining her idea with the input of others. Seeing the powerful influence of that unconscious, conditioned

value allows Jessica to choose a different course of action that will lead
to a better marketing idea and more learning for Jessica.

According to Argyris,

> There seems to be a universal human tendency to design
> one's actions consistently according to four basic values:
> • To remain in unilateral control;
> • To maximize "winning" and minimize "losing";
> • To suppress negative feelings; and
> • To be as "rational" as possible.[45]

Seeing these underlying values at play in our lives is an eye-opener,
especially when we discover that holding to them keeps us from achieving or experiencing what we say we want. (Sounds like the attachments
and aversions we introduced in Chapter 2!) The Teacher, then, in inviting the client to take a second look at what's motivating her, exposes
these gaps between conflicting desires and values. This must be done
sensitively and mindfully because for all of us, inner conflict may make
us feel defensive. The key, of course, is to support the client in discovering that a resolution is possible, that an alternative action might, in
fact, get her what she truly wants. Addressing this issue, Liane Anderson comments,

> Acting defensively can be viewed as moving away from some-
> thing, usually some truth about ourselves. If our actions are
> driven by moving away from something then our actions
> are controlled and defined by whatever it is we are moving
> away from, not by us and what we would like to be mov-
> ing towards. Therefore our potential for growth and learn-
> ing is seriously impaired. If my behavior is driven by my not
> wanting to be seen as incompetent, this may lead me to hide
> things from myself and others, in order to avoid feelings of
> incompetence. . . . If my behavior is driven by wanting to

be competent, honest evaluation . . . by myself and others would be welcome and useful.[46]

The coach as Teacher, then, works with the client on ways she can get what she has said she wants. The coach takes the client's commitment to these goals at face value, and when the client is acting in ways that don't move her in that direction, seeks to catalyze her awareness about the discrepancy. To do so by asking the client to come up with a different action, or suggesting one, is to encourage single-loop learning. It may or may not be successful. To engage the client in double-loop learning, the coach exposes her underlying thinking process, assumptions, and governing values, so that she is better able to fit her actions to her goals.

Pitfalls and Guidelines

The Teacher Voice is one of the Voices most likely to be overused. The coach should watch out for ways in which the teaching can become a way to either hide from the client or validate the coach's image of himself as competent and wise. These attachments invariably cloud the coach's ability to see the client clearly.

The Teacher is inherently neutral. There is no impetus from the Teacher toward action. (Enhancing a client's motivation to act, if and when this seems necessary, is the province of the action-oriented Guide, to be discussed in the next chapter.) The information the coach offers in this role must be relevant to the client's outcomes, and should be presented to the client concisely in the interest of fostering new perspectives and choices. The proportion of time spent using the Teaching Voice should reflect this.

This is because, if we accept the premise that our ultimate goal is to help the client develop his or her own ways to learn, reliance on us for easy answers may not further that goal. That is the basis for the critical distinction between appropriate and inappropriate uses of the Teacher Voice: does the imparting of *this* information to the client at *this* time, or challenging the client's thinking in *this* way, support his or her long-term ability to be effective and self-generating?

Here are some guidelines for staying mindful as the Teacher:

- Ensure that your teaching is serving a specific need or outcome that has been articulated by the client; don't confuse means and ends. The Teacher's contributions are not ends in themselves. To introduce a model or a piece of information because you find it interesting is not a productive use of coaching time; doing so as a way of enabling the client to see differently, and to illuminate new choices, is.

- Be aware of any developing dependency. The collusion of the client and coach around dependency is difficult; if you find yourself in the Teacher role a lot, it may be important to discuss this with the client and ensure that he or she is not leaning on you to an extent unhealthy for both of you.

- Watch for your identification with the Teacher role, as indicated by an energy charge or the feeling of being validated somehow by what or how you teach. Watch out for the feeling that it's "important" to share something or that you "should" teach it; this is a big clue to the presence of an attachment on your part. Come back to a fuller view of the client, and let that guide you as to what's important.

- Ask permission of the client before sharing information or models. Is it okay if I share a model that I think you might find helpful? is a question that will generally lead to agreement. Sometimes, though, a client will say no. A mindful coach is not attached to having every offering accepted.

- Keep your teaching concise and clear. Providing information and new language is a small part of most coaching. It is a laser-like intervention, done to increase the accuracy and understanding with which the client can perceive the landscape and his or her available choices. It is not, however, the primary work of coaching, which is to create change and forward motion. If overdone, teaching can become a diversion from the real work.

Summary

The Teacher Voice is an important one, in that providing information, language for interpretation, and insights into the client's thinking process can greatly enhance her ability to perceive both external and internal landscapes, and the possible choices that she can make to navigate them.

The Teacher Voice plays out in two Aspects. The first involves the providing of simple information or facts and the sharing of models and language that the client can then use to develop a fuller picture of his or her situation and possibilities.

The second Aspect involves inviting the client to examine his or her own assumptions and thinking process, by pointing out, for example, where he or she may be making faulty inferences that go way beyond the real data, or by helping the client explore the underlying values and assumptions that subconsciously guide his or her actions. This second function of the Teacher has some overlap with the role of the Investigator; the key distinction is that the Investigator works primarily through questioning, an eliciting stance, while the Teacher is primarily making statements that offer information, language, tools, and ways of thinking.

The Guide

*Advice is what we ask for when we already
know the answer but wish we didn't.*
—ERICA JONG

*I have found the best way to give advice
to your children is to find out what they
want and then advise them to do it.*
—HARRY S. TRUMAN

As the Guide, the coach provides impetus towards action, suggests possible directions for client action, or even makes recommendations for what a client might do. The Guide Voice can be exceedingly helpful when the client is feeling reluctant to commit, unclear, or simply at a loss. Generally, this Voice comes to the fore later in the course of a coaching conversation, after the territory of a situation has been explored and when the coach and client both agree that the coach's guidance and leadership might be appropriate and helpful.

The Guide is the third of the three sharpening Voices, supporting the client in finding answers to the three Investigator questions. The Guide can be instrumental as the client confronts that third question, What are you going to do?

The Guide Voice is the most directive of all the Voices, and therefore the most prone to being used in a way that undermines the client's authority, so particular attention needs to be paid to the balance between the client's legitimate need to see results and the ultimate goal that he take charge of his own unfolding growth and development.

On the one hand, the client is participating in a coaching program because he wants to be more effective, or wants his life or a specific situation to change—or because a third party has brought him there in an effort to achieve these goals. Bringing about these outcomes nearly always involves commitment to actions that will sometimes prove challenging to take, and this is where the additional encouragement and impetus of the coach as Guide can be enabling. On the other hand, an over-reliance on the coach can become a crutch, substituting for (and perhaps undermining) the client's ability to muster his own internal commitment. Some would argue that this doesn't matter, that the resulting action is the bottom line and that the benefits from acting make the source of the impetus moot. I hold that the ultimate goal of coaching is for the client to become self-generative, and that he accomplishes this by developing his own motivation and commitment to action in service to his own vision. This is why we must be careful what we say and do as the Guide.

About Time and Impetus

The more assertive nature of the Guide Voice carries with it more than the usual opportunity to confuse the agenda of the coach with the highest good for the client. Our very sense of identity as a coach may be intricately linked with how quickly our clients move into action. Some of us even hang out shingles saying something like "Mike: the Results Coach." And for all of us, seeing a client get stuck invokes questions about our own effectiveness. Our attachments, then, may mask our clarity about the client. A client can be *usefully* stuck. Sometimes we need to feel stuck for a while before we find the willingness to move on and try a new behavior. "Protecting" our clients from this discomfort by urging them on because of our own impatience to get movement, or because we assume that otherwise they're going to get lost forever, doesn't serve to help them get in touch with their own desires and purposes.

I struggled for some time with how to structure my calendar to write this book. On the one hand, it sounded great to devote several months to nothing but writing, and I felt I had something to contribute to the field; on the other hand, I had coaching and consulting clients, a number of other projects under way, and a short attention span. I knew I needed a lot of time to write, and I was committed to the book in principle, but in practice I was very anxious about actually blocking out weeks on my calendar when I'd be unavailable to work on anything else. After all, what if a favorite client really needed me for a couple of days? Or, worse, what if I committed the time and didn't produce a book at the end of it—who would I be then? I felt stuck.

My own coach was patient with my struggle. This was an issue that I had to work my way through, and it wasn't her issue. It took several weeks, but ultimately *I* had to get to the point of either allocating sufficient time to write or giving up the idea. It had to be my decision. If she had pushed me into committing the time, it would not have been fully my decision, and I wouldn't have gotten to it by having to face down my indecisiveness and work through the resistances that came up. Her willingness to let it be my struggle and my process while continually putting the choice in front of me was very important to my making a true and wholehearted commitment.

The key to using the Guide Voice well is the ability to suggest alternatives, or even to provide a timely nudge or two, without developing an attachment to the client's doing what *we* think is best for him. When we offer suggestions in our capacity as the Guide, there are no strings attached; we continue to see our clients fully and accept them whether they are stuck and aimless or purposeful and committed to action.

This doesn't mean that we don't care, or aren't committed to our client's success. It simply means that we don't confuse ourselves with them. It means that we seek to stay in our centered Master mind, seeing our clients clearly. It means providing impetus and/or direction when it's truly needed, and staying out of the way when the client is developing them on his own or needs to take some time to work through his own resistance to get there.

The Aspects of the Guide

G1 Encouraging client to take action
G2 Offering options and/or recommending courses of action

In the Septet scheme, the mindful Guide has two Aspects. The less directive is encouraging the client to take action. Here the guide is simply suggesting that movement is desirable and encouraging the client toward it. The client may have an idea (perhaps this emerged from an Investigator line of questioning) about what he would like to do next. In performing this Aspect of the Guide role, the coach encourages the client to act on that idea, but the idea itself came from the client.

In the second Aspect, the Guide may tell the client about what she has seen others do—involving specific actions or approaches or strategies—that has brought them success in similar circumstances. Or, if it's appropriate, she may speak from her own experience. Here the coach is providing examples of possible pathways forward. There's no push for the client to follow a specific pathway, but an action orientation is usually implied by merely presenting these as options or alternatives. If it seems to serve the client's needs, however, the uses of the Guide Voice may include suggesting or recommending that the client follow a specific course of action. The client is always at choice, of course, and the suggestion is usually framed as an invitation to try something. Still, this is the most directive of all the Aspects in the Septet.

Encouraging the Client to Take Action (G1)

Here the Guide is stating a bias for action. This is encouragement for the client to take the plunge, to move from considering a possibility to committing to it. The Guide isn't suggesting or contributing ideas for the action to the client, but she is an advocate for movement in a direction of the client's choosing.

Often the impetus for movement will come from the client, from dissatisfaction with the status quo, or from the excitement and energy generated by having a new picture of a desired future, or from a combination of both. The work has already been done, all the coach needs to do is provide encouragement and support.

But sometimes the client may resist taking action, even when he's thought it through and all the pieces are in place; here, additional impetus is helpful. This impetus is not a replacement for the client's ability to choose; rather, it's a nudge that enables him to do something he has already fundamentally decided to do.

CLIENT: It's hard to think about letting Jeff go. He's been with the company a long time.

GUIDE: Yes, he has. From what you've told me, he's made a big contribution.

CLIENT: Yeah. And I like the guy a lot. It's going to be tough for him. And for his family.

GUIDE: It's never an easy thing to do, even when you know it's the right thing. Have you explored every alternative, Dave? I want you to be sure that this is the right decision.

CLIENT: It is. I just don't want to. I know I have to do it, and sooner is better, but I really, really don't want to.

GUIDE: You've made your decision.

CLIENT: Yes, I've made it.

GUIDE: So now you have to move on it. It's time. [pauses] How do you think you'll feel after you talk to him?

CLIENT: Well, I'm sure I'll still feel sorry. But it'll also be a big relief, because I'm really dreading it.

GUIDE: Dave, we've been talking about this for a couple of weeks. You sound very clear about the need to let Jeff go. I know it's difficult, but it's time to take the plunge and do what you've already decided to do. Putting it off doesn't help anyone— not you, not Jeff, certainly not Jeff's staff.

CLIENT: You're right. It's time. I'll talk to him tomorrow.

Here the client knows what's ahead of him. The pathway is clear, the arguments back and forth have been weighed and decided upon. He's understandably reluctant, however, and appears to need some encouragement to initiate a difficult discussion. This pushing must be done with care. It's critical that it be the client who has made the decision. The coach is testing the client's commitment here, and asking him to be sure about his decision. Once the client is sure, the coach can encourage Dave to take action because *Dave* knows it's the right thing to do, not because the coach has an agenda about it.

Pushing a client into a decision that he's not yet ready to make, on the other hand, would not serve him well. The client's commitment must be explicit; the nudge serves to only to solidify it.

Besides the ethical and developmental arguments for ensuring that the decision is truly the client's, there are situations in which legal liability could be incurred should the coach be steering the client towards a decision with legal ramifications. Some coaches carry "errors and omissions" insurance, a policy standard with many consulting firms, to cover such eventualities. The best pedagogical and legal advice, however, is to keep the client in charge.

Offering Options and/or Recommending Courses of Action (G2)

Clearly, this Aspect of the Guide Voice requires that the coach know the territory. It has often been stated by people who are very knowledgeable about coaching that a coach does not need to be an expert in subject matter, that being a good question asker will suffice. This is sometimes true. Being a good question asker—a good Investigator—may fulfill most of a client's needs.

But some clients need more direction, and taking on this Aspect of the Guide role requires knowing the territory. This reality means that the unprepared coach will either be limited in the Voices available to her, or will extend her coaching beyond her expertise, which becomes an ethical issue. Knowing the territory can come from direct experience, or from having coached many clients in one industry or one area of development. The client certainly benefits from having a coach with broad experience across a number of related situations.

CLIENT: I'm interested in getting some process-improvement teams going in our company. We encourage suggestions, but we really haven't done anything systematic.

GUIDE: If it would be helpful, I can suggest a couple of approaches that have worked in other companies, and you can think about how they might fit.

CLIENT: That would be helpful.

GUIDE: Most of the programs I know about begin with some sort of pilot. The company trains a group of people in process improvement methods and tools. Then they identify some low-hanging fruit—some clear-cut problem that has a high likelihood of being solved pretty easily. The idea is to get an early success and build some commitment to the methodology. This seems to work better than taking on some huge issue and wrestling with it and the new process at the same time.

CLIENT: Makes sense. Who would be involved?

GUIDE: Depends on the issue. The people closest to the problem, I'd say. It would probably be a good idea to look at several issues. And pick a pilot team that includes people from different levels in the company—a few people you think of as leaders. Give them some training, pick an issue you think isn't too hard to solve, and get them on it. If they're successful they can bring what they've learned back to their departments.

CLIENT: That sounds very good. I want to do something like this. A pilot makes sense. Is this something that you can coach me through?

GUIDE: Yes, I could. And I could connect you with other resources that might be helpful. We will need to talk more about your goals, so you can think about what extra expertise you'd need and what decisions you'd have to make. When we flesh out a plan more, you'll have a better idea of what you'd be committing to, and what contraindications might lead you to decide not to do it for now.

Here the coach is laying out a scenario for how the client can accomplish the goal he says he wants, providing subject-matter expertise by drawing from the experience she's accumulated as a consultant, as someone familiar with the field, or as a coach for other clients that have gone through a similar process.

Notice that the impetus for action is coming from the client. The coach is laying out what she has seen work in other situations. She is neutral and does not *recommend* the approach to the client. In fact, she's slowing him down a bit and encouraging him to explore the possibilities in more depth before deciding. If there is implicit advocacy on the part of the coach here, it is for a sound decision based on good information, not for pursuing either a pilot or a full-blown process-improvement program. The client is in charge, and the coach is keeping him there.

Again, subject matter expertise and experience are necessary here in order for the coach's recommendations to have validity and credibility. Let's look at a much simpler scenario, one that involves both the Reflector and the Guide.

CLIENT: I just can't seem to get going on this finding-time-for–myself project.

REFLECTOR: Yes, you seem to be making it harder than it really is.

CLIENT: I think it'll get easier after the budget is in.

REFLECTOR: Probably, but I bet there will always be reasons for not finding time. We've talked about it before. That's the nature of the problem.

CLIENT: Yes, but this is a particularly challenging time.

GUIDE: That's why it's important to move on it right now—now's the time you really need the balance.

CLIENT: True enough, but how can I really get started when there's all this stuff I need to do?

GUIDE: You get started by starting. How about this? I want you to make a commitment to work out two times this week and take your wife out to dinner once this weekend—for a nice evening, not just a burger and back to work. That's it. We're not going to look at a whole program. We're just going for an initial success. Then we can talk again next week.

CLIENT: That's an evening and another couple of hours.

GUIDE: Yup. I think you added right. Do you want to do it or not?

CLIENT: Sounds like a lot.

GUIDE: Galen, many busy people wouldn't think that two hours in the gym and a date with their spouse over the course of a week was an overwhelming burden. You've been talking about this for a while now, but nothing's changed. It's time to get off the dime and do something. I recommend that you try a specific plan, but obviously it's your decision. What do you think?

CLIENT: Yes. Okay, I'm willing.

CONTRACTOR: So let's talk specifics . . .

In this case, the client appears to be rather stuck; he's talked about the need for balance in his life for some time without doing anything about it. The Guide recommends very specific actions and she pushes the client to take them. Both know that the client can follow through on these particular suggestions if it's important enough to him, and getting specific makes it more difficult for him to make excuses. An initial success will change things, and the conversation next week can build on these successes and look at what's next. On the other hand, if the client doesn't follow through, then next week's conversation can look at resistance and procrastination and explore whether the client is really committed to addressing the balance issue or not.

The coach here does not buy into the client's excuses about the budget cycle. Instead she's taking the lead to provide a short-term impetus until he's able to develop his commitment beyond the talking stage. In effect, she's testing him. To continue to provide this level of impetus would create dependency, but in this case the coach's judgment is that the client wouldn't move without a nudge, and at least *some* movement is what's necessary for the client to develop the energy to commit to what he says he wants.

Here's a more complex situation.

CLIENT: I want to come back to our conversation about the MBA. I just moved here, so I have no idea about what's available in the area. But I do think it's time to get started. Can you help me find a program?

GUIDE: Well, let's start with you. What are you looking for, exactly?

CLIENT: I'm not sure. I'd like to hear your suggestions, because I know you know a lot about business education. So tell me your ideas.

GUIDE: Okay. Here's the strategy I'd recommend. Start off by making a list of what's important to you and why. A set of criteria.

That'll help you evaluate what's available. But there might be other alternatives, too. We can take a look at the list in our next conversation if you want.

CLIENT: I can do that. I'll check it out with you next call.

GUIDE: Great. But you don't want to rush. You have to be very clear about what you're looking for. Then make another list, of all the programs you could do part-time, while maintaining your current job. Maybe half of those are distance-learning programs, and the rest are executive MBA programs within three hours from home. You'll need to think about the pros and cons of each. That can take a month or so, because you'll want to call them, get materials, and maybe follow up with a call to ask specific questions to determine how well they fit your criteria.

CLIENT: So you're telling me it won't be so quick. I need to do some research.

GUIDE: Yes, but you need some criteria to begin with. That's first.

CLIENT: Okay. And if I can, I think I should visit the final two.

GUIDE: Absolutely. The short list gets a more in-depth evaluation. Deciding between the last two will be more difficult, because that's where the commitment issues really come up. I think that's where I can be most helpful, by asking you tough questions against your criteria.

CLIENT: I like that approach, and you're speaking my language. I think for now the ball is in my court, where it should be. Then I use you to reality-check my thinking on the criteria and on how the final two stack up. Or maybe three if I'm feeling indecisive!

GUIDE: Yes. Is this how you'd like to proceed?

CLIENT: Yeah, this'll work great.

This is a pretty directive Guide interaction, but that's what the client is asking for. The client has pressed hard and the coach has provided the recommendations he judges to be most appropriate.

Again, the coach must be careful here if the overall pattern in the relationship is for the client to want a lot of this kind of specificity. If the overall relationship is balanced, though, and the client follows through well, there's no reason to hold back recommendations that he asks for. To do so could seem like playing games.

When the coach provides such specific recommendations, he or she must check to be sure that it's the client's decision, and that the client makes a specific statement of commitment. Sometimes it's just a check; in this example, the client is clearly on board already. At other times it will be very important to explore the client's commitment more carefully, to make sure the client isn't just going along with a specific plan without having to say, "Yes, I want to do this."

In this second Aspect, the Guide is providing suggestions for action. There is a continuum in directiveness from providing a possibility with no impetus (as in the example above concerning the process improvement program options), to providing a recommendation with specific ideas and an urge to action (as in the life balance and MBA program examples). The Guide must be constantly aware of the levels of energy and commitment around a client's contemplated change, and then choose where on that continuum it is most appropriate to coach.

Pitfalls and Guidelines

Those of us who like to solve problems and who get satisfaction out of helping others are in particular danger of overusing the Guide Voice. To the extent that we become attached to being a giver of advice, it becomes very easy to collude with the client by being more directive than is appropriate.

As coaches, we can also project on our clients. Sometimes we suggest a plan of action because we find it intriguing, or it's something we'd like to do. A test is, as with the other Voices, noticing if you experience extra energy or excitement as you move into this role.

It's easy for coaches to define their own success as getting the client to act, so we must beware of overdoing it. On the other hand, we may find ourselves at times reluctant to push and challenge. If that's the case we must ask ourselves if it's our own need to be comfortable and avoid the tension of challenging that holds us back. To hold back from pushing the client towards action can collude with the client's own desires to stay comfortable. We must balance the client's need for movement with his need to be grounded in that movement and in charge of the process. Always, the client's needs must provide the guidance for the pacing and direction of that movement.

Finally, we may seek to cover our lack of experience in a particular area by appearing more knowledgeable than we actually are. Speaking beyond our experience, or invoking a level of authority that we don't in fact possess is misleading to the client. It serves the client better to steer him towards knowledgeable resources than to pretend to have solutions that aren't, in fact, rooted in our experience.

It is the coach's role to challenge our clients and to encourage them to create movement in their lives. That is, generally, what they want and expect of us. Having clear outcomes and good agreements about how to work together creates the legitimacy for this challenging.

Use these guidelines to support your own mindfulness in the Guide role:

- Keep the client in charge. The Guide Voice slips quite easily into the coach's agenda. It can be difficult for both coach and client to know where the energy and direction are coming from, and who is responsible. Ask the client for an explicit commitment after making any recommendation. A simple lack of disagreement isn't sufficient. The client must proactively accept the proposed actions, or develop his own.

- If you're assuming the Guide Voice, ask yourself why. The Guide role is very helpful when used judiciously, but it should never be the default role. Going to the Guide Voice too easily may indicate that you're operating out of your own needs. Legitimate reasons for using this Voice don't include making the coach feel smart, getting the client to move at the pace the coach wants, or fulfilling the coach's desire to be of service. They do include the client's feeling stuck, lacking a strategy, or needing the coach's experience or encouragement to commit to a plan.

- Stay within the limits of your experience in offering suggestions for actions. That doesn't mean that you must have personally experienced every strategy that you suggest. It does mean that you should have a reasonable basis in personal experience, knowledge of others' experiences, or simply knowledge of your field, for believing that the strategy will make sense for your client. This seems obvious, but more than one coach has oversold her experience in the desire to "grow" her business.

- Ask permission before suggesting a strategy, especially if the suggestion is coming as a recommendation rather than as a neutral description of what might work. Ensure that you are really *asking*, not just jumping through the hoop to get the client to agree to what you've already decided he should do.

Summary

The Guide Voice is especially useful when the client is feeling stuck or doesn't have a sense of the right direction to go in. The coach can provide impetus by encouraging the client to take action. Or she can provide direction by sharing experience—her own and that of others—with successful approaches in related situations; this is done neutrally, with no impetus for action. Or, by recommending a possible course of action, she can provide both direction and impetus. Which of these she does will depend on the client and the situation.

Because the Guide is the most action-oriented of the coach Voices, it is the easiest venue in which to confuse the coach's investment in client action with the client's investment in their own action. As with any Voice, there is the potential for unhealthy identification, and mindfulness is required to stay attentive to the client's purpose and needs. The key is to be aware of any attachment to what the client does with either the impetus or the direction provided. To the extent that we are attached to what our client does with our recommendations, we are confusing ourselves with our client.

Properly employed, the Guide Voice can be enormously helpful. As the Guide, the coach can point the way when the client is feeling stuck. The Guide can give the client a little nudge when he knows what he wants to do but can't quite take the plunge. The Guide can be quite directive at times, recommending that the client take specific actions or try something new and different. The client never surrenders his authority, however. The contract between the coach and the client is such that the client is always at choice, always in charge. The Guide walks the fine line between providing impetus and/or direction but never overriding the client's ability to choose.

CHAPTER ELEVEN

The Contractor

Whatever you can do, or dream you can, begin it.
Boldness has genius, power, and magic in it.
GOETHE

Eliminate something superfluous from your life.
Break a habit. Do something that makes you
feel insecure. Carry out an action with complete
attention and intensity, as if it were your last.
PIERO FERRUCCI

*T*he Contractor is the coach in the role of providing psychological accountability for the client. Using this Voice, the coach develops, *with* the client, the structures of implementation, of action, of following through. These structures help the client take the work that has been done during the coaching conversation out into the world.

Obviously, the client is ultimately accountable only to herself. The Contractor, however, can be thought of as a link between her desire to move toward change and the actions that will make that possible. The Contractor helps the client construct an external pathway that enables her to go forward with direction and commitment, and with a minimum of anxiety and confusion.

When the coaching process creates new energy and new possibilities, the Contractor is the Voice that supports the client in anchoring these new possibilities in concrete action steps that change the situation "on the ground." The Contractor is hard-nosed, supportive, and practical all at once.

Who's Doing the Work?

Some clients are highly motivated and skilled at following through. When this happens, the Contractor part of the coach's job is easy. Sometimes, though, clients are resistant, disorganized, tentative in their commitment, or just plain feel powerless. They leave the coaching interaction saying the right things, but little or nothing happens. If this is the case, the role of the Contractor is even more important in following through and supporting the client in learning from what happened—or from what didn't happen.

The Voice of the Contractor is never adversarial: although the language of the Contractor is clear and focused on accountability, it is always in service to the client. In popular parlance, the Contractor can provide "tough love," but this is always grounded in self-awareness and respect for the client.

As with any Voice, there are ways in which the coach can overstep his bounds. In particular, the Contractor can get in trouble by becoming attached to the client's follow-through, confusing the client's "success" with his own. The mindful Contractor's respect for, and stance toward, the client is not affected by whether or not the client follows through according to the coach's standards of success. No matter what has happened in follow-through, the coach maintains an attitude of compassion and acceptance.

Any coach is well-advised to keep asking the question of whether the coach or the client is doing the work of commitment and follow-through. A well-coached client should be taking full responsibility for moving forward on what has been learned; excessive nudging and playing motivation games are signs of dependency.

The Aspects of the Contractor

C1 Establishing clear agreements about actions
C2 Exploring and resolving client doubts and hesitations
C3 Following up with client about agreed-upon actions

The first Aspect of this Voice involves establishing clear agreements about what the client will do to apply the work and insights from the coaching conversation. This framework provides both accountability and focus. The agreements developed here take the insights and good intentions from the coaching conversation and ground them in practical and specific commitments.

Second, the Contractor supports the client in understanding and working through resistances and hesitations about taking a particular course of action. While other Voices, particularly those of the Investigator and the Reflector, may come into play here, it's through the Contractor role that the coach helps the client take the risk of moving forward.

Third, the Contractor follows up with the client in subsequent coaching conversations to check in on results. Just knowing that the coach will be asking "So what happened when you . . . ?" reinforces the accountability the client feels to the commitments she has made to herself, and increases the likelihood of follow-through.

Generally, in relation to a specific course of action, that is the sequence in which the Aspects of the Contractor will be employed: developing a specific course of action, exploring resistances and hesitations and modifying the agreement if necessary, and later discussing what the client has or has not done and the results of the action or inaction.

Establishing Clear Agreements about Actions (C1)

Agreements for follow-through are most often driven by the client becoming clear about what she wants to do, how, and when. This is a logical outcome of the coaching process summarized by the three basic Investigator questions: What's the situation? What do you want? What are you going to do? The final question is practical and concrete. If the client has developed answers to this question with help from the three sharpener Voices (Reflector, Teacher, Guide), the Contractor's work is half done.

The Guide can sometimes be important in getting the client to that point of clarity. However we get there, though, at some point in the conversation we must address what the client is prepared to do. That's where the Contractor comes in. If the client is already clear, there is little to do but summarize what has already been said, or ask the client to do so. If it's still an overly broad course of action that the client is talking about, the Contractor helps narrow it down into immediate steps and practical, concrete commitments.

One of the challenges in coaching is to take "soft" behavioral changes and design "hard" measurable action steps to further them. There are extensive menus of alternatives for action resulting from a coaching conversation. Many major 360-degree review vendors (for example, Lominger Associates, Center for Creative Leadership and Personnel Decisions International, among others) have entire books of development suggestions keyed to specific competencies that are targeted by their assessment instruments. These resources can be valuable for the coach, whether or not the 360-degree review process is used. The danger, of course, is that these menus will be used as a cookbook for change, that the coach will substitute the ease and assurance of an "expert" system for his own judgment and his knowledge of the specific client.

While such models are excellent resources and their suggestions can obviously be shaped and customized, the most powerful development activities in my experience are ones that emerge from the coaching conversation itself. The client's new understandings of self and his situation become embedded in a specific course of action that either further increases awareness and understanding or shifts the situation itself.

Self-observation exercises are one way to do this. Other times, a specific action might entail a meeting with a particular individual, a phone call, a training class, or an experiment with new behaviors. For more complex courses of action that will take place over weeks or months, the client or the coach may write out an Individual Development Plan—or, better yet, the two of them will write one together—that outlines the steps that the client commits to taking. (See Exercise 13.23 on page 284).

The Contractor's role, then, is to work with the client to design the steps that make action specific, concrete, and measurable. These should be set in terms that avoid ambiguity about whether the client has accomplished the action step or not; this clarity provides the basis for revisiting the commitment in a later conversation and learning from whatever happened.

CONTRACTOR: So it sounds like you're pretty clear about your commitment to deal with the Rick situation.

CLIENT: Yes. I think it's important.

CONTRACTOR: Tell me again exactly what you're planning to do.

CLIENT: Well, you were right, I do need air cover from Anne on this one. It's too sensitive. So I'm going to meet with Anne and tell her that I'm worried about how other people might react if Rick has to leave. I'm going to ask for her support in putting him on probation, and tell her that I need her help in designing a damage control strategy if that doesn't work out.

CONTRACTOR: So when will you have this conversation?

CLIENT: Before next Friday for sure. She's out of town until Tuesday.

CONTRACTOR: Okay. Will you be able to get on her schedule?

CLIENT: Yes, no problem.

CONTRACTOR: What about your conversation with Rick?

CLIENT: I may not do that until the following week. Anne may want me to jump through a couple more hoops first. For now, I'm going to concentrate on involving Anne and completing that step by Friday. After that, the exact timing may vary depending on how that goes. I am committed to doing this, though.

CONTRACTOR: Good. Next time, let's talk about what happens with Anne, and make sure the pathway is clear from there. . . .

In this example, the client is already pretty clear about what he needs to do to deal with an impending personnel crisis. This conversation summarizes others he and the coach have been having, and anchors it in a very specific commitment. The client is clear that the first step needs to happen before he knows exactly what the next step will be, and the Contractor supports him in not adding further specifics at this time.

If the issue being addressed is very complex, it may be appropriate to schedule additional coaching time to work through the details. Alternatively, the client's action commitment may be to the creation of a plan; this work can take place step by step over the course of an agreed-upon amount of time.

CONTRACTOR: There's a lot on the table here!

CLIENT: Yeah. I feel energized, but I'm a little overwhelmed about where to begin.

CONTRACTOR: I understand. It's a great idea for a business, but bringing it into being will take time. Remember, it doesn't all have to happen at once.

CLIENT: So how do I figure out where to start?

GUIDE: Here's a suggestion. I think you start by organizing all the pieces we've talked about so far today. You'll also come up with some other ones as you go along. You have a project management challenge. Your first task is to make sense of the big picture. Then you begin to prioritize the bigger items and drill down to specific actions. We'll just take it one step at a time.

CLIENT: Good. I like that approach. So what do I need to do for next time?

CONTRACTOR: For next time I think you should make a list of everything you can think of that you'll need to do to get this business up and running. Eventually you can put it all into an outline that will become your master plan. For now, it's a way of making sense of all this. Don't worry about dates or specifics. Just do a data dump, and try to organize it by themes: business planning, financing, location, licensing. Then you'll be on your way to having a clearer picture.

CLIENT: Okay, I can do this. Next time, can we start talking about how to move forward based on that?

CONTRACTOR: Yes. We'll start sorting and making priorities.

CLIENT: It's exciting!

CONTRACTOR: It sure is. You're creating a new business. You'll learn so much. It just has to be done one step at a time.

Here, the "action item" is a placeholder of sorts for a more in-depth planning process. The initial action will begin the creation of a rough outline. Follow-up conversations will focus on fleshing this out into a detailed plan. After the plan is in place, the coach can provide support and accountability for its implementation.

Exploring and Resolving Client Doubts and Hesitations (C2)

Often resistance will surface just at the point where the client is getting ready to make a commitment. Everything sounds good until it comes time to take the plunge. Sitting on the precipice of change has a way of bringing up every doubt and question that's lurking in the background.

It's part of the coach's job as Contractor to ensure that the client's commitment is robust and full. This doesn't mean that all anxieties and resistances have been banished; it simply means that the client is fully committed to moving forward. To do this means acknowledging these feelings and doubts in the first place. Pretending they don't exist would seem easier on the face of it, but doing so may come back to haunt us later. The Contractor supports the client in naming and working through concerns with the goal of building commitment.

There are a number of approaches within this Aspect of the coach's role as Contractor. One involves looking at the resistance and concerns and addressing them. This is most often done cognitively, although some practitioners employ a range of other means such as visualization. A cognitive approach will often rely on questioning to work through the resistances. While this calls the Investigator Voice into play, the distinction is that the Contractor is focused on commitment to a relatively defined strategy.

Whatever the methodology, the tasks of the Contractor involve increasing awareness of resistance and blocks to action in the first place, and then helping to resolve them. The client's concerns are the foreground of our attention, but they are addressed in the context of a bigger picture. The proper relationship between the concerns and the outcome remains clear. Investing too much energy in exploring uncertainty and resistance may inflate them and dilute the sense of positive possibility and momentum. This can become a bit of a balancing act, but the mindful Contractor maintains awareness of the client's ultimate goals, steering clear of the tendency to get wrapped up in worries and fears as the whole subject of the discussion.

CLIENT: Well, I do think it's a good idea to get my team together for this planning session. We've never done this together, but I think it would be a good exercise for us. We're spread all over the country. We hardly see each other.

CONTRACTOR: Great. When will you begin?

CLIENT: In a couple of months. [pauses] Maybe. I'm pretty committed, but I do have some concerns.

CONTRACTOR: Okay, let's talk about them.

CLIENT: Well, one is that we don't actually have much practice in making joint decisions. This group has always been pretty top-down. I'll be taking a very different role from what they're used to with my predecessor. I expect them at best to be unenthusiastic, and they might not even want to participate. I'm the new kid on the block.

CONTRACTOR: So how will you get them on board? What can you do before you all get together to make them feel like they have a stake in this?

CLIENT: Well, I can try to give them all an idea about the process and what we're trying to accomplish. I can ask them what they think it's important for us to accomplish—sort of roll up their outcomes into the goals for the session. It'll take a bunch of phone calls.

CONTRACTOR: Okay, that makes sense. What else can you do?

CLIENT: I can put together a draft agenda early on, and I can say why I think it's important for us all to do this together. The truth is, I think we ought to be operating more closely together all the time. This is an opportunity to get that started.

CONTRACTOR: That sounds like something you feel strongly about.

CLIENT: Yeah. . . I do. And in order to do my job I need to be much
             more aware of what they think is important than I can be
             now. Mostly I get superficial acceptance, but I never really
             hear what they think. I do think I need to move on this.

CONTRACTOR: Good. So, now that you've anticipated some of the first steps,
             is there anything else before you're ready to commit to set-
             ting a date?

Here the Contractor is encouraging the client to explore her own
concerns and hesitations. Her overall commitment to change in this
case is pretty clear, but whether or not a commitment has already been
made, the concerns brought into the forefront by the *possibility* of
commitment are important. Unacknowledged concerns have a way of
undermining a client's best intentions. The Contractor asks the client to
go through her concerns and come up with ways of responding to each.
This is done in the foreground; the client's desired outcome provides
the background; the end result is a much fuller and more clear-sighted
commitment.

The Contractor can also encourage a client to move towards commitment by "trying on" a decision. Like trying on a new outfit in a
store, we wear it for a while, look in the mirror, see how it feels and
looks before making a purchase decision. We can do the same thing
for any decision we face. We "wear" the decision, pretending as if we
have made it, and we notice what surfaces. Generally, either the "Yes,
I like it" gains ground and we experience increasing energy and commitment, or the resistance gains ground, and we feel less and less like
making that choice.

Here's an example of a coaching dialogue built around trying on a
decision.

CONTRACTOR: So let's check in and see where you are with the VP opportu-
             nity. Have you made a decision?

CLIENT: Well, I'm pretty excited about the possibility. But I'm also concerned about the relocation and the demands of the job, with the acquisition that I'd be managing.

CONTRACTOR: Yes, that's a lot.

CLIENT: Jessica is very supportive, but neither one of us is totally sure about what it will really mean in terms of time. And, as you know, Jessica loves this city, and is very involved with a couple of local boards... she would have to give up a lot.

CONTRACTOR: Sounds like it raises some pretty significant concerns but you're still pretty fired up about it, too.

CLIENT: If I want to move up in this company, I can't turn this one down.

CONTRACTOR: When do you need to let Peter know?

CLIENT: I've really got a week.

CONTRACTOR: Let me suggest something that might help you decide. Pretend for four days that you've decided to go for the job. Talk to Jessica about it—she's your partner in all this and she gets to play this game too. Both of you act as if you were totally committed. Don't tell anybody else about it; it's just between the two of you. In fact, you haven't really yet decided, but you're pretending you have.

CLIENT: And what will that do?

CONTRACTOR: It'll give you the chance to see what making the decision feels like. You might find that you get clearer and clearer that this is what you want, and that all the rest seems manageable. On the other hand, you might find that your energy decreases, and the concerns seem to occupy more and more of your awareness. Same for Jessica. Either way it gives you what we in the trade call useful data. It's an experiment—together, you try on the decision and see what it feels like to wear it.

CLIENT: Okay. I'm willing to give that a try.

CONTRACTOR: The key is to pay attention, notice what you're feeling. We'll talk about it next time.

This approach doesn't deal directly with the resistances; here the coach as Contractor asks the client to temporarily sideline them, to try on a decision as a step towards committing to it. It's a trial run, an experiment, that will generate more information. The conscious attention is placed on the decision itself. The concerns are still there, of course, not having been resolved. The client is highly likely to notice that they will continue to come up during the course of the trial run. In fact, he's probably already working on them subconsciously. In some cases, the client's commitment to an action seems to firm up during this kind of trial period; the concerns that arise bring ideas for solutions along with them. In other cases, the impediments to taking the action loom larger and larger, and commitment seems to ebb. Either way, the experiment provides useful data that informs a final decision.

Generally, this approach is most useful when the client is on the brink of a big decision that appears to be a good thing; it's a way to help the client get past his or her initial resistance to change without spending lots of energy working through every little worry that arises.

The "trying it on" approach can also be coupled with a self-observation exercise. The following dialogue builds on the previous one.

CONTRACTOR: You know, there's a very simple self-observation exercise you could use as you try on the VP decision.

CLIENT: And what's that?

CONTRACTOR: You could just stop every couple of hours, and jot down what you've noticed about how it feels to assume you're going to go for it. It'll make you more attentive to what's coming up— how you're feeling about making such a big commitment at this point, whether you think it's overwhelming or whether you think you can handle the problems it will create.

CLIENT: How does this work? What do I have to do?

CONTRACTOR: It's simple. You're trying a mind experiment and the exercise just structures your observations. I can help you make a worksheet, if you want, with a couple of questions. You keep it in your organizer, and every two hours you take five minutes to notice and write. Jessica can do the same thing. At the end of four days, you and Jessica can review what you've both written. I think it'll help you decide about the job. You'll have another few days after this experiment before your deadline with Peter, right?

CLIENT: Yeah, I do. I think this will be interesting. I'm eager to try it.

Following Up with Client about Agreed-Upon Actions (C3)

The third Aspect of the Contractor Voice involves following up with the client in subsequent conversations to discuss what has happened. Sometimes the client has completed an action successfully and there's not much to be done other than to celebrate and anchor what's been learned. At other times, there may have been internal or external snags. If that's the case, the plan might need to be revisited and modified to make it more achievable in light of these circumstances, or it may need to be discarded and replaced with a new one.

Above all, the Contractor stands for a rigorous commitment to help the client follow through, look at whatever happened, and learn from it. It's the coach as Contractor who frames any results in terms of a larger perspective, moving beyond the apparent dualism of success and failure.

CONTRACTOR: So. How did it go with the first week of your training program?

CLIENT: It went pretty well! I worked out on my treadmill in the basement every morning before work. I'm just getting up half an hour earlier—no big deal. And I lifted weights at the gym three times this week. I've got a chart up on the refrigerator to track my work-outs. I'm checking it off every day.

CONTRACTOR: Nice going! How do you feel?

CLIENT: Great. I've got my benchmarks written down, and I've dropped four pounds just this week.

CONTRACTOR: You really are good at creating support systems. Didn't we talk about that as one of your talents?

CLIENT: Well, I do it well at work. This is new.

CONTRACTOR: So what else have you found out from doing it this week?

CLIENT: Well, obviously, it's not really such a big deal, this exercise thing. I just need to make it a priority and be willing to get out of bed. I guess that's true of a lot of things.

CONTRACTOR: That's it. Absolutely. That's important to see, and it does apply to many things. . . .

The Contractor is celebrating the client here, not only because she's been so successful in her very first week of a new program, but also to reinforce her insight and her sense that she has power in her own life.

Now let's look at the Contractor as he coaches a client who didn't follow through.

CONTRACTOR: Well, how did your conversation with Jeff go?

CLIENT: Not well. We met, but I didn't bring up the subject of the proposal.

CONTRACTOR: Did anything good happen at the meeting?

CLIENT: Well, we agreed to get together again to review progress on the payroll implementation.

CONTRACTOR: What kept you from bringing up the proposal?

CLIENT: I guess I didn't really want to hear what he had to say. I don't particularly respect his opinion. I bet he hasn't even read my proposal. He's had it for three weeks.

CONTRACTOR: That must be pretty frustrating. You really believe in it.

CLIENT: Yeah. Bottom line, though, I chickened out.

CONTRACTOR: So how are you going to get Jeff's feedback on the proposal?

CLIENT: Well, maybe I'll go through someone else.

CONTRACTOR: Last time we discussed how important you thought it was, for your relationship with Jeff, to bring this up directly with him.

CLIENT: I know. But I'm just sick of it. I always feel marginalized by him. I'm tired of meeting with him and feeling lousy afterwards. It's not worth it.

CONTRACTOR: Yeah, it would be easy to give it up. Do you still think it's important, though, to work on the relationship?

CLIENT: Yes.

CONTRACTOR: So, Michelle. How will you do that?

CLIENT: I guess I'm willing to give it one more try.

CONTRACTOR: Great. It's important to stay with what you trust is the right thing to do. This is actually a great learning opportunity for you. To think again and plan how to be powerful in a situation that's been pretty challenging so far, especially for your self-esteem. Can you see that? Can you see this as an opportunity?

CLIENT: Oh, sure. In principle. But I'd sure like to have fewer opportunities like this one!

CONTRACTOR: Yeah. We all would. Sometimes it's not easy to learn what we need to learn. Once we've learned it, of course, it's easy. Then the opportunities no longer appear!

CLIENT: Great. [laughs] How can I make that happen?

CONTRACTOR: By learning to stay centered and powerful in the face of someone like Jeff who pushes your buttons. Shall we talk about what you can do to increase the chances that you can do that next time you meet with him?

CLIENT: Yes, that would help. Let's get specific. I think if I have a more concrete plan, I can go in there and deal with it.

In this dialogue, the coach as Contractor is checking in with the client about an agreement they had made in their last conversation, and, obviously, she didn't follow through on a key action item. The Contractor provides accountability by bringing her back to the original commitment. Then the coach helps the client explore why she didn't do what she had said she would. Notice that there is no judgment or failure language. The client is being hard on herself; the Contractor acknowledges her feelings and empathizes, but doesn't add to the defeatism that the client is experiencing, moving on quickly to her overall commitment to address her problems in a difficult relationship directly. Rather than labeling her lack of action a failure, he helps her frame the whole experience as a learning opportunity, and one that she can master.

That reframing provides the motivation to go back in and re-plan for the same action item: a difficult conversation with Jeff. The potential failure becomes an opportunity, and the Contractor supports the client in responding effectively to the challenge. Michelle will go back out, seeking to do the same action as last time, but more cognizant of the challenge and better prepared.

Let's explore what this dialogue would look like if the client's experience with Jeff pointed her in a different direction. The italicized portion is identical to the previous conversation; where the italics end, the conversation goes in a new direction.

CONTRACTOR: *Last time we discussed how important you thought it was, for your relationship with Jeff, to bring this up directly with him.*

CLIENT: *I know. But I'm just sick of it. I always feel marginalized by him. I'm tired of meeting with him and feeling lousy afterwards. It's not worth it.*

CONTRACTOR: Yeah, it would be easy to give it up. Do you still think it's important, though, to work on the relationship?

CLIENT: Well, to tell you the honest truth, no. It became clear to me over the weekend that the price I'm paying just isn't worth it.

CONTRACTOR: That seems like a pretty significant shift. Talk more.

CLIENT: I've been living with this tension with Jeff for two years. I've tried a lot of things, but it's not getting better. I'm losing confidence, and it's easy to see he's not going to change. I'm ready to cut my losses. I've got too much to offer, and there isn't room to use it here.

CONTRACTOR: I hear that. You sound pretty fed up! Let's move away from Jeff for a bit. It sounds like you're thinking about making some sort of significant change. I'd say you need some more distance before making any irreversible decisions. But I also hear a clarity that deserves attention.

CLIENT: Yes, I think maybe I'm ready for a change. I'd like to talk about that.

INVESTIGATOR: Okay, let's talk. What alternatives are you thinking of?

This conversation begins the same way; the Contractor empathizes with the difficulties the client is having and then comes back to the commitment she made in their last conversation. This time, however, the client has made a significant shift and implies that she just wants to get out of what appears to her to be an impossible situation at work. It's possible that this presents a chance to move in another direction; it's also possible that the client is reacting very strongly in the moment and will see things differently in another couple of days. In either case, the coach responds by acknowledging the client's apparent clarity and taking her lead to explore what alternatives might look like.

This, in fact, moves the coach out of the Contractor Voice and back into the Investigator Voice. The conversation is no longer about the previous commitment, it has entered a new realm of exploration and discovery. The unfulfilled commitment has proven to be a catalyst that gets the client thinking about more radical change. While the conversation may well return to what the client can do to work on her relationship with Jeff, in the second version of our scenario the current energy is moving toward exploring other alternatives.

It's important to recognize that exploring alternatives is not the same as committing to them. In fact, fully imagining one's options may make the current situation look like a great opportunity for development and learning. As the Contractor, the coach helps keep the field of choice open for the moment, even as he assumes the Investigator Voice for the next piece of the conversation. In either case, the Contractor uses the client's lack of follow-through on an action item as an opportunity to open a deeper exploration of what she really wants.

Pitfalls and Guidelines

As with the Guide, one of the obvious pitfalls to taking on this role is the coach's identification with the client's results. In the endgame of a coaching conversation, the momentum is towards action. The Contractor must be careful not to compensate for a client's lack of movement by pushing for one action or another; to do so weakens the client in the long term because the commitment to action is coming from the outside.

In the Aspect of this role that is focused on exploring client hesitations, there's also a danger of pushing the client toward action before doubts and resistances have been adequately explored. While it is certainly possible to invest too much energy in this exploration, to the point where obstacles seem more immutable than they should, it often yields information that is useful to the client. To move through it too fast is to shortcut a portion of what could be important and valuable work. Keeping the balance requires mindful attention on the proper relationship between concerns and outcomes. Specifically, the client's concerns are what will need to be addressed in order to fully commit to the outcomes that the client wishes. The outcomes and actions are the most important thing. The concerns are addressed within that context.

Asking a client to report on actions with which she anticipated difficulty may prove uncomfortable for both the client and the coach. It's always more pleasant to think about the times we've been successful than the times when we feel we've failed. And of course, on some level, the coach may be confusing the client's feelings of failure with his own; to the extent we identify with our clients' successes, we are also likely to identify with their feelings of inadequacy.

The same danger exists when it comes to success. Of course we celebrate client successes. It's important to do this, and celebrating builds positive energy and confidence, which in turn leads to more success. Clients like to look good for their coaches, and this little boost in motivation may be a good thing, but it can sometimes lead to a kind of collusion in which the client and coach both have an emotional investment in the client appearing to perform more effectively than she is in fact doing. Naming what actually happened by using a Contractor-driven process of follow-through is critical to the kind of accurate, ongoing assessment that keeps the coaching relationship on an even keel, and to knowing what needs to happen next.

Here are some other guidelines for using the Contractor Voice well for the benefit of the client.

- Frame every experience as a success or learning opportunity. The client may see the lack of follow-through as a failure; the Contractor's job is to help him see the same experience in a larger context, and to support the client's learning from every attempt, no matter the results. Failure vs. success is often a false distinction that doesn't support the client's long-term development.
- Encourage accountability and discipline. Be diligent about writing down what the client commits to, and about following up about the results of these commitments.

- Simultaneously support change and accept the client as he is. These goals may appear to be in conflict, but they are not. Both accountability and discipline can be provided in the context of a fully accepting, supporting relationship.

- It is critically important for the coach to be aware of her own need for the client to get results. Like the Guide, the Contractor must be diligent in supporting the client's capacity to commit to outcomes and action plans. Noticing our own attachments and identifications with client results, and letting them go as they arise, is key to doing this; it is the coach's job to support the client, not to ensure client follow-through at the cost of the client's integrity and sense of self-reliance.

- Explore client resistance and concerns. Their nature is a valuable source of information, and addressing them is a key component of building commitment. At the same time, keep them in proper perspective. Resistances and concerns are areas of learning en route to the outcomes the client seeks, but they are secondary to the vision and results that the client wants, and must be kept in proportion.

Summary

The Contractor is the role that focuses on accountability and follow-through. In taking on this role, the coach supports the client in applying the work that has been done in coaching in very concrete, practical ways. The ongoing, iterative nature of coaching is one thing that differentiates it from other means of personal development. The Contractor makes coaching action-oriented and thereby effective in creating real and sustainable change.

The Contractor Voice manifests itself in three Aspects. First, the Contractor ensures that there are clear commitments to action. Generally, this happens at the end of each coaching interaction.

Second, where the client has resistance or concerns about a course of action, the Contractor explores these with the client, recognizing that addressing these, or moving past them, is central to the client's development of commitment.

Third, the Contractor follows up with the client in subsequent conversations to check in on the results of actions the client has taken. The Contractor endeavors to position whatever has happened as a success. If the client followed through as hoped, this is easy. If the client didn't follow through, or ran into unexpected difficulties, the Contractor supports the client in using this as additional data for learning and growth.

The Contractor is generally the final substantive Voice used in a specific coaching interaction, the one that helps set a tone of action-orientation and positive momentum. It is a key role that conveys support, accountability, and seriousness of intent, all at the same time.

PART

3

APPLICATION

CHAPTER TWELVE

An Integrated Model of Coaching

Life is a lot like jazz . . .
it's best when you improvise.
GEORGE GERSHWIN

Jazz is a very democratic musical form.
It comes out of a communal experience.
We take our respective instruments and
collectively create a thing of beauty.
MAX ROACH

*T*ogether we've looked at a lot of information. The first part of this book provided an overview of some of the core concepts that underpin mindful coaching. In the second part, we looked in depth at each of the seven Voices in the Septet and the various Aspects that make them concrete and specific.

Now it's time to revisit our model to talk about how to integrate all this information and put it into practice. In these final three chapters, we'll look at the details of the coaching process from a holistic perspective, focusing on the interrelationships between the Voices and the various Aspects of coaching that they represent. And, I offer a series of exercises to help you become more mindful and develop your skills as a coach, and a system of specific, data-driven means to ensure accountability to your client. Additional support for using the Septet Model to enhance your professional development, in the form of worksheets and on-line assessments, is available to the reader at http://septetcoaching.com.

A Second Look at the Model

While the development of our talents and capabilities is rarely a linear, step-by-step process, it's most useful, for both the coach and the client, to have a model from which to proceed. The model provides a basis for orientation, a compass for navigation through the sometimes confusing terrain of a conversation. Having such a framework helps us know where we are and where we're going.

Take a minute to look again at the model—Figure 4 on page 81— and maybe put a bookmark in at that page so you can refer back to it as we discuss the process it portrays.

Entry Points for the Client and the Coach

Coaching begins and ends with the quest for mastery. Coach and client both exist outside the coaching relationship. Each is on an individual quest for mastery. They conduct separate lives in separate worlds; the realm where their two lives overlap is the coaching relationship. Fortune, fate, or good intentions have brought each to this place, where their two worlds, for a brief period of time, intersect.

The primary purpose of this relationship is, of course, to support the outcomes that the client seeks, and it's the client's desire for change, to reach towards mastery, that provides the impetus.

The client enters the coaching relationship with a desire or a need to do things differently. This may be the result of dissatisfaction or anxiety about a specific problem; often, though, the client is driven by a dream, a goal, a desire to be more successful, however he or she defines it. Either way, the client enters with questions, with ideas, with choices to make and dilemmas ("stuck places") to resolve. Ideally, despite anxieties and resistances, the client enters the relationship as someone seeking guidance—as a learner.

For the client, then, the desired outcomes of any coaching interaction are new insights, new ways of seeing, and new courses of action. These feed the development of mastery, of competence and self-generation. Mastery, both in the subject matter in which coaching takes place, and in the learning process itself, is an outcome for the client.

Coaching requires mastery in the coach as well. Coach mastery enables the coaching process to happen, and allows it to be as pure as possible. The mindful coach is curious, present, and as open to learning as she expects the client to be. She carries three key questions that keep her fresh and attentive: Who is this client? Who am I as coach? How can I serve?

The coach's curiosity about these questions parallels the client's openness to learning. The first question requires being open to seeing the client freshly each time. It counters the tendency to think of the client's personality and patterns as fixed, requiring instead that the coach be flexible and responsive. The second question does the same with regard to the coach's inner life as a professional; it requires us to pay attention to ourselves, to what is arising, to what we can offer to the relationship. The third question reminds us that we have placed ourselves in service to the client, that the ways in which we can perform this service are many, and that it's our responsibility to choose which of these is most useful at a given time.

For the coach, then, mastery requires setting aside the comfort of thinking that we know what to do and have an easy formula for providing what the client needs. It requires a willingness to be influenced in the moment, to be taught both by the client and by the work that we do together. This stance serves both the coach's learning and the client's.

The coach emerges from each coaching conversation with new information about herself and about how she coaches. The mindful coach uses this information by reflecting on it and incorporating it as one input into her own ongoing process of learning. Each coaching interaction is a new experiment. The Septet Model supports this drive for learning in the coach while placing it in proper, subsidiary relationship to the primary purpose of serving the client.

The Crucible of Partnership

Both the coach and the client, then, enter the relationship with their own needs, wants, skills, and dreams. The initial task for both is to forge a partnership dedicated to the growth of the client. Again, the learning and growth of the coach is important, but secondary. There is, however, a convergence of interests, as the more skillful a coach becomes, the better he or she can support the client.

Coaching happens, and can only happen, within the container of a partnership. This partnership is created by the coach using the Partner Voice and working with the client to establish a vibrant, direct, and authentic relationship organized around achieving agreed-upon outcomes.

That's the beginning. But it's not as simple as the model suggests. While the Partner takes the lead at the outset, and there's a logic to the order in which I've presented the discussions of each Voice in Part 2 of this book, that order is an artifact of the model-making process, and our clients will not be well served if we adhere to it slavishly. The purpose of the model is just to keep us oriented, to help us become more mindful about what we're doing; within this context, we must respond flexibly to what the client needs and shift between Voices accordingly. For example, the Investigator Voice also plays a part in establishing the partnership since questions about the client's background and goals need to be part of the initial conversation. So as you read through these last three chapters, please remember that while distinguishing between the Voices will help you be more aware of what you're doing as a coach at a given moment, awareness of how and why you're coaching is the point, not sticking to a rigid sequence or losing focus on the client while parsing distinctions between Voices.

The Centrality of the Investigator

The three areas of Investigator questioning (situation, outcomes, action) lie at the heart of coaching. In fact, coaching can be thought of as a quest to help the client answer these three key questions: What's the situation? What do you want? What are you going to do? The power of coaching comes from the expertise that a skilled Investigator brings to probing the themes defined by these questions, as well as from the richness of experience that he or she can offer as Reflector, Teacher, and Guide, and as the advocate for accountability to the client represented by the Contractor.

While a conversation typically flows from situation to outcome to actions, the process can begin with any of the three questions. The entry point is really determined by the client, and the coach seeks to meet the client there. Sometimes the client will begin with a situation he feels stuck in, or excited about, or frustrated by: "I need to talk about something that happened yesterday." Here the Investigator will likely ask questions to explore the situation more deeply.

Another conversation might begin with something like "I'm so excited about moving to Fiji!" Here the Investigator will likely ask questions about how this fits in with what the client wants or hopes for, tapping into that excitement to get the conversation going.

Sometimes the client may be anxious or uncertain about something on the horizon: "By next week I have to decide . . ." Here the third Investigator question—What are you going to do?—provides a good starting point for helping the client explore the situation, think about what he wants to accomplish, and devise a strategy.

Whatever the starting point, all three questions will likely be helpful and relevant. Once the client has explored the territory of all three lines of questioning, the gap between the current situation and the desired outcome generates the tension that leads to change. The answers to the third line of questioning provide the direction for channeling this energy, as described in Chapter 7.

This investigative process provides the core and the touchstone for coaching. The coach will often recognize, in the pursuit of a line of inquiry, an opportunity to explore more deeply, or to expand the boundaries of the inquiry. This is where the "sharpeners" come in.

The Coaching Dance: The Investigator and the Sharpeners

Coaching is honed to a finer point with the support of the three "sharpener" Voices: the Reflector, the Teacher, and the Guide. Each lends a particular perspective and offers a particular gift. Each supports the client in discovering new and deeper answers to the Investigator's lines of inquiry. Each may, in fact, open or respond to new lines of inquiry.

As the Reflector, the coach is an advocate for the client's self-awareness. This can be very useful when the client doesn't appear to understand the impact of his behaviors, or when it would be helpful if he could observe himself more accurately. The Reflector provides feedback, helps the client see his full potential and all the capabilities he brings to the table, and encourages him to become more skillful at observing himself and identifying what he still needs to work on. Awakening this self-awareness helps the client respond more accurately to the Investigator's lines of questioning. It also enhances his ability to coach himself.

The Teacher provides missing information, adding to the client's understanding of the situation. The Teacher also provides language that allows the client to make new distinctions, to describe things more clearly and accurately; in this, the Teacher supports the client's skills of observation and information processing. Lastly, the Teacher challenges the client's thinking process, questioning his assumptions and inferences. All of these functions of the coach as Teacher are critical in developing truly useful responses to Investigator questions about the situation and the outcomes that the client wants.

The third sharpening Voice is the Guide. This is useful when the client appears stuck on what to do or feels uncertain about whether to move forward in addressing a situation. The Guide provides an impetus for action, suggestions for possible courses of action, or both. This role focuses the client toward action, supporting real movement and change. The Guide Voice is associated with the Investigator's third line of questioning, about what the client intends to do.

These sharpening Voices often bring up new questions, new lines of inquiry. Here's an example.

As my capacity as Investigator, I was asking a client named Jeff some practical questions about developing his leadership capacities in a very complex environment. Jeff was describing the challenges and the cross-currents of influence in the leadership team on which he served. This gave me an opportunity to refer to a recent 360-degree review in which Jeff had received feedback about being indecisive and slow to move, and a chance to use the Reflector Voice to help him examine his reactions to that evaluation. This also helped him see that he had the potential to move decisions along more quickly.

As I continued to reflect back to him what he was saying about the evaluation, Jeff recognized that he had a lot of anxiety about committing to decisions when the boundaries of his authority weren't clear. This was the time to speak as the Teacher to offer a distinction between decisions that should be delayed for further analysis and decisions that were being held up because of Jeff's own anxieties about being decisive in the politically charged atmosphere in which he was operating. This seemed to be a line of inquiry critical to observing and shifting a pattern of behavior that had negative implications for his leadership.

Jeff did recognize the need to become more aware of how he responded to various kinds of decisions that came across his desk. But when I asked him about what he could do differently, he got stuck. To try to help him break the logjam, I switched to the even more directive Voice role of the Guide, inviting him to consider doing a simple self-observation exercise that would help him pay attention to his gut reactions to the situations he was being asked to take the lead in resolving. This turned out to be very helpful. It took a while, but eventually Jeff got better and better at separating his own concerns from the practical issues at hand, and better able to make good decisions in a timely fashion.

The Investigator's lines of questioning, then, provide the core structure of the coaching process. The sharpening Voices are invoked as needed to support the client in doing the work of answering the Investigator's questions at the deepest level that the client is ready for. The end result is more incisive, powerful, and clear answers to the Investigator's questions. Generally, the conversation comes back to the Investigator's three-question framework, the touchstone from which coaching proceeds.

This process happens fluidly; the mindful coach will move easily and frequently between Voices as the client's learning process unfolds. The compartmentalization that we resort to in talking about the Septet is in a sense illusory, a construct that we use in order to see more clearly what we are doing. As we move toward our own mastery, our ability to use the Voices consciously and appropriately will increase and classification will become less important.

Anchoring Change in Action

Eventually, in this iterative process, it becomes relatively clear what's important for the client to consider or act upon prior to the next session. Often this emerges from the client as the energy that's released by her expanded perspective shifts smoothly into a clear picture of what's next to do. Other times, the coach leads with suggestions that the client comes around to seeing as useful. Either way, at some point the Contractor Voice provides the invaluable service of helping the client ground the insight, perspective, and impetus for action in very concrete, practical plans regarding actions to take in the near future. Sometimes these are obvious, as when the client knows she must face a difficult conversation that she has been avoiding. At other times, the partners must work harder together to shape exactly what the client will do.

The function of the Contractor is to help translate what has happened in the crucible of the coaching session into a clear course of action that the client can and will follow. Action agendas can include a wide range of concrete items, from the most mundane to the most ambitious: holding a conversation, committing to moving to another state, calling a meeting, putting together a business plan for a new enterprise, buying a plane ticket to Timbuktu. These are generally intended to achieve specific tactical results that move the client towards her stated outcomes.

Other, less narrowly targeted actions also qualify here. Self-observation exercises are action steps that offer a powerful means for a client to become more self-aware and see his or her situation more clearly. Skill-building practices and learning programs are a means to acquire or practice the skills and behaviors required for being successful in the client's field. Self-care practices sometimes seem tangential to the topic at hand, but may be important for developing the client's energy, well-being, and ability to manage time. Physical exercise, creative time, meditation, diet, etc., all bear on the client's quality of life. Individual Development Plans (IDPs; see Exercise 13.23, on page 284) are written development plans developed by the client, by the coach, or by the two of them together. Typically, an IDP delineates a longer-term series of actions and activities over the course of weeks, months, or even years. Actions may also involve seeking ongoing support, whether from friends, colleagues, or other professionals.

Finally, as the Contractor, the coach may encourage the client to "try on" a decision, especially a major one. "Trying it on" is a mind experiment that involves pretending that the decision has already been made and noting one's reactions and energy in relation to that assumption. As a technique, it is useful for feeling one's way through a difficult or complex decision.

Client Mastery

Ideally, the client emerges from a coaching interaction with specific ideas and plans that translate the inner work and awareness-building he's done into concrete actions and skills development. Thus focused, the client goes into the "practice field" of the rest of his life. There he experiments to practice what he has learned and learn from what he practices.

The right side of the model represents some of what happens in the realm of client mastery, which takes place outside the coaching relationship. The client will have successes and setbacks, experience resistances and feelings of triumph, as he uses what the coach has helped him discover: new perspectives and new information, skills, and tools for setting goals and making plans to achieve them.

The client will also have learned from the coaching process itself. By recalling and reflecting upon what the coach has done to support him, he learns to do the same for himself. He becomes more skilled at guiding his own development; not only has he acquired competence in the content area in which the coaching has taken place, he has also increased his capacity for self-generation—for taking personal responsibility for enhancing his own capabilities, for becoming more proactive. The client may engage the coach for a short time or a long time as support along this path, but eventually he will outgrow what the coach can provide and will move on to other arenas for learning. This is a good thing.

Of course there will be many challenges on the way. The client will run into unexpected obstacles, internal or external. He'll get stuck. He'll discover new questions. His successes will expand his capacity to dream. All of this is grist for the mill; one of the most important things a coach can help a client learn is that every moment is a clean slate.

Yesterday I had a conversation with Tom, a manager I'd been coaching for about four months. A year earlier, he'd received feedback from a 360 review about his strong tendency to be impatient and abrasive with his team. He had created a development plan to help him improve in this area, but hadn't really done more than just go through the motions. This time, Tom said, he was serious.

We had been holding weekly coaching calls and Tom did self-observation exercises, experimented with a range of self-management practices, and held some difficult conversations with his staff and peers. Each week we talked about the results of his experiments and observations. This time around he saw things working and reported that his staff seemed to be responding to him differently as a result of his efforts. This, in turn, increased his diligence and commitment.

Last week, Tom asked his staff to do a mini-360—and add written comments—on some of the questions that had provided troublesome data in the past. The results showed dramatic improvement. His people describe a notable shift in the atmosphere at work—and in their willingness to be open with him.

Tom has learned to manage himself more effectively. He still has to pay close attention; old habits die hard. The actual changes he made are, in the big scheme of things, pretty minor. Most importantly, however, Tom has learned that he does, after all, have the capacity to choose new behaviors and see the results. The second time around he has seen the power of his own commitment and has taken steps toward becoming engaged in life-long learning. For him, as for many people, the payoff from being coached extends far beyond the resolution of a single issue.

Coach Mastery

Let's look at the other side of the model. We've stated many times that coach mastery is also an outcome of coaching. Coaching provides a wonderful invitation for coaches to increase their own mindfulness and effectiveness and to shed old habits. Here's a vision of what that would look like in the best of all possible worlds.

The coach on the path to mastery recognizes that coaching provides a wonderful opportunity for her own learning. She learns from each session, reviewing what she's done and why. She creates structures and practices to increase her ability to observe and pay attention. Over time, by cultivating this attentiveness and acting on what is learned, she develops her professional skills and capacities.

The master coach also takes note whenever she sees herself reflected in her client. For many of us who serve as coaches in one venue or another, it's striking how often this happens. Our counsel to others seems like advice we should follow ourselves. Or our clients seem to have the same struggles that we do. ("Oh, look at that. He has a hard time saying no, too. Funny how I attract kindred spirits.") This isn't a metaphysical phenomenon about synchronicity and how we always meet just the right person; rather it illuminates our own tendency to see ourselves in others, to project onto others what we have experienced ourselves.

In pursuing her own mastery, the mindful coach recognizes potential entanglements and sets them aside to pay attention to later, coming back for the moment to the client. After the coaching session is over, on her own time, she explores what came up for her and what to do about it. As a learner, she recognizes the value of seeing how the client, and the coaching process, helps her work on her own concerns and values.

In committing to serve the client—to be present, flexible, and responsive—the coach herself becomes more present and alive. She enters the conversation awake and willing to discover something new about her client and about herself. She is open to new answers and the discovery that she doesn't yet know the answer. Perhaps most importantly, she is open to exploring who she is as a coach. She holds lightly to what she thinks she knows, recognizing that every conversation may provide a wonderful opportunity to coach in a way she never has before.

Intuition and the Flow of Coaching

Many coaches are fond of saying that they coach "intuitively." This is sometimes a way of describing a process that is highly skilled and internalized; unfortunately, it can also be a cover for not having a coaching model to work from and so not making conscious choices about how one is working with one's clients.

While intuition is a wonderful gift, there's a very fine line between intuitive wisdom and conditioned habits. Both arise from somewhere in our unconscious and appear, to approximately equal degrees, as urges or instincts that we then let ourselves follow. The fact that something derives from our unconscious doesn't by itself mean that it's helpful, correct, or even appropriate to the situation. Making our choices of role and behavior more explicit and conscious in our own minds fosters the self-awareness and discernment necessary to recognize the difference. It also makes it less likely that we will coach our clients out of conditioned habits while missing the essence of who they truly are and what they can actually use.

I believe in intuition, but I also hold that considerable rigor and discipline of practice is required before we can authentically claim to be coaching intuitively rather than naively. We must know what we stand for, what we represent, and, in very concrete terms, what we offer to our clients. This is what the Septet or any other rigorous model provides.

In the flow of coaching, we seek to become more mindful and discerning about what will truly serve the client and what roles we are playing at a given moment as we seek to provide it. This process can seem artificial and laborious. I can hear the critical reader say, this requires separating the mind into two parts, but doesn't being mindful really require integrating rather than separating? It's good to look at systems and theories critically, and that reader would be right about the ultimate goal.

I suggest, however, that using the Septet Model is simply holding up what you're already doing and making it more visible so you can examine it. Doing that will allow you to affirm or change how you serve your clients. The model is, of course, artificial and limited. We are creating a language that draws distinctions and chunks behaviors into somewhat arbitrary categories. But doing so also makes us more skillful observers, better able to adjust what we do to the specific needs of a client. As we become more mindful and learn to employ the whole range of the Voices and their Aspects without having to be self-conscious, we develop the concrete skills that ground our intuitions and ensure that they serve our clients rather than our own habits of mind.

After Tiger Woods's phenomenal early successes as a professional golfer, he took the time to re-learn his drive, changing habits acquired over years. Many wondered what on earth he was doing, how he could improve on perfection, but Tiger knew that some of his habits were limiting his game, and so he painfully deconstructed the nuances of his stroke and rebuilt it. Initially his tee shots suffered, but once he had mastered these new habits his drive became stronger than ever.

The Septet Model will be helpful as a means of deconstructing your coaching, seeing it more clearly, and then integrating the seven Voices back into a more intuitive, skilled, and responsive approach to meeting the needs of your clients. Here are some general principles that apply to all the Voices and Aspects.

- Clear your mind and your physical space before the conversation starts. Begin with a focus on the client, the outcomes he wants, and the potential that he has in the situation. Begin with a sense of optimism and acceptance.

- Pay attention to your own urges as they arise—the impulse to shift the conversation in a new direction, the desire to make a point. These are cues to what is going on inside yourself. Act on them only when you are sure they will serve the client rather than your own needs. In short, trust your intuition but keep yourself honest through self-observation.

- In particular, notice when your urges lead you to try a new Voice. This is appropriate when the client's needs change, when an opportunity arises for a new line of inquiry, or when it would be useful to the client to sharpen the existing line of questioning. The key is to become increasingly aware of these shifts, and to be able to articulate to yourself why you're moving into a new role.

- Keep the overall model in your awareness as a backdrop for the conversation. (You might even want to keep the representation of it—Figure 4—visible to use as a reminder of the roadmap and of the context within which you are coaching: your mastery and the client's mastery.)
- Maintain a portion of your awareness as the observer, staying on top of what you're doing and why.
- Ensure that each conversation is brought to a close at the end. The client should leave the session with a plan—actions, a practice, a self-observation exercise, even just some topics to think about— something that he can do to bring the work of coaching into the larger context of his life.
- Spend a few minutes reflecting on the session afterwards. (The next chapter, "Development Strategies for the Coach," will present some specific tools for doing this.) This post-conversation reflection is a key transition and link for the coach to learn from what happened, and to support her own mastery. The client emerges with an action plan developed during the conversation. The coach must structure the time to do this for herself if she is to derive the most learning from the coaching session.

The Septet Model serves as a general roadmap for entering a partnership and moving through a coaching interaction. To try to provide a list of "what ifs" and recommended responses for all situations would be impossible. Coaching is fundamentally an artistic, not a scientific process. Mastery in coaching, as in any other field, comes from experimentation and inquiry, not from pat answers and cookbook recipes. I don't mean to duck my responsibility here. Rather, I believe that you will benefit more from engaging with these ideas and practices, and from finding your own ways to apply them. The next chapter provides a range of specific tools for experimentation and application.

CHAPTER THIRTEEN

Development Strategies for the Coach

*What you are is what you have been, and
what you will be is what you do now.*
THE BUDDHA

*I*n this chapter I'll present a series of activities and approaches for
developing yourself as a coach. I encourage you to try out these tools
and learn to use them flexibly, experimenting with them to make them
as meaningful and powerful for you as possible. Think of them as games
or little experiments that you're conducting to better see what you're
doing as a coach, and to help you navigate as you explore the model.

I cannot prescribe a sequence for doing these exercises, nor is there
a curriculum around the Septet that will serve all readers. The bottom
line is that *you* are the curriculum. To follow a rigid process described
by someone else is to miss the point. At the same time, I hope you will
enter the inquiry process with a degree of faith that these exercises are

at the very least interesting and worth engaging with. Keep your mind open, but trust your gut instincts to help you discover which are most useful.

The model will take you as far as you want to go. Most of the exercises end with questions or additional practice suggestions. Your spirit of inquiry is the impetus behind your learning. The more curious you are about coaching and mindfulness, and the more committed you are to your own journey to mastery, the richer the results will be.

Each section of this chapter contains text describing a development strategy, plus exercises with sample worksheets to help you follow that strategy. I say "sample" because readability and aesthetic considerations have made it necessary to keep the spaces for answering questions, etc., quite small, and because in some cases you'll want multiple copies. The samples will show you the structure. You can easily create your own expanded versions, designed for quick notes that encourage self-observation and reflection on the activities to be observed, without adding much to the time required. Or, templates for each of these exercises can be downloaded from http://www.septetcoaching.com. You can customize these for your purposes, print out multiple copies, or create your own exercises by using them as models.

Read through this chapter to see what's here, then start with what seems interesting. Although you must be your own guide through this territory, I suggest that you begin with the first two sections, "Preparing the Place" and "Observing Yourself in Action." This will give you a solid beachhead from which to explore. Start now.

Preparing the Place

Setting up your coaching environment to support mindfulness makes everything else much easier. If you do most of your work from a distance, you are your only design constituent. But if clients come to see you face to face, you'll probably want to create a space in which to meet them that's welcoming and rich, but neutral rather than intimate. And if you travel to meet clients elsewhere, there may still be opportunities to choose or adjust the environment so that it's conducive to calm reflection.

This is very much an individual process, but design elements that seem to make for a good place in which to work include soft colors and reminders of nature, including artworks depicting natural scenes. (More than one coach who answered my general inquiries on this subject recommended a small water fountain; some advocated playing soft music or lighting candles.) Eliminating clutter helps: external clutter stimulates internal clutter. Plants are living things that encourage (and require) attentiveness in themselves. I have my office set up in a lovely spot overlooking the valley, with a view out the window past a silver maple tree to hawks circling above. It's an inspiring view and a constant reminder to be grateful and present, but a well-tended jade plant or geranium, a nice landscape photo, or a simple vase filled with dried flowers can serve the same purpose.

Don't underestimate the importance of your physical space in supporting your mindfulness. Exercise 13.1 invites you to look at, and enhance, your space so that it feels simple, comfortable, and inspiring.

The act of exercising control over your environment is in itself empowering. You are, by doing this, engaging in self-inquiry and acting on what you discover. This, of course, is the central premise of coaching and of cultivating mastery. Practicing this in one arena—discerning and creating what is required in your physical space—albeit a modest one, is a good beginning for doing so in other arenas as well.

Exercise 13.1: Creating a Mindfulness Environment

Instructions

Take a few minutes to simply sit in the physical space where you conduct your coaching. Notice what it feels like, what you like about it, and what tends to distract your attention.

Consider what you could do to

- simplify the environment (eliminate clutter, arrange or organize things harmoniously, remove unnecessary and/or distracting items, etc.),
- include objects of beauty (a candle, artwork, a better view from your window obtained by moving your desk or the client's chair),
- incorporate natural elements (plants, rocks, shells) or representations of nature,
- find a place for a memento or talisman that will serve you as a reminder to be present and mindful.

Make some changes and notice how the changes affect your mindfulness as you coach.

Make more changes.

Keep experimenting, recognizing that it will be an ongoing process to design your coaching space to be supportive of your practices as they evolve.

Observing Yourself in Action

A key to building your skills as a coach is to cultivate the ability to observe yourself in action. While you are fully engaged with your client, a part of your mind stands slightly apart and detached: you are observing yourself and observing the client at the same time. As in "The Raisin Meditation" (Exercise 2.1 in Chapter 2), there's a part of your mind watching what arises, watching how you engage in the task that you are doing. This "observer self" provides awareness in the moment and the vantage point from which to see many things, among them which Voice you are using and why.

About Self-Observation Exercises (SOEs)

While ideally awareness in the moment is to be cultivated at all times, self-observation exercises—or SOEs, called learning logs by some—can provide a very helpful structure for professional development. I have used them for years in my coaching practice, and in my own growth process. In his important book *Coaching: Evoking Excellence in Others,* James Flaherty explains the rationale for SOEs eloquently:

> All change begins with self-observation. People confuse self-observation with self-judgment. Judgment includes a critical element that is absent from self-observation . . . To self-observe means to not become attached to or to identify with any content of our experience, but to watch alertly, openly, passively. Many Americans hate the word passively—especially authors and advocates of self-help. Not acting allows self-observation to occur. We are already taking actions, be they physical or mental. The point in being passive is to have some power in intervening in the mechanicalness of thought, action, and speech.
>
> The general instruction for self-observation is to divide yourself into two people, one who acts in life and one who watches. Maybe this sounds simple to you, but you'll find in practice that it is quite difficult.[47]

Flaherty offers a number of SOEs from his own coaching practice, all designed to support the client in noticing his or her habits of mind and so create new choices. Of course (you can see this coming by now, can't you?) we learn best how to use a tool with clients by using it with ourselves first, and I've come to believe that SOEs are invaluable for improving one's coaching skills. Not only do they help us become more self-aware, they also help us understand the difficulties and resistances that our clients are likely to run into as they are coached by us using similar tools.

An SOE uses a template (a worksheet) or a journal for noting observations about our own behaviors, habits of mind, successes, or goof-ups. Some might be done as one-time experiments, but most are designed to be repeated on a regular basis, to be done at a regular time, usually tied to another event as a reminder. For example, most of the SOEs described here will ask you to observe yourself while coaching, and make a short entry at the end of each coaching session. Other SOEs might be done twice a day, at the end of the day before bedtime, once a week, or as triggered by a timer or specific kind of event to which the observed behavior is tied.

The point is to build accountability for paying attention to something subtle and behavioral by creating a structured practice around it. To be accountable to "listen better" or "use the Reflector Voice more" is so vague that it's difficult to know what it means. On the other hand, a person can feel very accountable to a specific deliverable like "complete a learning log," and this accountability makes us sensitive to specific targeted behaviors.

Beginning Exercises for the Coach

If you have not used SOEs before, doing at least some of those in this section of the chapter will give you a head start on others that follow.

In Exercise 13.2, you'll begin by dividing your coaching into two basic modes, questioning and telling. Obviously, there are many other ways to describe coaching, and lots of nuances within these two broad categories; the purpose here is simply to practice observing yourself, to begin to use your observer mind more deliberately. Try this; it's not so easy.

Like many SOEs, this exercise uses a physical analog; the physical act of moving a coin on a paper diagram—or from pocket to pocket, or of crossing and uncrossing your fingers—serves as a reminder of the behavior you're trying to observe. If one physical analog feels awkward, think of something else to do that's not too distracting; feel free to experiment and find one that fits you and your context. (With the

Exercise 13.2: Questioning and Telling

Instructions

Draw two circles on a piece of paper and label one "Questioning" and one "Telling." With your observer mind, pay attention to whether you're primarily questioning or primarily telling at each particular point in time. Use a coin, or any other small object that will stay put, and move it from one circle to the other as you coach, depending on the mode you're *primarily* in. (If you're coaching face to face, you can use a less distracting physical analog, like crossing fingers on your left hand for questioning and on your right for telling. The nature of the analog doesn't matter; just find something that will work for you in your context as a reminder to pay attention to which mode you're in.)

Don't worry about getting keeping a count or making mistakes. Stay gentle and relaxed; lightly pay attention but keep most of your focus on your client.

Do this for three or four sessions, and after each take a couple of minutes to complete one line of the worksheet. After observing and noting observations on the worksheet for a few sessions, answer these review questions:

- What did you learn about observing yourself in action?
- What surprises have there been for you from this exercise?
- What did you notice about your tendencies as you coach?

Sample Worksheet

Date/Client: Note the date and the client.

Questioning and Telling: Which mode did you notice yourself predominantly using during the session? Did you switch often?

Observations: In which mode were you most comfortable? What did you notice about the process of observing yourself?

Date/Client	Questioning and Telling *(Which did you primarily do? Did you switch often?)*	Observations *(What did you notice about your comfort level in each? About the process of observing yourself?)*

more complex SOEs, such as the ones in later sections, you'll likely find moving an object on the diagrams pretty helpful.)

Documenting your observations after each session gives you a solid basis for looking back and discerning patterns in your own behavior. Remember that this is about understanding: try to suspend self-judgment. The review questions after each SOE will help you cognitively process what you have been learning on a more subtle and visceral level.

Exercise 13.3 uses the same questioning/telling dichotomy. This time, though, you'll be paying more attention to the switches, the moments when you change from one mode to the other. Presumably, there's some sort of impetus that causes the shift, and this exercise asks you to pay close attention to which of your own attachments and aversions might be operating to influence your coaching choices.

Remember that attachments and aversions are our experience of the conditioned mind; the conditioning is always there, and always influencing us. Without self-awareness, we are hostage to our unconscious habits of mind, and our attachments and aversions will influence our coaching in ways we will be unable to see.

As your self-observation skills increase, you will become more alert as to when your own habits of mind are present, and more able to separate them from the work at hand. This in turn will help you make conscious choices about what you are doing as a coach, decisions based on a clear focus on the client rather than on unconscious influences from your own habits of mind.

You could redesign this exercise to focus on distinctions between any two Voices of the Septet, instead of between questioning and telling. Or between the Aspects associated with a particular Voice that you tend to overuse or underuse. Or on any other distinction in coaching or in other activities, for that matter. You get the idea. The area of attention that you choose determines what you will become more aware of, and where you will develop your skill and discernment. This SOE, like

Exercise 13.3: Attachment and Aversion

Instructions

Use the circles from the previous exercise, or another physical analog that works better for you, to track your use of questioning and telling as in Exercise 13.2.

After each session, take a couple of minutes and complete one line of the worksheet below.

After a week or two of doing this, answer these summary questions:

- How did your observations change over the course of this SOE?

- What did you learn about your attachments?

- What did you learn about your aversions?

- What questions come up for you that would be interesting to explore?

Sample Worksheet

Date/Client: Note the date and the client you were coaching at the time.

Observations: What did you notice about your balance between the modes of questioning and telling? When did you switch from one mode to the other, and why?

Attachment and Aversion: With hindsight, what attachments (pulls *toward* something—a sensation of increased energy, an emotional charge, a sense of "I know what to do," etc.) did you notice at times when you switched from one mode to the other? What aversions (resistance, or moving *away*—impatience, restlessness, negative judgment, feelings of inadequacy or being stuck, etc.) did you notice?

Date/Client	Observations *(balance between questioning and telling; switches)*	Attachment and Aversion *(What attachments and aversions did you experience?)*

any good tool, is a flexible one, to be used as the skillful developer of self chooses.

Another way to get information about what has happened in a session is to tape it, then review the tape afterwards. This, of course, is quite time-consuming. To completely review a session tape takes the same amount of time the session itself took, plus any extra time spent stopping and starting the tape, taking notes, etc. For busy people, this can be an obstacle. Still, because it's such a powerful aid to perspective and mindfulness, I do recommend Exercise 13.4 as something to do occasionally.

As in most of the exercises offered here, the review questions point to additional inquiry or practice. Each will raise additional questions in the ongoing process of experimentation and self-discovery that leads toward mastery.

Here are some general guidelines for using all of the SOEs in this chapter.

- Suspend any tendency that you may discover in yourself to evaluate, judge, or criticize. The point of an SOE is to become a better observer. This is best done from a neutral, objective perspective. An SOE could be constructed, for example, to observe yourself interrupting others, and to practice holding back until they are finished, acknowledging what they said, and then responding. It would then be tempting to be self-critical every time you notice yourself interrupting, but getting upset with yourself because you have not yet mastered an old behavior pattern is in fact just another conditioned habit which, in itself, undercuts your ability to stay focused. It's the noticing itself that's the key; coupled with a clear picture of alternative behaviors, it will lead naturally to behavioral change.
- Keep yourself fresh. These exercises are tools, not ends in themselves. When you commit to doing a self-observation practice,

Exercise 13.4: Reviewing Coaching Session Tapes

Instructions

Create an audio- or videotape of yourself as you coach. Ask permission of your client first, letting him or her know that the tape is only for your own use and you'll keep it confidential and destroy it when you're finished. (If you intend to use such a tape for any other purpose, of course, you'll need to get written permission. Those issues are beyond the scope of this book.)

Review the tape(s), using a clean worksheet for each taped session.

After reviewing the tape(s) to observe yourself in action, answer the following questions

- What patterns did you see in reviewing your tape(s)?
- What elements of your self-identity as a coach were apparent?
- What opportunity for increased mindfulness has been presented?

Sample Worksheet

Key Moment/Shift: What was a key moment, question, or comment that led to a shift between questioning and telling? (Later you could use this same structure to focus on shifts between the Voices or their specific Aspects.)

Cues and Observations: What triggered the shift? What opportunity did you see? What aspect of your identity did you observe? Were any attachments or aversions showing up within you? How did you confirm that the shift was indeed meeting the client's needs?

Session Tape Review Template

Date:

Client:

Key Moment/Shifts	Cues and Observations *(triggers for the shift, attachments and aversions)*

commit for a specific and limited period of time. Most often, this will be between a week and a month. Once that time is up, you can review what you've learned, take a break for a while, and/or try another exercise to focus on something new. This keeps the process alive and interesting. The same, of course, holds true if you are using SOEs with your clients.

- Commit yourself to the process of self-discovery and change. There's a certain discipline in following the structure of a self-observation exercise that comes easier to some than to others. Think of it as a practice. It will change the way you notice yourself, and ultimately it will change the way you coach for the better. It does, however, call for the kind of willingness and commitment that are the keys to any self-development activity.

- Use the exercises and worksheets as templates to design your own program. I'm a believer in designing structures to support me in paying attention. For me, a meditation practice is the ultimate exercise for bringing myself to attention. It's simple, I do it in the quiet hours of the morning, and then I go into the rest of my day. After my work day begins, though, my business life is busy, demanding, and fragmented. The structure of a more focused template that I can print out and put in my organizer or in front of me as I coach is immensely valuable as a visible reminder of the specific things I'm working on this week or this month—a trick, if you will, that you can use to direct your attention for the benefit of your own professional development and ultimately your client's.

Finally, self-observation exercises can be written into a client's, or a coach's, development plan. They increase clarity and accountability—the person either completes the SOE or doesn't—and provide fertile ground for follow-up. If the person completes the exercise, there will be interesting data to reflect upon and discuss. If she doesn't, that will provoke a useful conversation about motivation, the appropriateness of the exercise, and/or external factors that stood in the way.

Self-Assessment Tools

Whether or not you feel ready to commit yourself to the Septet Model, the following two self-assessment exercises will give you a great deal of information about where your strengths as a coach lie and which aspects of your coaching you might want to pay more attention to.

The patterns that emerge from a thoughtfully completed self-assessment can be fascinating and informative. Any method of self-assessment assumes a reasonable level of self-awareness and honesty on the part of the person entering into it. When it comes to a self-assessment, of course, there is no one to lie to except ourselves. It does not serve us to paint an idealized picture of ourselves; only we are watching anyway.

Self-awareness is another issue. Coaches may be unaware of the degree to which they underuse or overuse a behavior, as appropriate levels of use are ultimately measured against the degree to which they address the needs of the client. These self-assessments, then, measure the *coach's* perception of his or her use of Aspects and Voices, subject to the limitations of his or her self-awareness. Additional assessments in a later section will include the client perspective in the assessment process, making the comparison rich indeed. You may start with the self-assessment included here in Exercise 13.5, or take the more robust self-assessment on line.

The scores at the bottom of the page indicate your apparent comfort level with each of the seven Voices in the Septet; the individual items, of course, are the twenty Aspects. These numbers will give you some information about your general tendencies as a coach—including which roles or coaching behaviors you may be overly identified with or may underutilize. These numbers are only numbers, of course; they do not provide a complete picture, nor does any specific score, whether high or low, necessarily mean that you overuse or underuse a specific behavior. (Determining this requires the perspective of clients.) Still, they point to lines of inquiry that may help you grow as a professional. Use the scores to generate questions; for example:

- What do my responses confirm to me about my strengths?
- Which (if any) strengths, identified by higher scores, *might* I tend to use in service to my own attachments and identity, rather than the needs of my client?
- What behaviors here could I potentially develop and seek to use more?
- Which Aspects am I curious to learn more about?
- How can I design this learning for myself?

Exercise 13.5: A Brief Coaching Self-Assessment

Here is a brief self-assessment that measures your comfort level with the 20 behaviors represented by the Voices and Aspects of the Septet Model. It is not a substitute for the on-line self-assessment available on the Septet website, which is more accurate and addresses nuances of mindfulness through completely different scales. It will, however, provide you with basic information about your coaching style in relation to the governing model of the Septet system.

Instructions

Complete the assessment below, filling in each white box in the matrix to the right with a number from one to five, according to this scale:

5: I am entirely comfortable and skillful in using this behavior.

4: I use this frequently and well.

3: I do this sometimes.

2: I occasionally do this, but am somewhat awkward and new at it.

1: I rarely do this or don't really understand what it means.

Then total each of the seven columns down to the row at the bottom of the matrix. Divide by the number shown to get an average for that group of behavior; a calculator may help.

Exercise 13.5: (cont'd)

Aspect Behavior	Enter scores in white boxes						
Helps the client to articulate desired outcomes							
Maintains self-awareness							
Provides "expert" information, tools, and language							
Encourages self-observation and reflection							
Encourages the client to take action							
Explores and resolves client doubts and hesitations							
Chooses which of the operational Voices to use at a given time							
Makes explicit, clear choices with the client about the coaching process							
Asks questions that deepen a client's understanding of the situation							
Listens with focus and presence							
Provides direct and honest feedback							
Challenges and stimulates client's thinking process							
Models learning and growth							
Establishes clear agreements about actions							
Directs the client's attention towards his/her capabilities and potential							
Offers options and/or recommends courses of action							
Embraces the client with compassion and respect							
Asks the client to generate courses of action							
Establishes and honors an explicit structure for the coaching relationship							
Follows up with client about agreed-upon actions							
Total of scores from boxes in this column							
Divide by:	5	2	3	3	2	2	3
Average score for this Voice:							
Category initial:	M	P	I	R	T	G	C

Exercises 13.7 and 13.8, below, will be helpful in following the lines of inquiry that you've identified.

The Septet website (http://septetcoaching.com) includes a more detailed self-assessment tool that you can complete on line. After taking the self-assessment, you'll receive a detailed report about your relative use of the Septet Voices and each of the twenty Aspects of the model. Exercise 13.6 will guide you through the process of taking and using the tool. The on-line process provides supporting materials to help you interpret the more detailed data you've gathered.

Both of the Septet self-assessments give you an opportunity to see what your overall coaching style looks like. Given that overview, you can take a closer look at those Aspects that tend to stand out, either because they're over-utilized or because they're under-utilized. Then, for each of these Aspects, you can cultivate the curiosity of an observer who might say, for example, "Oh, how interesting! This coach (read: you!) tends to overuse the Aspect of providing expert information. She does it with a couple of specific clients with whom she can feel intimidated. I wonder what that's about."

Possible lines of inquiry, then, might center around what the coach is experiencing at the times he or she takes on a particular Voice or plays out a particular Aspect within the range of available possibilities. This leads us back to self-observation exercises, which provide a logical means to explore questions raised by a self-assessment or a particular interest in a specific Voice or Aspect. Exercise 13.7 can be used around an area of curiosity, to notice more closely the circumstances around a coach's use of a Voice or an Aspect, including the feelings or habits of mind that arise at moments of choice between the use of one or another.

Here the coach is practicing self-observation in relation to one specific Voice or Aspect. By paying attention, the coach becomes more aware of herself as she uses that specific role. She learns to discern, in the moment, what the source of the impetus for using the role is.

Exercise 13.6: An On-line Self-Assessment

Instructions

Go to http://septetcoaching.com, and follow the links to the self-assessment. Instructions will be at the site, and the final screen will tell you how to obtain your results.

When you get the results back, look at your scores, and read the explanatory information on the scoresheet, which will help you interpret the numbers. Identify three or four interesting scores for:

- Aspects of the Master Voice that are *lower* than your typical scores.
- Aspects of the six operational Voices that are *either higher or lower* than your typical scores.

Complete the worksheet below. (After the assessment, you will be provided with a ready-to-use electronic version. Please use a journal format if that works better for you.)

Sample Worksheet

What does the self-assessment tell you about your core strengths? How would you describe your approach to coaching, given the Aspects that are most typical of your results?

Aspects with Interesting Scores	Concrete examples of overuse or underuse of this Aspect	Line of inquiry: What would you like to discover about yourself in relation to this Aspect?

What self-observations or other development exercises will be helpful for you in following the lines of inquiry above?

Sometimes this impetus may derive from her attachments and aversions arising around the use of the role. At other times, the impetus may be from an attentive observation of her client and what the client needs. With practice, this kind of SOE will greatly increase her ability

Exercise 13.7: Self-Observation on a Specific Voice or Aspect

Instructions

Choose a Voice or Aspect that you want to pay attention to. This might emerge from client feedback, from a self-assessment, or from any other source of curiosity.

Make copies of the worksheet below to use with one or more clients. Following each coaching session, complete one row. Do this for several weeks.

At the end of each week, review your completed worksheets, and answer these questions:

- What did you learn about yourself from observing how you used this Voice/Aspect?

- What are the cues and observations that tell you when you are using it mindfully and in service to the client?

- What cues and observations tell you if there is some need in you that's being addressed?

- What do you want to change or pay closer attention to moving forward?

Sample Worksheet

Date/Client: Note the date and the client.

Examples: Note two or three times, in the session you just completed, when you used the Voice or Aspect.

Cues and Observations: Were you aware of the choice at the time? What led you to use the Voice or Aspect? Did your use of it respond to a need of your client? How did you know? Were you aware of any need or impetus (attachment or aversion) within you that led to that choice?

Date/Client	Examples *(Use of Voice/Aspect)*	Cues and Observations *(Awareness of choice and responding to client, impetus)*

to know the difference. This is a very useful SOE for exploring any Voice or Aspect in more depth.

You may find it useful to choose another of the Voices and experiment with similar exercises that you design yourself to focus on its Aspects or on other areas of particular interest. An SOE can be constructed around any behavior, coaching related or not, that you wish to pay more attention to. Since SOEs are useful for clients as well, it will add greatly to your coaching repertoire to be comfortable creating them, and to have experienced how using the structure works for you. Exercise 13.8 takes you through the process of constructing an SOE with a structure similar to that of others in the book.

The power of a self-observation exercise stems in part from using the cognitive information gathering process, but, more importantly, the simple act of non-judgmental observation brings more light and attention into our use of the behavior in question and increases our mindfulness. Committing to an SOE is a gentle reminder to pay attention to a specific behavior.

SOEs can take very different forms, and can be done with no template or note-taking at all. For the purposes of providing consistency and sufficient structure to get the reader started with self-observation, I've used similar templates throughout, but I do not mean to imply that this is the only way. The structure is simply a means to an end. There are countless other tools that work; mindful attention is the end that we're after. Play with these first, then try other approaches and learn what works for you. Infusing your coaching with a mindset of experimentation and openness to learning will benefit both you and your clients.

Exercise 13.8: Constructing a Self-Observation Exercise

Instructions

Choose an area of inquiry and self-observation that is of interest to you. This could be a specific behavior related to coaching (use of an Aspect, managing distractions, making eye contact, using reflective listening, etc.) or something completely unrelated to coaching (telling your kids you love them, listening deeply to music, watching yourself around compulsive eating, etc.) The purpose of the exercise is to construct and use your own SOE; the specific behavior to be observed is less important than that the behavior is governed by habits of mind about which you wish to cultivate mindfulness and attention.

Determine

- the specific behavior around which you want to observe yourself,

- the circumstances under which the behavior is to be observed,

- the frequency or trigger for using the SOE format (this could be a daily reflection, or something that you do after specific events, or several times a week, as determined by you), and

- the underlying questions that you seek to answer through the self-observation.

Construct an SOE worksheet for writing your notes. Create a template like that below, or download the formatted one from the website. Use the information generated above to add detail to the generic column headings in the worksheet and guide your observations.

Construct a short set of review questions to help you look back over your SOE notes and reflect on what you've learned. These should be meta-questions about a *set* of observations, rather than questions for the observations themselves. Questions might be modeled after these examples:

- What patterns do you notice in your observations?

- What has surprised you in doing this SOE?

- What have you learned about what helps you be mindful in the behavior, or about what keeps you from doing it?

- What is next for you to learn in relation to this behavior?

Use the SOE for what seems to you an appropriate period of time, taking brief notes as determined by the frequency or trigger you described above. Then answer the review questions.

Exercise 13.8: (cont'd)

Sample Worksheet

Event: Note the date, time, or circumstance.

Examples: Note examples of your use of the behavior.

Observations: Note observations relevant to the questions being explored.

Event:	Examples:	Observations:

Navigating the Whole Model

Once you have some experience with focusing on specific Aspects or behaviors, the next step is paying attention to which roles you're using when, and how you are moving through the Septet Model as a whole. The first two exercises in this section will focus on the three core Investigator Aspects: the first step is noticing when you're using each of these Aspects and when you depart from questioning to use one of the sharpener Voices; the next is paying attention to the impetus behind these choices. Later in this section we'll expand this approach to include the entire operational portion of the model.

Exercise 13.9 zeroes in on the central role of questioning. Remember from Chapter 7 that the interplay between the three lines of Investigator questioning—What's the situation? What do you want? What are you going to do?—is what establishes the creative tension that leads to change. This exercise, then, supports your self-observation of the core process by which this tension is established by attending to which line of questioning you're following as the Investigator, and when you

Exercise 13.9: The Investigator Aspects

Instructions

Keep this template in front of you, or re-create it on a separate piece of paper. Consider the four areas shown: the three Investigator Aspects, as represented by the three questions, and the three undifferentiated sharpener Voices, collectively called Telling. With your observer mind, pay attention to where you're working in at each particular point in time. Use a quarter, or any small object, and move it as you coach, keeping it in the spot that *primarily* represents the mode you're in. Don't worry, for now, about distinctions between sharpener Voices.

After each session, take a couple of minutes and complete one line of the chart below.

After a week or two, answer these summary questions:

- What did you learn about the nature of observing yourself?

- What did you learn about when and why you switch from questioning to telling or vice versa?

- If you were going to continue but modify this exercise, what would be interesting to pay attention to in learning more about questioning and telling?

Sample Worksheet

Date/Client: Note the date and the client.

Investigator Aspects: Of the four roles, what did you notice yourself primarily doing during the session? What switches did you notice?

Observations: What did you notice about your use of these four ways of working? Which were you most comfortable? What else did you notice in observing yourself?

Date/Client	Investigator Aspects *(What did you primarily do? Switches?)*	Observations *(Use of four ways of working? Comfort? Other observations of self?)*

switch to using a sharpener Voice. Don't seek to change the way you're coaching; simply observe lightly what you're doing, then reflect on it afterwards.

You may recall that a conversation can begin with any of the Investigator Aspects. Learn to pay attention to moments where it's useful to switch between the Investigator Aspects, or to bring in a sharpener. This is a particularly rich exercise for becoming more observant of your use of questioning.

In Exercise 13.10, you'll seek to *stay* with questioning, to focus in turn on the client's situation, clear outcomes, and action ideas. The artificial restriction that you stay with questioning, of course, brings the urge to do otherwise into sharp focus. As you do this exercise, you'll most likely notice impulses to shift to one or another of the sharpener Voices. These impulses aren't necessarily off-base; in fact, they may well be on target. The purpose here is to simply to notice the impulses, stay with questioning anyway, and practice moving flexibly among the three Investigator Aspects to evoke creative tension. Here you will experiment with how to work with artful questions to do the work of coaching, and to begin to discern whether the impetus to move to more directive sharpening voices comes from your own needs or from an intuitive sense of what the client needs. Again, pay attention to the attachments and aversions that influence your choices.

(I suggest that you don't do this with a client unless the client is experienced, and you have an explicit agreement to experiment together. Although it will be highly useful to you, the constraints of the exercise will mean that for the moment the client doesn't receive the benefit of your full range of abilities as a coach. As an alternative, you could ask a non-client to do the exercise with you.)

While cumbersome, doing Exercise 13.10 over the course of several conversations will provide much insight into what's going on in those transition moments that are usually either intuitive or unconscious.

Exercise 13.10: Focusing on Questions

Instructions

This exercise requires the cooperation of someone—an experienced client, a colleague, or a friend—who has agreed to support you in the experiment. Because you will be paying more attention than usual to your own attachments by artificially restricting your coaching to one Voice, you will not be providing the full range of your coaching to the "client" in this session.

In your coaching, seek to stay with the Investigator Voice, asking questions of the client around the three Aspects. It may be useful to keep the Septet Model in front of you. At each point in your coaching session where you notice an impetus to depart from your Investigator questioning, notice which Voice or Aspect you are drawn to. Stop the action long enough to check out where the impetus is coming from. Perhaps an attachment? An instinct about what the "client" needs? Ask the "client" which Aspect would be in fact be most helpful to her at that moment.

Use the worksheet below to jot quick notes about your self-observation, either during or immediately after the session. After doing this for two or three sessions, use a journal to explore these questions for yourself:

- What patterns did you notice about what triggers your urge to switch out of the Investigator Voice into a sharpener Voice?
- How can you increase your ability to discern accurately whether your switches between Voices are serving the client?
- What practice can you take from this to use in actual coaching sessions to become more mindful in your transitions?

Sample Worksheet

Impetus to Shift: Each time you notice the impetus to shift, stop the action and note which Voice or Aspect you're drawn to.

Cues and Observations: What was the feeling you had as you experienced the impetus? Was there an attachment within you? An aversion? How did you check out whether it would have served your client's needs? What did your client say if you asked her?

Date/Client:

Impetus to Shift (to):	Cues and Observations *(Feelings, attachments, aversions, observations about where impetus comes from)*

With this in mind, let's go back to considering the entire model. Exercise 13.11 asks you to go beyond the "questioning and telling" distinction to pay attention to your use of all the operational Voices of the Septet in a given coaching session. Since there are six of them, this may seem a bit daunting. As you coach, I suggest that you do your mental labeling lightly and quickly, without worrying too much about fine distinctions. Remember to keep your attention primarily on your client; self-observation is a parallel activity in which we pay constant but light attention to where we are within the model. Beware of any attachments that you might have to doing this well; think of it as a game in which you are a beginner and have something to learn.

This exercise is complex, and getting the most out of it will take some practice. If you stay with it for a while, though, you'll find that it becomes easier and easier to keep a balance of attention between the observer mind and the coaching mind. This is important in learning to manage your use of different Voices. (I suggest that you practice this exercise for at least a couple of weeks before moving to the next one.)

Several of the previous exercises asked you to go beyond the "navigation practices" of simply noticing if you are questioning or telling and/or observing where you are on the coaching map. In Exercises 13.3 and 13.10, for example, you began to look at the impetus (which can include your own attachments and aversions) behind your shifts between questioning and telling and behind moving from the Investigator to any of the sharpener Voices. Exercise 13.12 applies the same discipline to the entire model. While sometimes these shifts are driven by habit or an instinctive reaction to something, at other times they are an appropriate response to the changing needs of the client or to the discernment by the coach that there is an opportunity to deepen the conversation. It's important to notice what's triggering your shifts in Voice in order to become more mindful about using them.

Exercise 13.11: Observing Your Coaching Flow

Instructions

Review each of the Voices briefly, so that the distinctions are clear in your mind. (See "An Overview of the Voices," in Chapter 4.)

Keep the central portion of the Septet Coaching Model in front of you. You may use the diagram below, download a full-page version with the exercise from the website, or sketch your own. Coach as you usually do, but, with the second, observer part of your mind, maintain a portion of your awareness on constantly orienting yourself relative to the model. Focus on the six operational Voices you are using, moving a game piece or a quarter to the location in the model that fits the Voice that you are currently speaking in.

Don't let it be too complicated; do it lightly, with a portion of your awareness. (Be aware of your own attachment to doing this well, and let it go; it will only get in your way.) After each session, take a couple of minutes and complete one line of the worksheet below.

After doing this for a week or two, answer these summary questions:

- What did you learn about the nature of observing yourself?

- What are your tendencies? Where are you most comfortable? Where are you least comfortable?

- If you were going to continue but modify this exercise to focus more closely on something, what would be interesting to pay attention to?

Sample Worksheet

Date/Client: Note the date and the client you were coaching at the time.

Observations: What did you notice about your use of the Voices? Where did you spend the most time? The least?

Exercise 13.11: (cont'd)

Comfort Level: What did you notice about staying present with the client while observing where you were on the model?

Date/Client	Observations *(What did you notice about your use of the Voices?)*	Comfort Level *(What did you notice about staying present with the client while observing?)*

Exercise 13.12: Observing the Impetus
Behind Your Coaching Flow

Instructions

Review each of the Voices briefly, so that the distinctions are clear in your mind. (Again, see the overview in Chapter 4.)

Keep the central portion of the Septet Model in front of you. You can use the diagram in Exercise 13.11, download a full-page version with the exercise from the website, or sketch your own. Coach as you usually do, but with the second, observer part of your mind, maintain a portion of your awareness on orienting yourself relative to the model. Focus on the six operational Voices you are using, moving a game piece or a quarter to the location in the model that fits the Voice that you are currently using.

Following each coaching session, complete one row. Do this for 2-3 weeks. At the end of each week, answer these summary questions:

- What have you learned about both the internal attachments and aversions, and the external cues from your client, that tend to trigger your shifts between Voices?

- In which ways do you tend to use Voices in habitual ways that aren't mindful, and don't serve your client?

- What do you want to pay closer attention to as you coach?

Exercise 13.12: (cont'd)

Sample Worksheet

Date/Client: Note the date and the client.

Shifts Between Voices: Describe two or three significant shifts from one Voice to another during the just completed coaching conversation.

Cues and Observations: With hindsight, what did you notice about when you switched? What were the triggers or cues that told you when to switch? Was it an intuition on your part? Some message from the client? Was the new Voice appropriate for what was needed at the time? As you look back, what attachments or aversions might have been showing up?

Date/Client	Shifts Between Voices *(describe two significant switches)*	Cues and Observations *(What did you notice about your shifts? Cues? Attachments? Aversions?)*

Here you are invited to observe what is *behind* the choice of Voice—to make explicit and conscious that which often is subterranean or unconscious. Certainly there are intuitive choices that arise in us. But before shifting to a new approach with a client, or heading down a pathway about which we have a "good feeling," it's important to inquire where the impetus comes from and to discern whether it's simply a conditioned, intuitive response to our own attachments and aversions or is truly in service to the client. (Often it will be helpful to check out our discernment verbally with the client by presenting a choice point about which way to go in the session.)

Obviously, there's a lot to pay attention to here. You have sufficient tools and experience from what has been covered to this point to occupy your observer self for some time to come. I encourage you to experiment with a series of simple navigation SOEs first, and then to inquire into the impetus behind your shifts and choices of Voice and Aspect. Doing so will make you a vastly more mindful helper of others.

Learning from Your Reflection

While we often seek to act as mirrors for our clients, reflecting back to them what we hear and observe about their concerns and behavior, our clients are also mirrors for ourselves. The more we see ourselves in our clients, the more compassion we are able to hold. But it is also true that the more we see ourselves in our clients, the more likely it is that we'll project our own concerns onto them or otherwise blur the boundaries between our issues and theirs. The reflection of ourselves in our clients is both a source of connection and a challenge to our mindfulness practice. The three exercises in this section will support you in getting clearer about these connections.

Remember, from our discussion of projection, that the things that we resist in others tend to be things that we have not yet resolved within ourselves, that specific traits we dislike in others are often those we dislike within ourselves. Exercise 13.13 involves recognizing how we tend to project on our clients, and how our clients, in fact, reflect us to ourselves. This exercise, then, is asking you to discover and "own" parts of yourself that you might rather pretend were not there. It's not supposed to be easy. It will, however, open new doors to compassion for yourself and for your clients.

It is key to be able to see what a client, particularly one we have some difficulty with, is showing us about ourselves. Recognizing the projection is the first step, then comes the question of what to do about it.

As a coach, even though I seek to be compassionate, I can occasionally feel impatient with clients who don't seem to "get it" or who

Exercise 13.13: Recognizing Your Projections

Instructions

Choose one or two clients with whom you experience some level of resistance or judgment. Perhaps you feel impatient with this person's defensiveness, or you just don't understand why he can't follow through. Base these choices on your observations of your own reactions to the person.

Make a copy of the worksheet below for each chosen client or clients. Following each coaching session with the client(s) you've chosen, complete one row.

Do this for several conversations with each. At the end, review the completed worksheets and answer these questions:

- What did this exercise show you about yourself and the source of your reactions to others?
- What can you do to become more compassionate towards yourself in relation to that trait?
- What is important to adjust in your coaching as a result of what you learned?

Sample Worksheet

Date/Client: Note the date and the client.

Observation of Trait in Client: Note one or two traits in the client that you judge, resist, or struggle with. Be as specific as possible, and provide an example.

Observation of Trait in Self: How does the same trait manifest in you? What do you do, or how do you behave, that is similar to what you resist or judge in your client?

Date/Client	Observation of Trait in Client	Observation of Trait in Self

struggle to follow through on commitments that seem simple enough to me. The next exercise addresses the problem of the ways in which we ourselves fall short of "walking the talk." The world is full of missed opportunities. Self-acceptance and compassion require being forgiving of others and of ourselves.

Exercise 13.14 is loosely based on the Tibetan Buddhist practice of *tonglen*.[48] Here, on each in-breath, the coach visualizes the trait of the client about which he has resistance or judgment. On the following out-breath, he focuses on compassion and acceptance. This exercise, done with mindfulness and attention, expands the coach's compassion and acceptance, both of the client and of himself. While it is beyond the scope of this book to go further into meditation practice, the reader is encouraged to explore this further. The Buddhist literature includes a wealth of very practical information about increasing one's own mindfulness.[49]

Whether or not you go further into breathing practice, this simple exercise is very powerful in expanding the compassion and empathy you have for your clients. It will help you to experience, rather than simply intellectually acknowledge, the commonalities that you share. It will also help you accept the parts of your client that you resist, and, by extension, those parts of yourself.

Our common ground with our clients, and our human tendency to project onto others that which we are denying in ourselves, leads to an interesting phenomenon. It is sometimes astounding how often, speaking in the Guide Voice, I provide my client with just the advice I myself need to hear. Or how often an action plan that my client has just committed to somehow seems like it would be the perfect thing for me to do myself. If only I were my own client, being coached by me, I'd know what to do! Often it is only our own conditioning that limits us from using what we already know to full advantage. (Lest we become arrogant, it's important to remember that exactly the same is true of our clients!)

Exercise 13.14: Finding Compassion and Acceptance

Instructions

Choose a client with whom you seem to have particular difficulty, judgment, or resistance.

Following each coaching session with this person, complete one row in the worksheet below, *except for* the column titled "Breathing Observations."

After you complete the first three boxes in the row, sit in a comfortable relaxed posture in silence for five to ten minutes. As you sit, be aware of your breathing. During each in-breath, visualize your client, and specifically the aspect of your client that you resist or that somehow reflects you. During each out-breath, imagine that your breath is flowing out and wrapping your client with compassion and acceptance. Be gentle with yourself as you do this; if your attention wanders, you feel irritated, or you find yourself thinking about something else, simply notice that and bring your attention back to the breathing practice.

Gently bring your attention back to the worksheet and note what you experienced in the "Breathing Observations" column.

Do this in relation to this particular client several times. Then review the worksheet and answer these questions:

- What did you notice about what is reflected in you?
- What was your experience during the breathing practice?
- What changes did you experience over the course of the exercise in your perception of your client and the trait that you have difficulty with?
- How did your experience of the trait in yourself change over the course of this exercise?

Sample Worksheet

Date/Client: Note the date and the client.

Trait of Client: Note one or two ways in which your client showed you something about yourself. It could be that she did something that you would do, or responded in a way that you characteristically would. It could also be that she is in a situation that is similar to one you face, and you felt empathetic.

Reflected Trait of Self: What aspects of yourself did your client illuminate about you? What do you see more clearly in yourself?

Exercise 13.14: (cont'd)

Breathing Observations: What did you notice in your experience with breathing? Did your feelings change in relation to the client? In relation to yourself?

Date/ Client	Trait of Client *(what you saw in client that you related to)*	Reflected Trait of Self *(the aspect of yourself that you saw)*	Breathing Observations *(What did you experience in the breathing?)*

Our clients, and our conversations with them, lay out before us an entire curriculum for professional and self-development. Exercise 13.15 will help you take a closer look at what you could be learning about yourself from your clients.

Doing this exercise can help expose a range of opportunities for our own learning and development; it can also expose ways in which we live vicariously through our clients, or avoid our own issues because we are, on some level, working them through in our interactions with our clients. In either case, it's designed to help you become more mindful of what you're doing as you coach, and of what you can learn from the process that fosters your own development.

Exercise 13.15: Taking Your Own Advice

Instructions

Make several copies of the worksheet below and keep them on hand as you coach your clients. After any coaching session when you've noticed yourself being directive or giving advice (as the Guide or Teacher in particular), complete one row. This is simply an observation; taking notes doesn't mean that you can, or should, follow through on it. You're simply collecting data.

Do this for 2-3 weeks. At the end of each week, review the completed worksheets and answer these summary questions:

- What did this exercise show you about yourself and your development opportunities?
- Are there areas in which you are living vicariously through your clients? (And, if so, is supporting them in taking action somehow removing energy from your taking similar action in your own life?) How are you projecting? What are you avoiding?
- Is there anything you want to adjust in your coaching as a result of what you see here?
- Has doing this exercise reminded you of something you yourself want to act on?

Sample Worksheet

Date/Client: Note the date and the client.

Recommendation/Client Action: Note one or two things that you suggested, or that the client ended up committing to, that somehow resonated for you as relevant to your own situation.

Possible Action/Practice: What possibilities does each trigger in you, in relation to your own development? (This may be very similar to what your client does, or it may be quite different; the focus here is on what gets triggered within you by the client's work.)

Date/ Client	Recommendation/ Client Action *(that seems relevant to your life)*	Possible Action/Practice *(that you could apply yourself)*

Obtaining and Listening to Client Feedback

Our clients are our single best source of information on how we coach. They have a vested interest in our effectiveness, and they see us in action regularly. While we may find ourselves resistant to doing this, a proactive cultivation of feedback will help us make our coaching more valuable to each given client, and will contribute to our professional development at the same time.

Your clients are also your customers, whether you're a paid coach external to an organization, a manager coaching a subordinate, or an educator coaching a teacher. Most well-run businesses provide means for their customers to give them feedback. Complaint systems, customer satisfaction surveys, partnerships with customers to enhance service delivery—these are standard practices. In coaching, however, while many coaches tell their clients that they're open to feedback, most don't systematically gather or analyze it, and most don't insist that their clients actively influence and shape how they are being coached. I think that they should, and that you should as well. This section of the book will give you some tools for doing so.

Informal Feedback

Informal feedback is all that's necessary in many situations. Many coaches ask questions of their clients, especially towards the end of the session: What worked best for you in this session? What were the most important ways in which I was helpful to you? These are useful questions because they provide a preliminary check for both people about whether or not the process is working. They are also affirmative questions, in the spirit of appreciative inquiry, that direct the attention of both parties to the positive aspects of what they're doing together. This is a good thing to do on a regular basis, and it does provide information that helps us adjust what we're doing to better fit the needs of each specific client.

Even more powerful, however, is to state an observation about your coaching relationship, or about how you are coaching, and ask for feedback and discussion about that specific issue. For example, I could say something like "Jessica, I've noticed that in our last three conversations you've asked me for my ideas on issues about which you're more informed than I am. So I think I might be shortchanging you and shortcircuiting your own thinking process by providing my ideas so quickly. What do you think?"

By surfacing a potential difficulty in the way we work together with clients, we invite them to help us coach them more effectively. We also send a clear message that we are committed to their fullest development.

Exercise 13.16 offers an SOE that will structure your attention regarding asking for informal feedback from your clients. By simply observing yourself around this behavior, you'll find yourself doing it more often and more consciously.

While any feedback is useful, and patterns may be evident, the most valuable outcomes of obtaining feedback are the ensuing conversations with the client. Observing yourself in any arena of life will change the way you do it. Here, while the SOE doesn't explicitly track the conversations themselves, the exercise asks you to pay attention to the specific behaviors that are the catalysts for the feedback and conversations; doing so will change the way you interact with your clients.

Formal Feedback and Data-Based Assessment

While your clients may not be sophisticated about coaching at the outset, it's in your mutual interest to have them become more insightful as your relationship evolves. A primary reason is that a skilled client will be more able to take advantage of what you really have to offer. She will also move more quickly toward independence and self-generation.

Secondly, the more skilled your client is, and the more informed she is about your coaching process, the more able she will be to give you

Exercise 13.16: Asking for Informal Feedback from Clients

Instructions

Make copies of the worksheet below for use with several (if not all) of your clients. Following each coaching session, consider which actions you've taken to ask for feedback on that session, and enter the responses in the third column.

Do this for 2-3 weeks. At the end of each week, review the completed worksheets and answer the following summary questions:

- What patterns did you notice in the feedback?
- What did you notice about the attention that you pay to asking for feedback?
- How has this SOE changed your relationship with your clients around feedback?

Sample Worksheet

Date/Client: Note the date and the client.

Actions Taken: Check the boxes for the practices you did in this session; add notes as necessary.

Feedback Received: Summarize the feedback you received.

Date/Client	Actions Taken	Feedback Received
	❏ Asked what worked well ❏ Asked what else would be useful ❏ Asked what client needed ❏ Raised issue; asked for feedback ❏ Other:	
	❏ Asked what worked well ❏ Asked what else would be useful ❏ Asked what client needed ❏ Raised issue; asked for feedback ❏ Other:	

useful feedback that will help you become a better coach and in turn give her the benefit of more skillful and sensitive coaching. This is one of the foundations of a strong partnership.

The Septet website, at http://septetcoaching.com, offers an on-line tool for obtaining formal feedback from a particular client and comparing that client's assessment of you against your own self-assessment. Ideally, this will be someone you have been coaching for some time and for whom more transparency in your coaching will be of benefit. It will also be helpful to go through this process when you know that you could be coaching a client more effectively and want a common language with which to explore what might be needed.

The client logs onto the website using a procedure provided by you, and completes the single-client assessment tool, which is designed to track the appropriateness of your use of each of the twenty Aspects in relation to her specific needs. Both you and the client will then get a graphic report that compares your self-assessment with her assessment of you. This is a way to hold up the relationship, and your coaching approach with that specific person, for the scrutiny of both. The data provides a good reality check of your own perceptions. Exercise 13.17 describes the process and provides a worksheet to prepare both of you for a subsequent conversation about the results.

Exercise 13.17: On-Line Single-Client Assessment

Instructions

Select a client with whom to conduct this process, and ask for her willingness to participate. Explain that the purpose is for you to strengthen your partnership, fine-tune the way you are working with her, and make her a more informed partner.

Log onto http://septetcoaching.com. Follow the links to set up a Single-Client Assessment. In the process, you'll take the Septet Self-Assessment on yourself; *you should answer the questions with this specific client in mind.* You will receive directions to provide to your client, so that she can then take the Single-Client Assessment on you.

Exercise 13.17: (cont'd)

You and your client will receive electronic copies of the worksheet below, and a report summarizing and comparing your respective responses to the assessment items. Ask your client to review the results, fill out the worksheet, and be prepared to discuss the results together in a scheduled conversation. You will also review the results of the assessment and fill out a copy of the worksheet.

Once you both have reviewed the results and completed the worksheets, set aside thirty minutes to an hour with your client to discuss the questions together. Depending on the nature of the relationship, you may or may not charge for this session. An alternative approach is to discuss the results of the assessment in pieces spread out over several conversations.

Discussion Questions

- What are the ways in which you work well together? Discuss this in some depth, so that both of you are clear about the effective core of the relationship.
- What discrepancies do either of you see between the two assessments? To what do you ascribe these discrepancies?
- Consider each Aspect that one or the other deems useful to discuss in light of the following questions:
    - How could increased/decreased use of this Aspect benefit the long-term development of the client?
    - How can both partners share responsibility to guide the coach's use of this Aspect?
    - What agreements can you establish to make your partnership as responsive as possible to these ideas as you move forward?

Sample Worksheet for (coach) and (client)

- What areas of strength and appropriate use of coach roles in this coaching relationship does the assessment point out?
- What discrepancies do you see between your assessment and the other person's that might be interesting to explore?

Specific Aspects that you believe the coach might better use more, less, or differently	Concrete examples where more or less of this Aspect will be helpful to the client

The follow-up structure recommended in the exercise is just a suggestion; there are lots of other questions that might occur to either of you for addressing what this shared assessment brings to light. And many of the tools provided earlier in this chapter can be used by the coach to explore opportunities identified by the assessment. The power of this exercise stems from the fact that it provides data-based neutral ground for discussing the relationship; it may also uncover issues that both the client and the coach have overlooked. Involving both parties in observing and discussing the ways in which coaching unfolds can only deepen the relationship.

The Septet website also offers a multi-client (180-degree) feedback tool for use with all, or a significant sub-set of clients. (The minimum number of clients is three.)

While the results of the single-client assessment go to both parties (since its purpose is to enhance the relationship between the coach and a single client), with the multi-client assessment the feedback is anonymous and the results go to the coach and not to the clients. The coach works with the feedback "off line" and will not necessarily spend time processing it with the clients during sessions.

This is a powerful means to obtain a whole picture of your coaching practice. Again, you will need to select a group of clients to participate, explain how the process will support your development and ultimately your coaching of them, and obtain their willingness to participate. Exercise 13.18 explains the process.

There are three key things to do following the receipt of your data. The first is to spend some time reviewing the information and thinking about what it means to you. Identify the questions and hypotheses that will lead to new lines of inquiry. Look for examples from actual coaching situations that make these questions more real.

Second, create a learning plan to follow up on some of these lines of inquiry. Completing the worksheet will provide the elements of that learning plan. Make it concrete, however. You may find many of the

Exercise 13.18: On-Line Multi-Client Assessment

Instructions

Log onto http://septetcoaching.com. Follow the links to set up a Multi-Client Assessment. Take the Septet Self-Assessment if you have not already done so. You will be informed of the procedure for your clients to follow. Ask all, or a group, of your clients to take the Multi-Client Assessment for you. Explain that the purpose is to develop your capabilities and awareness around the Septet Coaching Model. Explain that the data will be collected and compiled anonymously, that you will not see their individual responses, and that the results from a minimum of three clients will be averaged together to present a whole picture. Provide the log-in procedure to your clients.

After at least three clients have participated, and you have provided permission to close the process, you will be sent the results of the assessment and an electronic copy of the worksheet below. Review the results, then print and complete the worksheet below. Use it to shape a development plan for yourself.

Once you have reviewed the results and completed the worksheet, you may wish to discuss the results with the clients who filled it out. See the book text for suggestions.

Sample Worksheet

- What areas of strength and appropriate use of coach roles do the client assessments point out?
- Where do you see significant discrepancies between your assessment and those of your clients?
- What Aspects are notable because of either high or low ratings by clients?
- What Aspects are notable because of either high or low variability in client response?

Specific Aspects that raise questions	What do you suspect might be true about you in this Aspect? What examples provide evidence of this?	How can you test this, or learn more about yourself in this area?

- What are your next steps for development using this information?
- What conversations might be useful to hold with all clients who responded to the survey?
- What conversations might be useful to hold with specific clients that could enhance your partnership with them?

tools in other sections of this chapter useful in zeroing in on particular lines of inquiry, especially Exercises 13.7, 13.8, 13.12, 13.19, and 13.20. Let your own curiosity be your guide.

Third, after you've sketched out the broad outlines of your development plan, consider what to share with your clients about the assessment. You can do this in a general way, by thanking them and telling them about some of the key learning points that emerged for you. It's always appropriate to do this, and it closes the loop with valued clients who have given their time for your learning.

In addition, the multi-client assessment may present other opportunities. For example, some clients may find it less risky to bring up an issue with you based on general data rather than their specific concerns or feelings. This is especially true if the assessment is done in an organizational context. In addition, you may recognize opportunities to change the way you coach specific individuals based on what you have learned; in this case, it is advisable to involve the client by sharing what you feel you could do differently and asking the client if he or she would find it helpful.

Developing Your Weaker Voices

Self-assessments, client feedback, or your own self-reflection will likely indicate Voices or Aspects that you tend to underuse. Underuse, remember, assumes meaning in relation to the needs of the client; this means that you are sometimes not using the role in situations where it would be helpful, and therefore are underserving the client. The logical approach, then, is to increase your competence and/or your confidence in that realm.

Choose a Voice or an Aspect that you think needs attention because a client brought it up, because self-observation has led you to believe that developing it would benefit your clients, or because its underuse showed up in a formal assessment. Ask yourself some questions. For example, you might ask, Am I resistant to playing the Teacher role? Is there some aspect of the Teacher that doesn't fit with how I think of myself? What do I feel comfortable teaching about? What not? How do I know what it means to teach well?

Then, based on your answers to those questions, either use Exercise 13.19 or design a self-observation exercise around that role. For example, after each coaching session you might note examples of openings when speaking as the Teacher would have been helpful but you didn't take that role. The point of this exercise is to increase your ability to see these opportunities as they arise.

After doing this exercise for a week or two, if you identify unhelpful patterns you can design a development plan for yourself to address them. This might include reading books, practicing specific skills, designing a more narrowly focused self-observation tool, getting feedback from other coaches about how they do it, etc. Establish goals and timeframes for yourself, then follow the structure that you've established. (Exercise 13.23, below, is designed to help you formulate a development plan.)

Exercise 13.19 is written to encompass both times when you do and times when you don't use opportunities to practice the skill or behavior. You may find it helpful to modify the "Increasing the Use" exercise to emphasize the times when you *do* rather than those when you don't. Either way, of course, the point of using the SOE is simply to keep the role in the forefront of your attention.

Exercise 13.19: Increasing the Use of an Aspect

Instructions

Choose a Voice, Aspect, or specific behavior that you think you're not using often enough for maximum benefit of your clients. Following each coaching session, complete one row of the worksheet below.

Do this for 2-3 weeks. At the end of each week, answer these questions:

- What did you learn about yourself from seeing missed opportunities in hindsight?

- What is important for you to pay attention to in becoming more fluid in this Voice/Aspect?

- How did the self-observation practice change the way you noticed opportunities as they arose during coaching?

- What is next for your development in this area?

Sample Worksheet

Date/Client: Note the date and the client.

Opportunities: Note two or three situations, from the session you just completed, when either a) you acted on an opportunity to use the behavior, or b) there was an opportunity to use the Voice or Aspect that you are seeking to develop, but you didn't use it. Remember, no judgment, just observation.

Cues and Observations: What cues told you that there was an opportunity? Were you aware of the opportunity at the time? If so, what led you to use or not use the behavior? If not, where was your attention when the opportunity arose?

Aspect or Behavior to be Observed:

Date/Client	Opportunities (to use the behavior)	Cues and Observations (awareness of opportunity, what led you to use/not use?)

Using Stronger Voices Mindfully

As coaches, we all have Voices that we use comfortably and frequently. That's the good news. The bad news is that these same Voices, which we may think of as our strengths, can often be overused in a way that doesn't serve our clients as best we could. Your mind, following a well-worn groove, may lead you to what's easiest for you and serves your needs best, even though it's not what your client most needs at the moment.

My own most pressing habit is to move to the Teacher role rather quickly. I like concepts and models (this should be apparent to you by now!), and I enjoy providing my coaching clients with new ways of seeing and interpreting their situations. My habit of mind is to teach, and I do it well. While this is often fine, it sometimes represents a misdirection of my energy relative to what my client needs; when used unconsciously, it can deprive the client of the opportunity to do her own work. I'm aware of this, and I work on being conscious about using this strength sparingly and at times when it will really be useful to the client.

Self-assessments, your own self-observation, and feedback from your clients will identify similar tendencies that are habitual for you. With skillful observation, you'll also likely recognize a pull or an attachment as you step into certain roles—an increase in your energy level or a subtle emotional charge. These are signs that your emotional needs are being met. There's nothing wrong with that, of course. It's just that the meeting of your needs isn't the purpose of the conversation.

It also can be true that the Voice that's habitual for you is *exactly* the one that is needed at that particular moment in time. Paying attention and being mindful and attentive to your client doesn't necessarily mean that you need to change what you're doing. As always, self-observation is the key to noticing what's going on beneath the surface.

Exercise 13.20 is designed to increase your awareness of how you use your stronger Voices and/or Aspects.

Exercise 13.20: Using Stronger Voices Mindfully

Instructions

Choose a Voice, Aspect, or specific behavior that you tend to overuse, and that you want to use more mindfully and less habitually.

Following each coaching session, complete one row of the worksheet below.

Do this for 2-3 weeks. At the end of each week, answer these questions.

- What attachments or aversions tend to drive your habits in relation to these roles?
- What practices will help you address or let go of these attachments and aversions in order to be more mindfully present in serving your client?
- What's next for you in becoming more mindful about the use of this Voice/Aspect?

Sample Worksheet

Date/Client: Note the date and the client.

Situation: Note two or three situations from the session you just completed. Consider times you found yourself using this particular Voice or Aspect and you suspect you might have been using it just out of habit. Remember, no judgment, just observation.

Cues and Observations: Were you aware of the possibility of overuse at the time? Looking back, what feelings or cues might have been there to pay attention to? What attachments or aversions might have triggered your habit?

Alternatives: How could you have checked out whether the Voice/Aspect was serving your client? What alternative approach might there have been that would have met the client's needs better?

Date/ Client	Situation *(use of Voice/Aspect)*	Cues and Observations *(awareness at time, attachment/aversion)*	Alternatives *(what else might have worked, making joint decision?)*

Keep in mind that each time you notice a habit is a small awakening and a real increase in your self-awareness. This is absolutely true even if you're noticing an unhelpful habit and you see it only in hindsight. Suspend any self-judgment, remembering that self-judgment is just another especially unhelpful habit of mind. Practice the neutral observation of your habits at play. Tap into your boundless curiosity to learn about what makes you tick.

Take the time to review and summarize what you've learned from this exercise, then act on this information to devise an action plan for yourself. The action plan might include such steps as actively cultivating a different approach to use in the situations that trigger your slipping into a certain role, a practice of checking in with the client before moving into the Voice that you overuse, or recording a coaching session and getting feedback from a mentor coach. It might also involve some personal work on your part to address any issues that trigger the habitual use of one particular role. The goal is to make conscious choices rather than operate on auto-pilot.

Paying attention to these small awakenings, to your exercise of choice over habit, will lead to more awakenings. It is very much a cumulative process. The more you pay attention, the more times you will replace an unconscious habit with a conscious choice.

Making Your Coaching Model Explicit with Your Clients

Sharing your coaching model with your clients is a great way to ensure that you are accountable to them. It also creates a common language through which to build your partnership and jointly shape the coaching process. Ultimately, understanding the process allows your clients to become independent and take charge of their own development.

Coaching is always happening on two levels simultaneously. The first is the level of content, of the issue that the client is addressing. The second is the process of coaching itself. In most coaching, this second level remains the rarified territory of the coach. While the coach is presumably aware of his approach to a greater or lesser extent, it is often not shared explicitly with the client. I suggest that this shortchanges the client, maintains a subtle level of dependency, and limits the ability of the client to become self-generative.

Many clients have never used a coach and don't really know what coaching is. It is up to the coach to talk about what he does and how he does it in order to create a reasonable set of beginning expectations. Beyond that, however, there's a lot of room for deepening the shared understanding of what coaching is as the relationship progresses.

In the Septet Model, the purpose of the Partner Voice is, of course, to build an informed and trusting relationship that allows responsibility for achieving desired outcomes to be shared. Sometimes this is simply establishing the structure of the relationship. However, while coaching I often move from the content at hand to discussing the process for brief periods of time, to make that process explicit. This means shifting from the Investigator or whatever sharpener Voice is being used to the Partner role for a few minutes. Generally this shift is pretty obvious—and that's the point. In my coaching conversations with clients, I want us *both* to become skilled and aware enough that we recognize which Voice is being used at a given time.

Any coaching model is complicated, and it's neither necessary nor appropriate to give your clients a crash course in how you practice your profession. Still, a certain amount of transparency will enable you to communicate better.

A good starting point is to introduce the three core questions of the Investigator—What's the situation? What do you want? What are you going to do?—at the outset. This provides a great basic introduction to the coaching process, as well as the foundation for a reasonable conversation to hold as you're feeling out whether or not to work together. There's certainly no need to go into the Voices at this point, but explaining how a coach helps a client to discover answers to these three questions is a good premise for beginning.

Once the relationship is up and running, there will be other opportunities to deepen the client's understanding of the coaching process. The most logical way to do this is simply to share the model by giving the client copies of Figure 4 and Table 4 (both are to be found, you'll remember, in Chapter 4). Some clients won't be interested. That's fine, let it end there. For others, especially those who are learning to become coaches themselves, talking about the model at the beginning and revisiting it at other times may be useful. Let your client's interest be your primary guide, but be mindful that attention and interest to this area both serves her long-term development and enables you to support her more deeply.

Exercise 13.21 focuses on putting the client in the driver's seat vis-à-vis the model, by identifying choice points and asking her to set the direction. The model will sometimes provide the language for these distinctions; other choices will simply be between two different content areas or lines of questioning. Either way, the client is assuming increased responsibility for navigating the coaching process.

This exercise, of course, involves the Partner Voice, in particular the Aspect of making explicit choices about the coaching process. This is always a good thing to do; the more a client understands what it means to become self-generative, the more she will bring to the conversation the energy and curiosity that makes these exchanges exciting.

Bringing the model to life can also be done by using shifts between Voices or Aspects as reminders to briefly touch base between client and coach. The outcomes are several. First, the coach becomes more mindful of his Voice selection process in relation to that specific client. Second, the client becomes a more conscious and skilled partner in the coaching process. Third, the relationship is strengthened by an ongoing conversation about a specific aspect of the relationship.

Exercise 13.22 is an advanced exercise that you can do with a select client to enlarge his or her understanding of the process. It assumes

Exercise 13.21: Asking the Client What's Next

Instructions

Choose a client with whom to do this exercise. Share the exercise with your client, and ask her to work with you on shifting responsibility to her for shaping the direction of the coaching conversation.

Seek choice points in each coaching conversation where it appears to you that there are two or more ways to proceed. These choices might be between content areas, e.g., questioning about different facets of a situation, or between different Voices.

When these choice points arise, specifically ask your client what would be most useful at that point. You may or may not find it helpful to name the alternatives that you see. Eventually, however, you want the client to become more skillful at discerning what she needs, without suggested alternatives from the coach. When you and the client have worked together to decide this direction, then follow it.

At the end of each coaching session, take a couple of minutes to review this aspect of your session. Do this together. Discuss what each of you learned from the process.

- How did it serve your relationship to discuss the client's needs during the previous few sessions?
- How did it shape the coaching process to do this?
- What did you learn about sharing responsibility for identifying the client's needs?
- What are ways in which you can use this approach to support the client's ability to take increased responsibility for driving the coaching process?

that the client is familiar with the overall structure of the coaching model and with the basic function of each of the Voices. While most clients are more focused on getting the results of coaching than on the process, this exercise will be powerful for clients who are serious about understanding the nuances of the coaching process for their own self-development, or who are themselves learning to coach.

Exercise 13.22: Discussing Voice Shifts with Clients

Instructions

Invite a client to do this exercise together. Ask her to share responsibility with you for identifying shifts from one Voice or Aspect to another. Both should have the Septet Model available during the session.

While coaching, pay attention to the Voices you're using, and let the client know when you are changing Voices and why. Invite her to identify Voice shifts as well. Use Voice shifts as a reminder to quickly check in with the client and ensure that each shift fits, moving her in a useful direction relative to the overall coaching roadmap.

At the end of each coaching session, take a couple of minutes to review this aspect of your session. Do this together. Discuss what each of you learned from the process. Consider these questions together:

- How did it serve your relationship to discuss these Voices shifts with each other?

- What did you learn about sharing responsibility for identifying and choosing Voices?

- What are ways in which you can use this approach to support the client's ability to take increased responsibility for driving the coaching process?

The coaching process begins with the coach asking questions, offering choices, perspectives, and information. With practice and attention, however, clients will become more and more able to know what they need from the coach, and eventually they will be able to fill those needs for themselves. This is self-generation, our goal for our clients.

Approaching this goal doesn't necessarily mean that we will no longer coach a client. It does mean that she will *need* us less and less, that we will have become free to coach her in new ways that are responsive to her newly increased capacities, and that we have committed to her independence.

Planning Your Own Development

Becoming mindful is the antidote to functioning mechanically—the key to making conscious choices about how we coach and about how we live the short lives we are given. A cognitive approach to identifying and working with issues is a very useful thing, but because behaviors are deeply rooted and often driven by assumptions and paradigms that we're not even aware of, real change requires mindful and consistent practice over time.

In a recent coaching workshop, the participants and I reviewed a short list of coaching competencies with the goal that each person would choose one to develop. I chose to do the exercise as well. Since listening was so key, and my listening had been suffering as a result of a distracting work environment and too much to do, I chose to construct a development plan for myself around that activity. My plan, developed after some thought, included uncluttering my coaching space, creating a new system to manage client files, and designing a self-observation exercise to be completed through brief journal entries after each coaching session. And it worked, but not exactly as I had expected.

For me, the very act of constructing the SOE brought forth an increased awareness of how I was listening and when lapses occurred. I found myself listening better. My span of attention increased significantly, and I found myself "actively" listening more regularly and consciously.

Well and good, but on review of the SOE after two weeks, other patterns became clear as well. I tended to listen less well when the desired coaching outcomes with a specific client were unclear, and, because of how I was scheduling clients, I often had insufficient time to complete the centering practice before each session that my development plan called for.

This review then opened the door to new practices. I went back to a couple of clients with whom I had been feeling stuck, to re-clarify goals for our coaching together. I started scheduling clients differently to provide more breathing space in between sessions, and dedicated a small but solid block of time for doing my own pre-session preparation. Soon some of these new practices became habits and I no longer needed the SOE to pay attention to them.

The cognitive review and planning portions of this cycle support and guide the SOEs and the practices that make up the core of the behavioral change program. But it's the mindful practice, self-observation, and adjustments based on those observations that fuels real change. When cognitive processes and mindfulness are coupled, we greatly increase the chances for success.

In his book *Primal Leadership*, Daniel Goleman writes,

> Improvement plans crafted around learning—rather than performance outcomes—have been found most effective. For instance, in a program to improve communication skills, a learning agenda resulted in dramatically better presentations; a performance agenda tended to make people react defensively—not wanting to "look bad"—while neglecting to give them concrete steps to improve their actual performance.[50]

As with your clients, in planning for your own development it makes sense to design learning practices that reduce performance anxiety and increase commitment and motivation. Designing how to learn, how to observe yourself, how to practice—these actions lead to increased competence and increased performance. This is the purpose of most of the exercises in this book. Self-observation is done from a neutral frame of mind. There is no failure.

Exercise 13.23 presents a simple tool that can incorporate a range of learning activities into an integrated, practical plan to address any theme you wish to develop. This, if you have been using the exercises in the book, is likely to relate to an aspect of the Septet Model. But such a plan can address anything else that you wish to develop, from quitting smoking to launching a business to developing supervisory skills to enhancing intimacy with a spouse.

Exercise 13.23: Creating a Development Plan

Instructions

Choose an area of development for yourself. Download, copy, or re-create the development plan worksheet below. Use the plan as a framework to hold yourself accountable to following through.

Sample Worksheet

Development Theme: Choose a general area in which you want to focus your development activities.

Strategies: Pick a couple of approaches to address the identified theme. Generally, these will be learning strategies. Approaching the same theme from a variety of learning angles is a good idea. For example, in addressing listening skills, strategies might include a self-observation exercise, reading or other cognitive learning about listening, and getting feedback from others.

Action Steps: Identify specific, concrete actions tied to dates and times that will provide the structure for moving forward and link easily to your calendar or organizing system.

Resources: Other people, books, tools, training materials, movies, etc., that will be helpful or critical in succeeding at the action steps.

Development Theme:

Strategy	Action Steps (Specific, Measurable, Action-oriented, Realistic, Time-bounded)	Support/Resources
	1. 2. 3.	
	1. 2. 3.	
	1. 2. 3.	

Very concrete practical changes are relatively easy to map using this format. I use the tool extensively with my own coaching clients; it is a tool for the Contractor to use in supporting the client's efforts to design concrete steps for his or her development. However, the structure that it provides is also enormously helpful when dealing with elusive changes around behaviors, and especially about becoming more mindful about behaviors in the first place.

In the realms of change that we have been discussing in this book, which really involve unwrapping long-practiced unconscious behaviors to expose new choices, success begins with learning to see conditioned behaviors that might not be helpful. Each moment of noticing a habit is in itself a small win. Following these glimpses, success becomes learning to see, in the moment, opportunities to do something more effective in a given situation. Lastly, success is acting on the new, more effective behaviors.

The reality of busy lives is that we often take the path of least resistance. The development plan is one way of creating a structure to support continuous learning. SOEs and other learning activities can be built into a system that coach and client both use to track learning activities and pay attention to follow-through. A development plan takes good intentions and translates them into a practical roadmap for learning and paying attention.

Practicing Mindfulness

I strongly recommend some sort of mindfulness practice independent of your coaching. This can be nearly anything that will build your self-awareness. Like any physical muscle, self-awareness grows stronger through repetition and exercise. Meditation, of course, is the activity most purely designed for mindfulness practice, and a wide range of meditation approaches are available, with or without religious contexts. The muscle of self-awareness can also be developed through

physical exercise, yoga, golf and other sports, martial arts, quiet con-
templation, journaling, time in nature, or in almost any arena of life
that requires the cultivation of attention and presence. The shift in
attention that converts ordinary activities into mindfulness practice is
that you dedicate that time to becoming a student of your own mind
and how it works. What does it feel like when you're aware and mindful? What triggers your mind to be distracted, to seize upon ideas or
fears, to judge or criticize? What works—for *you*—to center yourself
and be awake with a full appreciation of the present moment? Your
mind is a marvelous creation, and it is a life's work to come to know it
intimately.

In my daily meditation practice I sit for twenty-five minutes in the
early morning and seek to still my mind by focusing on my breath,
counting to ten, and then starting over. As thoughts arise, I seek to simply notice them and let them go. Of course, I tend towards a busy mind.
Frequently, when I sit, I notice myself obsessing about future plans, or
my daily lists, or yesterday's mistakes. For me, this meditation is simply
about noticing where my mind is wandering and gently bringing my
attention back to the present.

Once, on a silent retreat, I wrote down a caricature of my mind in
meditation:

> [Ding! . . . . . the bell rings to begin meditation] OK, I'm
> really going to do it right this time. . . . . . I'm going to
> count and be really disciplined. . . . . . I know I can do this.
> . . . . . Things come easily to me. Oh, there's an attachment!
> I'm attached to doing this well. There I go again. . . . . .
> My postures about being competent. . . . . . Let it go. . . . .
> You don't need to be good at this. . . . . . Just be! Oh, yeah,
> . . . . . this is meditation time. [Breathe] . . . . . . One . . . . . .
> [Breathe] . . . . . . Two . . . . . . There you go, that's good!
> I'm starting to get it now! I can do this. Careful, when you
> congratulate yourself, you're taking yourself away. Ooops!

There I went again! [Breathe] . . . . . . One . . . . . . [Breathe]
. . . . . Two . . . . . But I have to be an observer. . . . . . I have
to notice what's going on. . . . . . I have to pay attention. I'm
doing all right now. You know, this retreat is pretty cool!
. . . . . I'd love to have Jessica come. I'd like to have her see
me in this context. I'd like to lead people to this. . . . . . Oh,
there's a bit of ego! I want to be seen as the serene Buddhist!
That's pretty funny. Oops . . . breathe, stupid! [Breathe]
. . . . . . One . . . . . . I'm really not very good at this.
I should be better at this! My monkey mind is at work. . . . . . Oh,
yeah, I'm supposed to be meditating! [Breathe] . . . . . . One
[Breathe] . . . . . . Two [Breathe] . . . . . . Three. . . . . . I can't
even count to ten without losing my focus! Well, it's just the
skandhas arising. I KNOW that, but I should at least be able
to count to ten. . . . . . I've been doing this for years! I pretend
to be this wise spiritual person, but I'm actually really rather
a mess. . . . . . Oops! [Breathe] . . . . . . One . . . . . . It's pretty
quiet in here. . . . . everyone else is quiet. . . . . . I wonder how
they are inside themselves. . . . . . I bet they're all very serene.
. . . . every one else does this well, but I feel pretty frenzied.
. . . . . Oops! [Breathe] . . . . . . One . . . . . . [etc, etc!]

This is fairly typical of my meditation experiences. Obviously
I have a long way to go before I'm sitting serenely, free of obsessive
thinking! Practice, however, not attainment, is the point. Practice
is the path by which we learn to see how our minds work. Practice
means seeing our ego arising, over and over, and learning to accept
it. Practice means recognizing the games we get caught up in, and
letting them go. Practice means learning to bring our attention back,
time after time, to the object of focus, and not losing patience. Being
perfect at it isn't the goal. Just noticing, and accepting, is. Gradually,
over time, we become more and more able to keep our attention gently
on what we're doing.

A client of mine that who had tendencies to become very anxious at work, and worried about how people perceived his competence, was also an avid golfer. He loved the game and brought a fierce competitiveness and high performance standards to it. We designed a mindfulness practice around golf that would help him at work.

While work is a complex, constantly changing environment, with lots of other people and dynamics involved, golf is comparatively pretty simple. Mostly, it's you and the ball out there; golf provides a wonderful opportunity to practice mindfulness and attention. It also becomes immediately obvious when you're not present, as the golf ball defies every known law of physics to land in the woods. For a while this client's coaching assignment was to play golf, and to stay relaxed and present as he did so. While he was to be attentive and focused, he was also to practice not being invested in a particular score, and he was to notice when self-doubt, self-judgment, anxiety, or competitiveness arose, and just come back to the present moment. It was a great practice, helped him enjoy his golf game more, and showed him much about how his mind worked. What he learned on the golf course was also immensely helpful in learning to notice what arose for him in the more complex surroundings of work.

Whatever you do for a living and for recreation, you have daily opportunities to practice paying attention in the fullest sense of the word. Choose at least one venue for your mindfulness practice. It could be meditation, prayer, or yoga. It could be playing a musical instrument or writing poetry or singing. It could be public speaking or mediating conflicts. It could be golf or tennis or almost any other sport, because every sport has an "inner game." (See also the "Basic Tools for Cultivating Mindfulness" section of Chapter 2.)

Whatever venue you choose, it's important to recognize that using it as mindfulness practice adds an entire dimension to the activity beyond simply trying to practice your serve or play a new song, or being good at the activity. Your work is to stay in the present and cultivate your ability to notice what's going on in your own mind. The simple act of doing one thing and paying full attention to it is the key. The emphasis is on practice rather than accomplishment, and on quality of attention over performance. Practicing mindfulness will pay huge dividends, not just in your coaching, but in every other aspect of your life as well.

CHAPTER FOURTEEN

Toward Mindful Service: A Pathway to Mastery

*A human being . . . experiences himself, his thoughts
and feelings, as something separated from the rest—
a kind of optical delusion of his consciousness. This
delusion is a kind of prison for us. . . . Our task must
be to free ourselves from this prison by widening our
circle of compassion to embrace all living creatures
and the whole of nature in its beauty. . . . The
striving for such achievement is, in itself, a part of
the liberation and a foundation for inner security.*

ALBERT EINSTEIN

*Believe those who are seeking the truth.
Doubt those who find it.*

ANDRE GIDE

*I*t is in serving others that we cultivate our own mastery. Mastery is not
something to be achieved, it's a search through which we find meaning.
The search requires recognizing and setting aside our own self-imposed
limitations, and dedicating ourselves to serving others.

Recognizing and moving past limitations in order to achieve higher
levels of success is, of course, what coaches often sell to clients. It follows
that coaches with integrity demonstrate the same levels of introspection
and commitment to their development as they expect of their clients. In
coaching others, the coach encounters the perfect practice field for his
own journey toward mastery.

Service has many definitions. For our purposes, the most useful include "work done for another; respect; attention; devotion; helpful, beneficial, or friendly action or conduct; giving assistance or advantage to another."[51] All these are directed toward another person, are for the benefit of another. That doesn't mean, as we've said before, that the coach doesn't take care of her own needs; the coaching agreement is set up to be a win/win arrangement. But it is the needs, aspirations, and fulfillment of the client that are at the center of coaching and provide the guiding energy for the process. The coach is there as a resource and a catalyst. It's all about the client.

Mindful service means that the coach is paying attention as she coaches. She seeks to be awake during coaching, to be selfless enough to be attentive to the client and his changing needs. This requires recognizing and moving above the relentless calls of her own ego and her insecurities. In order to do so, she practices becoming aware of her self and letting go, for the moment, of what does not serve the client. This is the central premise of mindfulness.

Mindful awareness is not about trying to become someone we're not. It's really about cultivating curiosity about ourselves and who we are.

Pema Chödrön describes it this way:

> The point is not to try to change ourselves. . . . Practice isn't about trying to throw ourselves away and become something better. It's about befriending who we are already. The ground of practice is you or me or whoever we are right now, just as we are. That's the ground, that's what we study, that's what we come to know with tremendous curiosity and interest. . . . The idea isn't to get rid of ego but actually to begin to take an interest in ourselves, to investigate and be inquisitive about ourselves.[52]

Remember that in the Septet Model, the coach enters each coaching session with three questions: Who am I as a coach? Who is this client?

How can I serve? The commitment to mindful service keeps these questions at the forefront; seeking the answers is our curriculum.

Service becomes the mirror in which we see ourselves reflected. Our dedication puts our ego needs—our attachments, aversions, and conditioned habits—right there in our face to look at. Sometimes we like what we see and choose to keep it. Sometimes we don't, and we choose to change or try something new. Either way, the act of committing ourselves to truly serving another guarantees that we will see ourselves more clearly, which in turn creates unlimited opportunities to learn.

Dependency and Service

A good way to check in with yourself to see if you are truly serving your clients' needs is to ask about the ways in which you may be fostering their dependency on you. If we jump in to provide information and suggestions, perhaps that helps the client make an immediate decision, but perhaps doing so will make him less capable of finding the information on his own the next time he has a question, and more dependent on you for help. There's no clear answer on this one, and no guidance that will reliably lead you to the "correct" balance between empowering your clients and creating dependency. However, the search for that balance must be undertaken responsibly and explicitly by the coach if the coaching process is truly to support the long-term growth of every client.

In a coaching relationship, the client looks to the "expert" coach to provide information and knowledge. The ability to serve an apparent need is satisfying to the coach, and part of the work that pays the bills, no matter the specific profession in which the coach is engaged. Both may collude in this mutual dependency.

The bottom line here is that the client's long-term effectiveness and capacity for self-generation define the success of the coaching process. The more explicit the coach is about how she is coaching, the more informed the client becomes about the coaching process itself. This means that the client learns to use the coach ever more wisely, and that through coaching he learns how to do for himself what the coach had been doing. This reduces dependency and leads to a client who is increasingly able to be self-generating.

In the words of James Flaherty,

> Well-coached clients can observe when they are performing well and when they are not and will make any necessary adjustments independently of the coach. By keeping this criterion in mind, coaches can avoid the big temptation of becoming indispensable and, instead, work to build the competence of their client. . . . We can always improve, and well-coached people know this and will continually find ways on their own to do so.[53]

Coached well, toward specific outcomes, a client will know he has been successful when he has reached the desired outcomes he stated at the beginning of the relationship and has, in parallel, become fully capable of guiding his own development in the future. He's then ready to dispense with the services of the coach, and this is certainly the goal most coaches will say they are working toward. What's often not openly acknowledged is the subtle potential for a conflict of interest between the coach and the client that this outcome raises. The client has become self-sufficient. The coach, on the other hand, seeks to make a living. Creating dependency in clients is a form of job security for coaches. Coach and client would appear to be working at cross-purposes.

This conflict of interest is inherent to all the helping professions, from psychotherapy to consulting to healthcare. Coaching is no exception. The mindful coach will examine her own motivations and attachments and observe honestly the benefits she is deriving from each coaching relationship. This includes any number of things, such as money, satisfaction, or appreciation and validation from the client.

Within an organization, a coach also derives benefits from coaching others: improved performance, kudos from the client, appreciation for her efforts from higher-ups. If coaching is truly done in primary dedication to developing the long-term capacities of the client, the coach in any venue must be willing to subsume all of these as drivers of coaching to the needs and aspirations of the client. She must be willing to let them all go if that's what serving asks of her.

It is our job as coaches to do our jobs so well that our clients no longer need us. This is what integrity and mindful service demand, and is the test of true service. If we truly serve our clients' interests, their testimony about the benefits of our services will generate all the demand we could desire.

Strategies for Building Accountability

Here's a review of key practices discussed elsewhere in the book. Using these as practical guidelines will help you be accountable to your client, an essential part of the practice of service.

- Create a structure for your partnership that enables you to keep the dialog open about how it's working for both of you.
- Educate your client about how to use you as a coach.
- Make your coaching model explicit with clients.
- Provide opportunities for your clients—even shy or reticent ones—to give you feedback about your performance as a coach.
- Commit to each coaching relationship but make it clear to each client that he or she can end that relationship at any time.
- Make yourself accountable to the client's outcomes. Define these outcomes together, and in such a way that they are as measurable and explicit as possible.
- Make it clear that the end result of your coaching is client independence.

The Nature of Practice

Outside the coaching relationship, we are required to practice mindfulness in our own choices and lives. This "earns us the right" to coach, a right not automatically conveyed by an authority-based relationship, by the paying of fees, or by formal or informal agreements. Coaching is not a set of techniques that we apply to our subject. It is a way of interacting, a discipline.

As a practical matter, we cannot teach that which we do not know. When we practice mindfulness, when we learn to lead our own lives in an effective and fulfilling way, we are mastering that which we bring to the table as coaches. By practicing our own mindfulness, by being students of the territory of learning, growth, and change, we become seasoned, more able to be of service to others in their own process of fulfillment.

You may notice the word "practice" being used often. Practice, as it's often used in our culture, implies what we do to learn a new skill before we do it for real: it's the piano lesson that gets us ready for the recital, but in our minds we know it's the recital that really counts.

Here we use the term "practice" differently. Practice is the whole thing; we are always practicing. It's what we do, how we lead our lives. The path itself is the goal. There is no point at which we will arrive when we've done sufficient practice, because there is no limit to what there is to learn. As George Leonard says, in his classic book *Mastery,*

> The people we know as masters don't devote themselves to their particular skill just to get better at it. The truth is, *they love to practice-* and because of this they do get better. . . . Ultimately, practice is the path of mastery. If you stay on it long enough, you'll find it to be a vivid place, with its ups and downs, its challenges and comforts, its surprises, disappointments, and unconditional joys. You'll take your share of bumps and bruises while traveling—bruises of the ego as

well as of the body, mind, and spirit—but it might well turn out to be the most reliable thing in your life. Then, too, it might eventually make you a winner in your field, if that's what you're looking for, and then people will refer to you as a master. But that's not really the point. What is mastery? At the heart of it, mastery is practice. Mastery is staying on the path.[54]

The joys and rewards of the path are to be found along the path itself, not from arriving at a predetermined destination. Everything that we do is part of the practice. As coaches, we practice mindfulness in each coaching session, noticing what arises, seeking to stay present and to serve our clients as fully and selflessly as possible. When we're not coaching (which is most of the time!) we seek to practice mindfulness and effectiveness in all the other realms of our lives. We learn to accept that we won't get it right all the time; as they say in Alcoholics Anonymous, "Seek progress, not perfection." Being hard on ourselves for our shortcomings just increases our suffering.

This stance provides tremendous freedom. When we see all of life as practice, and take pleasure in the practice itself, we begin to recognize that the pressure for perfection is just another habit of mind that gets in our way. No matter the perceived stakes in an interaction or event, we can choose to view it as nothing more than yet another opportunity to practice. As Leonard says, "Practice *is* the path."

The Spirit of Inquiry

Whatever your profession, you are in it for more than a paycheck. Whether you are an executive, a therapist, or an educator, a health care professional, a social worker, or a coach, you would not have read this far without both a zest for learning and a commitment to serve those for whom you have assumed development responsibility. The book has been written in the hope and belief that the development of people is a venture that inherently enriches both the coach and the recipient of coaching. It is a wondrous privilege to be invited to support the growth of others. In accepting the invitation, you will be most authentic, effective, and ultimately fulfilled if you enter each engagement with the same spirit of inquiry into which you invite those you are coaching.

It is the asking of questions and seeking of answers that catalyzes learning. I invite you to become more curious about your mind, about your clients, about the world. It is through this exploration that we find meaning and purpose.

The Voices described in this book are simply a way to see, another mirror that reflects us to ourselves. Like any model, the Septet is a means for increasing awareness and understanding of what we're doing and why. Some readers will have a tendency to learn about the Voices and Aspects of the Septet and seek to fit them into an existing cognitive framework that they hold about what coaching should be. Others may adopt the Septet as their coaching model and fit other ideas into that framework.

I invite you to use this approach expansively, as a way of opening doors. As you play with and explore the material in this book, questions will arise. What does it mean to *me* to be mindful as I coach? How can I remind myself, in the moment, to be present? I think I overuse the Reflector Voice—why is that? How can I learn to catch myself as that urge arises? What am I trying to reassure myself of when I tell others about how effective they are? What would it mean to truly be dedicated, fully, to my clients' growth? What would I have to give up?

These questions are inherently interesting. Answering one raises others. Follow them where they lead you. Mastery is a quest, rooted in the practice of chasing questions, of being relentlessly curious. Try on this mindset, this attitude toward learning, and see where it takes you.

This work is the work of the Master. The Master is part of, essential to, and bigger than the one who coaches. By engaging fully in our own work of mastery, we earn the right to work with our clients. This is how we coach.

Committing to consciously serve others is a pathway through which we discover our own mastery.

The Ten Thousand Things

"A person can hold seven items in the mind at once."

I think (one) to write about these seven things
my mind can hold: (two) a slice of cold Mutsu,
the quick spurt (three) of tart-sweet juice,
(four) the thought of taste budding on my tongue's
nubbly surface (five), to seek to find the certain
word for fruit dissolving in the mouth,
or something (six) not apple, like the truth,
or sunlight pouring amber (seven) through a curtain.
By the time I've come to know of these, they're gone;
but words they spawn wing through my mind, following
the leader over the edge of moment like wild geese:
one sea, its drops—one field, a million spikes of grass—
a sky of unseen stars are jumbled in the time
this poem took to write: what flocks, what birds, have flown?

ANN SILSBEE

Notes

1. "Long term development of effectiveness and self-generation" borrows from James Flaherty's work, which has been very influential in my own. See Flaherty, *Coaching: Evoking Excellence in Others* (Boston, MA: Butterworth-Heinemann, 1999).

2. James Flaherty, *Coaching: Evoking Excellence in Others* (Boston, MA: Butterworth-Heinemann, 1999).

3. Daniel Goleman, *Primal Leadership: Realizing the Power of Emotional Intelligence* (Boston, MA: Harvard Business School Press, 2002), p. 39.

4. The Five *Skandhas* are described in many works on Buddhism. Two particularly lucid and accessible explanations are found in Thich Nhat Hahn's *The Heart of the Buddha's Teaching* (Berkeley, CA: Parallax Press, 1998), pp. 164-171; and Lama Surya Das's *Awakening the Buddha Within: Tibetan Wisdom for the Western World* (New York, NY: Broadway Books, 1997), pp. 80-82.

5. Thich Nhat Hahn, *The Heart of the Buddha's Teaching* (Berkeley, CA: Parallax Press, 1998), p. 168. In the teachings of one school there are fifty-one specific types of mental formations, each with its own distinct characteristics; while this may be somewhat overwhelming to the Western mind, such is the precise nature of Buddhism's description of what goes on inside each of us.

6. The Eight Worldly Influences are also referred to as the Eight Worldly Winds, or Dharmas. Good explanations of these concepts can be found in Lama Surya Das's *Awakening the Buddha Within*, pp. 239-242, and Pema Chödrön's *When Things Fall Apart: Heart Advice for Difficult Times* (Boston, MA: Shambhala, 1997), pp. 46-52.

7. Lama Surya Das, *Awakening the Buddha Within*, p. 241.

8. Pema Chödrön, *When Things Fall Apart*, p. 48.

9. Lama Surya Das, *Awakening the Buddha Within*, pp. 301-302.

10. *Webster's New Universal Unabridged Dictionary* (New York, NY: Simon and Schuster, 1983).

11. In this book, we will consider the observation of self as a developmental activity, a practice for cultivating mindfulness. In learning to be self-observant it may be useful to think of ourselves as both the observer and the subject of inquiry, but from a rigorous point of view, when we are truly mindful there is no observer. Observer and subject are artificial separations. As you try out the practices presented here, think of the distinction as a learning device designed to increase your awareness. If one is fully present—fully mindful—it disappears.

12. James Flaherty, *Coaching: Evoking Excellence in Others* (Boston, MA: Butterworth-Heinemann, 1999), pp. 62-63.

13. Ibid., p. 62.

14. Nancy Spence, *Back to Basics: An Awareness Primer* (Bryson City, NC: Inner Vision, 1995), p. 19.

15. Ellen Langer, *Mindfulness* (Reading, MA: Addison-Wesley Publishing Company, 1989), p. 43.

16. Shunryu Suzuki, *Zen Mind, Beginner's Mind* (New York, NY: Weatherhill, 1970), p. 22.

17. From Lama Surya Das, *Awakening the Buddha Within*, pp. 348-350. Used by permission.

18. Books with very practical basic instruction in meditation are included in the "References" section of this book. I recommend the books by the following authors: Thich Nhat Hahn, Lama Surya Das, the Dalai Lama, and Bhante Henepola Gunaratana. The reader can take or leave the Buddhist context within which the practices are presented; they stand on their own. On the other hand, exploring this context will greatly deepen the reader's understanding of why meditation works.

19. *The Relaxation Response*, by Herbert Benson with Miriam Klipper, (New York, NY: Morrow/Avon, 2000) is a good introduction to meditation from a medical perspective, with no religious trappings whatsoever. First published in 1975 and since updated and reissued, the book is a classic in the field of the mind/body connection; Dr. Benson is a Harvard-affiliated cardiologist whose extensive research clearly demonstrates the health benefits of meditation on, for example, blood pressure and heart disease. *Zen and the Brain: Toward an Understanding of Meditation and Consciousness*, by James H. Austin, M.D. (Cambridge, MA: MIT Press, 1998) is an up-to-date and thorough exploration of the field.

20. Hanh, Thich Nhat, *Present Moment, Wonderful Moment: Mindfulness Verses for Daily Living* (Berkeley, CA: Parallax, 1990), p. 34. Other breathing meditations by Thich Nhat Hahn appear in *The Miracle of Mindfulness: A Manual on Meditation* (Boston, MA: Beacon Press, 1975), starting on p. 79, and in most of his many excellent books on meditation.

21. The classic book on the subject is W. Timothy Gallwey's *The Inner Game of Tennis* (New York, NY: Random House, 1997), first published in 1972. A precursor to the burgeoning field of sports psychology, Gallwey's book draws from Zen and psychology in presenting methods for increasing self-awareness and focus. While ostensibly about tennis, these lessons are translatable to many activities.

22. Julia Cameron's book *The Artist's Way* (New York, NY: G.P. Putnam's Sons, 1992) provides a wonderful roadmap for anyone seeking to discover their creative side.

23. Based on an exercise described by Rick Ross, in Peter Senge, *The Fifth Discipline Fieldbook* (New York, NY: Doubleday, 1994), pp. 108-112.

24. An assessment tool that allows clients to provide detailed feedback to their coach is available at http://septetcoaching.com.

25. The list included here is excerpted from the ICF's Code of Ethics. The ICF Code of Ethics, including the ICF Philosophy and Definition of Coaching, and Ethics Pledge, may be viewed in their entirety at http://www.coachfederation.org/ethics/code_ethics.asp. Guidelines are reprinted here by permission of ICF

26. Darya Funches, *Three Gifts of the Organization Development Practitioner* (Seattle, WA: The REAP Gallery Unlimited Corporation, 1989), p. 157.

27. Laura Whitworth, Henry Kimsey-House, Phil Sandahl, *Co-Active Coaching: New Skills for Coaching People Toward Success in Work and Life* (Palo Alto, CA: Davies-Black Publishing, 1998), pp. 17-18.

28. Flaherty, *Coaching: Evoking Excellence in Others*, p. 53.

29. Whitworth et al., *Co-Active Coaching*, pp. 34-39.

30. Darya Funches, *Three Gifts of the Organization Development Practitioner*, p. 157.

31. Pema Chödrön, *When Things Fall Apart*, pp. 78-80.

32. Flaherty, *Coaching: Evoking Excellence in Others*, p. 51.

33. Merilee Goldberg, *The Art of the Question* (New York, NY: John Wiley & Sons, 1998), p. 3. This excellent book on the use of questions in therapy has lots of value for coaches as well. While the examples are clinical, the discussion of questions and language, and the uses of questions to shape learning, are powerful and applicable to the distinct process of coaching.

34. See Robert Fritz, *The Path of Least Resistance: Principles for Creating What You Want to Create* (Salem, MA: DMA, Inc., 1984); and Peter Senge, *The Fifth Discipline: The Art and Practice of Learning Organization* (New York, NY: Doubleday Currency, 1990) for two good descriptions of creative tension.

35. Fritz, *The Path of Least Resistance*, p. 66.

36. Richard Wiseman, *The Luck Factor: Changing Your Luck, Changing Your Life: The Four Essential Principles* (New York, NY: Miramax, 2003).

37. See Diana Whitney and Amanda Trosten-Bloom, *The Power of Appreciative Inquiry: A Practical Guide to Positive Change* (San Francisco, CA: Berrett-Koehler Publishers, Inc, 2003), which provides a good overview of the field.

38. Sue Annis Hammond, *The Thin Book of Appreciative Inquiry* (Plano, TX: CCS Publishing Company, 1996), pp. 7-8.

39. Peter Senge, *The Fifth Discipline*, p. 250.

40. Roger Fisher and William Ury, *Getting to Yes: Negotiating Agreement without Giving In* (New York, NY: Penguin Books, 1981), p. 40.

41. This model draws from Loy Young's unpublished relationship awareness work; personal communication with the author.

42. Flaherty, *Coaching: Evoking Excellence in Others*, p. 9.

43. Chris Argyris, "Teaching Smart People to Learn," *Harvard Business Review*, 1991.

44. Chris Argyris and Don Schön, *Theory in Practice* (San Francisco, CA: Jossey-Bass, 1974), p. 638.

45. Argyris, "Teaching Smart People to Learn."

46. Liane Anderson, *Argyris and Schön's Theory on Congruence and Learning* (1997). Available at http://www.scu.edu.au/schools/gcm/ar/arp/argyris.html

47. Flaherty, *Coaching: Evoking Excellence in Others*, p. 163.

48. *Tonglen* is described in more detail in Lama Surya Das, *Awakening the Buddha Within*, pp. 161-165. Surya Das describes *tonglen* as "a way of transforming the recalcitrant hardened heart into a heart softened by love and empathy" and as "the taking on of burdens without feeling burdened." The application described in the exercise is a simplified adaptation of this powerful and advanced mind-training technique. Karen Kissel Wegela, *How to Be a Help Instead of a Nuisance* (Boston, MA: Shambala, 1996), pp. 136–143, has another good description.

49. Thich Nhat Hahn's *The Miracle of Mindfulness* (Boston, MA: Beacon Press, 1975), 79-98, is a good starting point for some basic mindfulness techniques, and Bhante Henepola Gunatarana's *Mindfulness in Plain English* (Boston, MA: Wisdom Publications, 2002) is an excellent introduction to sitting meditation.

50. Daniel Goleman, *Primal Leadership: Realizing the Power of Emotional Intelligence* (Boston, MA: Harvard Business School Press, 2002), p. 141.

51. *Webster's New Universal Unabridged Dictionary* (New York, MA: Simon & Schuster, 1983).

52. Pema Chödrön, "Loving Kindness," in *Entering the Stream: An Introduction to the Buddha and His Teachings*, edited by Samuel Bercholz and Sherab Chödzin Kohn (Boston, MA: Shambhala, 1993), p. 166.

53. Flaherty, *Coaching: Evoking Excellence in Others*, p. 4.

54. George Leonard, *Mastery* (New York, NY: Plume, 1992), pp. 75-80.

References

Argyris, Chris and Don Schön, *Theory in Practice: Increasing Professional Effectiveness* (San Francisco, CA: Jossey-Bass, 1974).

Auerbach, Jeffrey E., *Personal and Executive Coaching* (Ventura, CA: Executive College Press, 2001).

Austin, James H., M.D., *Zen and the Brain: Toward an Understanding of Meditation and Consciousness* (Cambridge, MA: MIT Press, 1998).

Batchelor, Stephen, *Buddhism Without Beliefs: A Contemporary Guide to Awakening* (New York, NY: Riverhead Books, 1997).

Bell, Chip R., *Managers as Mentors, Building Partnerships for Learning* (San Francisco, CA: Berrett-Kohler Publishers, 1998).

Bench, Marcia, *Career Coaching: An Insider's Guide* (Palo Alto, CA: Davies-Black Publishers, 2003).

Benson, Herbert and Miriam Z. Klipper, *The Relaxation Response* (New York, NY: Morrow/Avon, 2000).

Bentley, Timothy and Esther Kohn-Bentley, *Leadership Coaching for the Workplace* (Toronto, Ontario: Irwin Publishing, 2002).

Bercholz, Samuel, and Sherab Chodzin Kohn, eds., *Entering the Stream: An Introduction to the Buddha and His Teachings* (Boston, MA: Shambhala, 1993).

Bianco-Mathis, Virginia, Lisa K. Nabors, and Cynthia H. Roman, *Leading from the Inside Out: A Coaching Model* (Thousand Oaks, CA: Sage Publications, 2002).

Brandon, Nathaniel, *The Art of Living Consciously: The Power of Awareness to Transform Everyday Life* (New York, NY: Fireside, 1997).

Brown, Byron, *Soul Without Shame: A Guide to Liberating Yourself from the Judge Within* (Boston, MA: Shambhala, 1999).

Butler, Gillian, *Managing Your Mind: The Mental Fitness Guide* (New York, NY: Oxford University Press, 1995).

Cameron, Julia, *The Artist's Way* (New York, NY: G.P. Putnam's Sons, 1992).

Chödrön, Pema, *When Things Fall Apart: Heart Advice for Difficult Times* (Boston, MA: Shambhala, 1997).

Crane, Thomas, *The Heart of Coaching: Using Transformational Coaching to Create a High-Performance Culture* (San Diego, CA: FTA Press, 1998).

Dalai Lama, *How to Practice: The Way to a Meaningful Life* (New York, NY: Atria Books, 2002).

Das, Lama Surya, *Awakening the Buddha Within: Tibetan Wisdom for the Western World* (New York, NY: Broadway Books, 1997).

Dass, Ram and Paul Gorman, *How Can I Help? Stories and Reflections on Service* (New York, NY: Alfred A. Knopf, 1996).

Davis, Brian L., Carol J. Skube, Lowell W. Hellervik, Susan H. Gebelein, and James L. Sheard, *Successful Manager's Handbook: Development Suggestions for Today's Managers* (Minneapolis, MN: Personnel Decisions International, 1992).

de Beauport, Elaine, *The Three Faces of Mind: Think, Feel, and Act to Your Highest Potential* (Wheaton, IL: Theosophical Publishing House, 2002).

Fisher, Roger, and William Ury, *Getting to Yes: Negotiating Agreement Without Giving In* (New York, NY: Penguin Books, 1981).

Flaherty, James, *Coaching: Evoking Excellence in Others* (Boston, MA: Butterworth-Heinemann, 1999).

Fritz, Robert, *The Path of Least Resistance: Principles for Creating What You Want to Create* (Salem, MA: DMA, Inc., 1984).

Funches, Daryl, *Three Gifts of the Organization Development Practitioner* (Seattle, WA: The REAP Gallery Unlimited Corporation, 1989).

Gallwey, W. Timothy, *The Inner Game of Work* (New York, NY: Random House, 2000).

Goldberg, Marilee C., *The Art of the Question: A Guide to Short-Term Question-Centered Therapy* (New York, NY: John Wiley & Sons, Inc., 1998).

Goldstein, Joseph, *Insight Meditation: The Practice of Freedom* (Boston, MA: Shambhala, 1993).

Goleman, Daniel, Richard Boyatzis, and Annie McKee, *Primal Leadership: Realizing the Power of Emotional Intelligence* (Boston, MA: Harvard Business School Press, 2002).

Grant, Anthony, *Coach Yourself: Make Real Changes in Your Life* (Cambridge, MA: Perseus, 2002).

Gross, Ronald, *Socrates' Way: Seven Master Keys to Using Your Mind to the Utmost* (New York, NY: Jeremy Tarcher/Putnam, 2002).

Gunaratana, Henepola, *Mindfulness in Plain English* (Somerville, MA: Wisdom Publications, 1994).

Hammond, Sue Annis, *The Thin Book of Appreciative Inquiry* (Plano, TX: CCS Publishing Company, 1996).

Hanh, Thich Nhat, *Essential Writings* (Maryknoll, NY: Orbis Books, 2001).

Hanh, Thich Nhat, *Present Moment, Wonderful Moment: Mindfulness Verses for Daily Living* (Berkeley, CA: Parallax Press, 1990).

Hanh, Thich Nhat, *The Heart of the Buddha's Teaching: Transforming Suffering into Peace, Joy and Liberation* (Berkeley, CA: Parallax Press, 1998).

Hanh, Thich Nhat, *The Miracle of Mindfulness: A Manual on Meditation* (Boston, MA: Beacon Press, 1975).

Hargrove, Robert, *Masterful Coaching Fieldbook: Grow Your Business, Multiply Your Profits, Win the Talent War!* (San Francisco, CA: Pfeiffer, 2000).

Hudson, Frederic M., *The Handbook of Coaching: A Comprehensive Resource Guide for Managers, Executives, Consultants, and Human Resource Professionals* (San Francisco, CA: Jossey-Bass, 1999).

Kegan, Robert and Lisa Laskow Lakey, *How the Way We Talk Can Change the Way We Work: Seven Languages for Transformation* (San Francisco, CA: Jossey-Bass, 2000).

Langer, Ellen J., *Mindfulness* (Reading, MA: Addison-Wesley, 1989).

Langer, Ellen J., *The Power of Mindful Learning* (Reading, MA: Addison-Wesley, 1997).

Learner, Harriet, PhD, *The Dance of Connection: How to Talk to Someone When You're Mad, Hurt, Scared, Frustrated, Insulted, Betrayed, or Desperate* (New York, NY: Harper Collins, 2001).

Leonard, George, *Mastery* (New York, NY: Plume, 1992).

Mipham, Sakyong, *Turning the Mind into an Ally* (New York, NY: Riverhead Books, 2003).

O'Neill, Mary Beth, *Executive Coaching with Backbone and Heart: A Systems Approach to Engaging Leaders with Their Challenges* (San Francisco, CA: Jossey-Bass, 2000).

Ornstein, Robert, *Multimind* (Boston, MA: Houghton Mifflin, 1986).

Ornstein, Robert, *The Evolution of Consciousness: Of Darwin, Freud, and Cranial Fire: The Origins of the Way We Think* (New York, NY: Touchstone, 1992).

Restak, Richard, *The Brain Has a Mind of Its Own: Insights from a Practicing Neurologist* (New York, NY: Crown, 1991).

Richmond, Lewis, *Work as a Spiritual Practice: A Practical Buddhist Approach to Inner Growth and Satisfaction on the Job* (New York, NY: Broadway, 1999).

Seligman, Martin, *Learned Optimism: How to Change Your Mind and Your Life* (New York, NY: Pocket Books, 1998).

Senge, Peter, *The Fifth Discipline Fieldbook: Strategies and Tools for Building a Learning Organization* (New York, NY: Doubleday Currency, 1994).

Senge, Peter, *The Fifth Discipline: The Art and Science of the Learning Organization* (New York, NY: Doubleday Currency, 1990).

Shafir, Rebecca Z., *The Zen of Listening: Mindful Communication in the Age of Distraction* (Wheaton, IL: Theosophical Publishing House, 2000).

Spence, Nancy, *Back to Basics: An Awareness Primer* (Bryson City, NC: Inner Vision, 1995).

Stone, Douglas, Sheila Heen, and Bruce Patton, *Difficult Conversations: How to Discuss What Matters Most* (New York, NY: Viking Penguin, 1999).

Suzuki, Shunryu, *Zen Mind, Beginner's Mind* (New York, NY: Weatherhill, 1970).

Thondup, Tulku, *The Healing Power of Mind: Simple Exercises for Healthy, Well-Being, and Enlightenment* (Boston, MA: Shambhala, 1996).

Wegela, Karen Kessel, *How to Be a Help Instead of a Nuisance: Practical Approaches to Giving Support, Service, and Encouragement to Others* (Boston, MA: Shambhala, 1996).

Welwood, John, *Toward a Psychology of Awakening: Buddhism, Psychotherapy and the Path of Personal and Spiritual Transformation* (Boston, MA: Shambhala, 2002).

Whitney, Diana, and Amanda Trosten-Bloom, *The Power of Appreciative Inquiry: A Practical Guide to Positive Change* (San Francisco, CA: Berrett-Koehler Publishers, Inc, 2003).

Whitney, Diana, David Cooperrider, Amanda Trosten-Bloom, and Brian S. Kaplin, *Encyclopedia of Positive Questions, Volume One: Using Appreciative Inquiry to Bring Out the Best in Your Organization* (Euclid, OH: Lakeshore Communications, 2002).

Whitworth, Laura, Henry Kimsey-House, and Phil Sandhal, *Co-Active Coaching: New Skills for Coaching People Toward Success at Work and in Life* (Palo Alto, CA: Davies-Black Publishing, 1998).

Wiseman, Richard, *The Luck Factor: Changing Your Luck, Changing Your Life: The Four Essential Principles* (New York, NY: Miramax, 2003).

Zander, Rosamund Stone and Benjamin Zander, *The Art of Possibility: Transforming Professional and Personal Life* (Boston, MA: Harvard Business School Press, 2000).

Index

About the Author

Douglas K. Silsbee, an internationally known consultant and executive coach, has been a catalyst for change for more than a quarter of a century. A master teacher, he has taught in eleven countries on four continents, working with leaders in Fortune 100 companies, non-profits, and government. Doug integrates his Buddhist practice and personal commitment to growth into the work that he does in leadership effectiveness, organizational change, and performance management.

Formerly a uranium geologist and Director of Corporate Programs at North Carolina Outward Bound, he has worked independently since 1986. Selected recent projects have included global training for product development teams at United Technologies, diversity training for US WEST Communications, and teaching coaching skills at PricewaterhouseCoopers, the American Red Cross, and Taiwan Semiconductor Manufacturing Company. Among many other clients, he has coached faculty members at the Central American Institute of Business Administration, executives at GE and Sara Lee, and ministers of the Cabinet of Nicaragua. Doug also teaches coaching skills at professional conferences and public multi-day workshops.

With his wife Walker, Doug owns a retreat center on 63 acres of beautiful mountain land north of Asheville, North Carolina. They have three teenage and grown children. More about Doug's work can be found at http://septetcoaching.com.